ALEXANDER BEDWARD

ALEXANDER BEDWARD
THE PROPHET OF AUGUST TOWN
RACE, RELIGION AND COLONIALISM

DAVE ST AUBYN GOSSE

The University of the West Indies Press
Jamaica • Barbados • Trinidad and Tobago

The University of the West Indies Press
7A Gibraltar Hall Road, Mona
Kingston 7, Jamaica
www.uwipress.com

© 2022 by Dave St Aubyn Gosse

All rights reserved. Published 2022

ISBN: 978-976-640-908-1 (print)
978-976-640-910-4 (ePub)

A catalogue record of this book is available from the National Library of Jamaica.

The University of the West Indies Press has no responsibility for the persistence or accuracy of URLs for external or third-party Internet websites referred to in this publication and does not guarantee that any content on such websites is, or will remain, accurate or appropriate.

Dedication

To my two women: my wife Deirdre and daughter Mckayla

Contents

List of Figures / ix

List of Tables / x

Introduction: Lies, Distortion and Colonial Memory / 1

1. Revivalism and the Birth of Bedwardism, 1860s–90s / 15
2. The Fundamental Pillars of the Jamaica Native Baptist Free Church / 44
3. The Arrest and Trial of Alexander Bedward / 57
4. Bedwardism, Revivalism and the Jamaican State / 81
5. Judgement Day: Tearing Down the White Wall / 111
6. The Impact of Bedwardism / 143

Appendix 1: Berry, the Independent Stream Flowing from a Huge Rock / 167

Appendix 2: The Rock from which Bedward Preached Many of His Sermons / 168

Appendix 3: Remnants of Union Temple, Shown from Three Angles / 169

Appendix 4: The Churches of the Jamaica Native Baptist Free Church, 1920 / 171

Appendix 5: List of Males Who Marched with Bedward and Were Imprisoned / 174

Appendix 6: List of Twenty-five Females Who Marched with Bedward and Were Imprisoned / 177

Appendix 7: Rules and Report of the 1920 Convention / 178

Appendix 8: Bedward's Manifestation into Kingston in 1921 / 182

Notes / 183

Bibliography / 203

Index / 209

Figures

Figure 1   Increase/decrease in people sent to Bellevue, 1885/86–1925/26 / 86
Figure 2   Recovery rate per cent at asylum, 1885/86–1925/26 / 89
Figure 3   Prisoners versus inmates at Bellevue, 1911–19 / 90
Figure 4   Causes of insanity, 31 December 1922 / 91
Figure 5   Age-group profile of those sent to the asylum, 1903–04 / 93
Figure 6   Cross and Crown in Rules and Report / 126

Tables

Table 1 Admission of Persons to the Jamaica Lunatic Asylum, 1885/86–1925/26 / 85
Table 2 Persons Deemed as Lunatics across the Island Acquitted up to 1902 / 88
Table 3 Contrasting Patients at Bellevue with Prisoners, 1911–19 / 90
Table 4 Age-Group Profile of Persons Sent to the Asylum, 1903–04 / 93

Introduction

Lies, Distortion and Colonial Memory

Revisiting and interpreting the past is extremely important for societies like Jamaica, which have experienced over three hundred years of brutal British colonialism. A by-product of such colonial rule is the dissemination of lies and propaganda by the colonial state and its allies as an important measure in maintaining that colonial rule. The French scholar Michel Foucault argues that the language of the powerful ruling elite usually becomes the normal discourse in societies, as they "construct, define and produce the objects of knowledge in an intelligible way, while excluding other forms of reasoning as unintelligible".[1]

This explains the reason the Bedward movement of August Town, Jamaica, in the latter nineteenth century has been so largely discredited by the Jamaican colonial elites as religiously unauthentic. They characterized Alexander Bedward as a mere madman and developed stories about him for entertainment purposes. For Jamaicans who have heard of Alexander Bedward, most will recall humorously the colonial myth that Bedward climbed a tree to literally fly to heaven, fell and was taken to the lunatic asylum as a madman. As a further testimony to Bedward's marginalization, the majority of younger Jamaicans most likely have never heard about Alexander Bedward, his movement or the cultural songs about him, such as "Dip dem, Bedward, dip dem, dip dem in the healing stream". Ironically, Bedward was one of Jamaica's important religious leaders and a most significant nationalist.

To demonstrate the lies, distortion and discrediting of Bedward and his movement, some of the writings of pro-colonial figures, such as white European and North American missionaries to Jamaica, are good examples.

One such North American missionary, the Reverend George Olson, field secretary of the Church of God Mission, described Bedward as a false prophet, a false Christ and a lunatic. Olson, in his extensive critique on the popular charismatic prophet, notes:

> The Scriptures warn that before the coming of the Son of Man, false Christs and false prophets shall rise, and shall show signs and wonders. In other times and in other lands, false Christs have appeared, but I believe this is the first time in the history of Jamaica that one has arisen here.

Around twenty-seven years ago, a new religious sect among the lower orders of the people was started at August Town. August Town is a peaceful village about six miles from Kingston, nestling in a valley between the mountains, through which flows a portion of the Hope River, the river which affords the main water supply of Kingston. The leader of this religious movement was one Bedward, a black man of sturdy and portly dimensions. He discovered, so he alleges, and his followers believe, that God had imparted peculiar healing properties to the water at that place. Of this he took advantage, and since that time thousands have been baptized by him and his elders, or shepherds, in the healing stream. Bedward himself was styled "Shepherd" or "Prophet" by his numerous followers, and so it is said, has made a considerable profit from selling the waters from this river, insomuch that he has been called in sarcasm "profit" Bedward.[2]

At the time of the earthquake in 1907, which it is said he predicted, Bedward received a large accession of followers; many of whom were frightened by that occurrence and applied to him for baptism; hundreds were immersed by him at one time. All his baptisms took place at August Town. These baptisms, which were held at intervals, were always preceded by fervid religious exercises and preparations in which fasting and lighted candles played a prominent part. Each candidate was charged one shilling at the time of baptism. His followers were generally dressed in white and were distinguished by white turbans. Their creed was the usual Christian formula, similar to Baptist doctrines, but mingled with much superstition and fanaticism. Several things contributed to the ascendancy Bedward gained over the minds of his superstitious followers. First, he discovered that he could stare at the sun without blinking or getting injured. Then, early in his career, he was arrested and tried by a Kingston jury for sedition, but was adjudged to be of unsound mind and detained for two days in the asylum. The reason for this short stay was that his lawyers proved that the law did not allow a man to be committed to the asylum on a charge of sedition. This no doubt added to Bedward's prestige with the ignorant masses. So, for years, Bedwardism was preached until several thousand accepted the faith.[3]

The climax came at last, rather suddenly. A short time before Christmas, startling rumours were circulated that, with mingled exhortation and cursing, Bedward was predicting his own ascension to heaven and the judgement of the world. These reports were scarcely believed at first but soon confirmed. The erstwhile shepherd and prophet had developed into the "King of Kings" and "Lord of Lords" and had to be addressed as "Lord and Master" by his devoted followers, or a stick, sturdily wielded, would be used on them. He first announced his ascension to take place on Friday, 24 December 1920, but then changed it to a week later, the last day of 1920.

Kingston would be destroyed by fire! He was not to be gone long, however, only going to prepare a place for his followers, in the realm of the blessed, and then to return for them on Monday, when the judgement would take place. The following message was sent out to all his followers: "Come, the day of judgement is at hand, wonders are going on here; come at once – everybody try to come."[4] And his followers came by the twos and the dozens and the scores, from various parts of the island, and some even from across the seas, from Cuba and Colón. They had been instructed to dispose of everything they had, as they would no longer need it. Houses, lands, livestock, furniture and jewellery were sold at a sacrifice. Their meeting house at Annotto Bay was sold for £13. To the number of five or six thousand, they gathered at August Town to witness the ascension of their master, a frenzied, singing, praying crowd.[5] To be prepared for the great event, they arrayed themselves in all-white garments, white socks and white turbans. A tailor's shop was kept working early and late to prepare garments for all. At last all was ready!

To be prepared in case of trouble, the government authorities stationed 150 men of the Sussex and West India regiments about two miles away. Nearer at hand, about a mile distant, forty armed policemen were stationed at Mona. The gates of the large church were guarded by a dozen Bedwardite men to prevent any but the faithful from entering to witness the great event. These guards were called "The Angels", and they were dressed in white. Still farther in were other guards called "The Seraphims", and within were still more called "The Archangels", to hustle out any intruder should he gain entrance. An eyewitness described the scene on Friday: "The services began at 4:30 in the morning. Bedward entered the church and from the platform cried, 'Father, I am coming home today.'"[6]

The time until 7 a.m. was occupied with singing. Then Bedward retired to prepare for the event. He came out dressed in full white: a white turban, white gauntlets on his hands and bearing a white flag. He seated himself in front of the veranda of his cottage in a chair with white cushions, specially prepared for the occasion. This chair was the chariot in which he was to ascend. All the people were singing. At 10 a.m., the hour appointed for the event, there was a great silence, and all eyes were watching him. He was heard to say something, and it was announced that the ascension was postponed to noon. Later, it was again postponed to 3 p.m., then to 10 p.m. From Saturday to Sunday, his despondent believers all took their departure in groups for their various homes. "They were a sad and dejected and sullen looking lot, as they returned weeping, jeered and mocked by the lower elements along the road. In returning from a meeting in St Mary in my motorcar, I met a group of them. They had parted with all their earthly possessions and had met with bitter disappointment."[7]

To reinforce his point on the seeming insanity of Bedward, Olson further alleges that Bedward's excuse was that God had specially commanded him to remain on earth for another seventeen years to continue to spiritually guide his flock. Olson writes:

> The masses of the people, of course, have had no sympathy with this deluded prophet and his movement. Only about one out of every one hundred and sixty of the population of Jamaica has been identified with it. But even then it is sad to think that five thousand people should listen to the deluded ravings of this man. Surely there is need for proper religious and ethical instruction when such an event can take place. As for Bedward himself, the proper place for him, no doubt, is in the insane asylum.

Olson's categorization of Bedward, as a false, deluded prophet who belonged in the asylum, was shared by fellow European missionaries of other denominations, who supported the Jamaican colonial state. Anglican Bishop Enos Nuttall, while not outright issuing a formal denunciation, believed that this wave of fanatical superstition would run its course and eventually dissipate. He nevertheless advised that those Anglicans who were followers of Bedward should be prevented from partaking in communion.[8] The Right Reverend Bishop Gordon, of the Roman Catholic faith, went much further, by issuing a proclamation to be read in every Catholic Church and school in Jamaica, forbidding Roman Catholics to visit Bedward's healing stream or encourage others to do so.[9] Gordon's proclamation in 1893 read as follows:

> It having been brought to our attention that scenes of the most indecent, degrading and superstitious character are being enacted at August Town in the vicinity of Kingston. We, in virtue of the authority committed to us by the Apostolic See, hereby ordain and command that all Catholics refrain from visiting the waters of August Town, from using them, or encouraging others to use them, until this restriction be withdrawn. We, moreover, direct this notice to be read at all the services on Sunday Sept 17 and Sept 24 and at all the Catholic schools on Tuesday Sept 19 and 26.[10]

While there were several religious groups with demonstrably African rituals, the Bedwardites were the most threatening, as they had the largest following.[11] Bedward's popularity, particularly among the poor black masses of Jamaicans, caused fear of another major riot or rebellion. Building upon a culture of resistance pioneered by their enslaved ancestors, disgruntled sugar-estate workers, for example, struck for better wages in various parts of the island in 1867, 1868, 1878 and 1901. These disturbances did not imperil the colonial state, but they were an expression of the discontentment of the people and a clear indication that challenges to an oppressive economic and social order could occur at any time.[12] Would Bedward's popularity among the masses ignite a black nationalist agenda, given the country's history, especially the Morant Bay War, which was still fresh in the minds of many?

Historian Edward White describes the levels of hysteria among such colonial advocates surrounding Bedward's popularity. He writes:

> Journalists, government officials, and social reformers inquisitive or prurient enough to attend a service looked on aghast, and in almost universal agreement that this was nothing other than mass lunacy. Explanations were advanced from various branches of Victorian pseudoscience as to the root cause of this medieval insanity, including the size and shape of the worshippers' brains. Some suggested there must have been something in the water and urged chemists to analyze the Hope River to isolate the chemical responsible. And as the number of Bedwardites grew, so the roll call at the asylum got longer and longer.[13]

Bedward's mass meetings, despite their religious nature, were always a concern for colonial officials, not only for their sociopolitical implication but also because of their "indecent" and traditional African religious practices. Historians Brian Moore and Michelle Johnson describe one such mass healing meeting where Bedward had an audience of close to twelve thousand people in attendance. When Bedward arrived and blessed the water at 9 a.m., "every consideration of decency was lost" as the very foundation of Victorian codes of "decent behaviour" was overturned:

> Women undressed on the bank and went into the water stark naked among the men and women . . . the banks were crowded with women; on the left naked men and women bathed together indiscriminately. . . . The spectacle was a most discreditable one and it is safe to say there is more harm done in five minutes at Hope River than can be undone by all the preachers in Jamaica in five years.[14]

This embarrassment among many middle- and upper-class Jamaicans over Afro-Jamaican religions such as Bedwardism was quite understandable.[15] Such Jamaicans subscribed to colonial norms and values and to the European civilizing mission of refining and Christianizing Africans away from their barbaric and heathenish behaviours. The healing services of the Bedwardites were a most painful reality of the country's regression into backwardness and darkness, according to these colonial advocates. Large numbers of Jamaicans went to August Town carrying bottles, calabashes, demijohns, cans or some other utensil, in fact, anything capable of holding water, while near the site of the healing stream the scene baffled description:

> Stalls, booths and small shops had been created at intervals where coffee, tea, chocolate, pudding or beer could be obtained by the thirsty traveller. Higglers were present in hundreds selling bread, fish, fruit and everything else necessary for the refreshment of the inner man . . . there was a constant stream of buggies, buses, horses, mules, donkeys, pedestrians passing along in the direction of the river . . . there were lepers, people with running sores, the crippled and deformed, blind, consumptive, asthmatic and in fact every complaint known in the medical world was well represented.[16]

Members of the medical profession even lobbied the government's chemist to take samples of the water in Bedward's famous healing stream, to prevent a public health crisis, as they were certain that the water which the Jamaican masses were given as medicinal water was contaminated. The chemist's analysis, they concluded, showed that it was ordinary river water with no special chemical property.[17] Since Bedward was the cause of such mass lunacy in the island, an example had to be set. He had to pay the price and become the sacrificial lamb if Jamaican colonial society was to be preserved.

Interpreting Bedwardism

Why was Bedwardism so popular from the 1890s to the early twentieth century that it boasted a membership of thirty-six thousand nationally and internationally?[18] Was Bedwardism a religious movement with political ambitions, sowing the seeds of nationalism, or was Bedward a con artist, playing on the emotions of vulnerable Jamaicans who were praying and hoping for a religious/political messiah to deliver them? Was Bedward an insane individual who best belonged in a mental institution where he could be healed? These are germane questions in any study of Alexander Bedward himself and his movement.

One of the major problems in interpreting these questions, however, is that Bedward did not personally record his thoughts or sermons for posterity. What has been attributed to him as his ideas and his sermons is the perspective of various witnesses and journalists. The Bedwardites themselves did not sufficiently record their own history, except for A.A. Brooks's publication in 1917 and interviews given in the 1980s by prominent Bedwardites to the African Caribbean Institute of Jamaica.[19] Thus many of the sources on Bedwardism are primarily biased: either sympathetic to Bedward or critical of him and his influence. Nevertheless, when read critically they provide valuable insights into Alexander Bedward and Bedwardism.

The *Daily Gleaner* newspaper is a prime example. The paper, which started publication in Jamaica in 1834, was highly critical of Bedward, and its editorial comments on Bedward were usually sensational, intended to embarrass the movement. It is the *Daily Gleaner*, for example, which informed much of missionary Olson's views. One of its sensational headlines and commentaries on Bedward is: "The Prophet of August Town, Bedward – Reformer and Blasphemer" by Rudolph Williams. He writes in his opening paragraph: "This is the story of the man who seemed to bewitch so many – regarded as saint, imposter and a mere madman."[20] Williams ends his article by characterizing the nature of Bedward's madness and making the point that even in his obvious state of insanity, his beloved followers were so deluded that they could not recognize the obvious signs of his madness. Williams writes, "Bedward raised a wooden dais and sat thereon, while his followers passed before him and bowed down. He spat at them, he kicked at them, he cursed them, indulging in the vilest obscenity. They bowed and shouted, 'Ail, Lard.'"[21]

Another journalist, although attempting to write a balanced account of the rise, spread and decline of Bedwardism, was still prejudicial to Bedward's insanity. The headline reads, "'On a certain day a will fly away to heaven, go sell your sins and come': Many Await the Return of Bedward."[22] From sections of the article, you could not help but conclude that Bedward was indeed insane. For example, the reporter writes:

> The Shepherd immensely enjoyed the sight of his converts washing their sins away and, in his desire, to make sure they were properly washed, he developed a weakness – an almost fatal one. He had the habit of hesitating a few seconds with converts held under the water, and there were many cases where people came splashing and struggling with mouths filled with water and lungs empty of air. If anyone dared to wipe his face the Shepherd would promptly grab such a one and dip him under the water again. It was reported that he once ducked a woman so enthusiastically that she drowned. It turned out, however, that the woman in fact passed out temporarily. Bedward believed that this was because she lacked faith.[23]

According to another report in 1921, Bedward told his flock that if they had enough faith they could fly. Bedward had taken a sudden liking to birds and became obsessed with the idea of flying. Initial experiments, however, did not involve his own person; instead, he convinced two female members of his flock that if they had faith, they would be able to fly. One Sunday morning, the two women climbed to the top of a tree and perched themselves on branches like birds. It is uncertain what type of tree the two women climbed. Some say it was a breadfruit tree, others say it was an ackee tree. Bedward waited anxiously to see what would happen. At the magic moment, the two women launched their bodies into the vastness of space, flapping their hands like the wings of a bird. But instead of soaring up like birds they went crashing to earth, suffering broken legs and bruises. Thompson then concluded that for the moment, Bedward's idea about flying was placed on hold.[24]

Martha Beckwith, an American folklorist and ethnographer, who interviewed Bedward on the morning of 26 December 1920, four days before his alleged flight into heaven on 31 December, believed that Bedward was insane and his movement was cultic. She wrote that Bedward kept dreaming of the impossible to the point that he duped even himself and deluded his followers. One result of this delusion was changing his title from "Shepherd" to the very incarnation of Christ. He was to be addressed in the 1920s as "Lord". Bedward further insisted, "I myself is Jesus Christ, I was crucified," as he pressed this point with a touch of asperity.[25] She further claimed that Bedward was visibly upset with the white colonial system, as several times he applied for his own pastors to be recognized as marriage officers, for the fees to be received within the church, but each time, his request was denied. As a result, Bedward was so infuriated that he was bringing the world to an end.

Stories even circulated in magazines and journals implicating Bedward and his madness in ruining the lives of many poor Jamaicans who were climbing out of poverty. One such story, in the *West Indian Review* of 1950, chronicles the life of one Alexander Thomas, a former Bedwardite living in St Thomas. Thomas gave his interview as a dirty, derelict beggar living on the streets. Bedward was the cause of his plight, as his wife had persuaded him to sell their little farm and hand the money over to Bedward, as "Judgement Day" was really near and they would have no need of their property. When they realized their mistake, his wife killed herself and he was left homeless, without food or shelter.[26]

While most of the colonial narratives on Bedward reinforced the idea of his insanity, post-colonial scholars have sharply questioned those narratives as biased. Bedward is viewed by such scholars as a significant black nationalist who built a well-organized and well-orchestrated movement. Such a robust movement of national resistance could not be led by an insane individual. Veront Satchell, for example, argues that Bedwardism was a political movement taking a religious form and that Bedward was a proto-nationalist leader in the context of Jamaica's rigid socioeconomic configuration. Thus Bedwardism was a challenge to the economic oppression and the social and political inequality of the black majority, as he challenged the status quo on behalf of the oppressed.[27] Barry Chevannes agrees with Satchell and opines that Bedward virulently denounced the oppression of blacks in Western societies and taught his people a black revolution. Among other things, he explained to his followers how in the nineteenth century, two of Jamaica's national heroes, Sam Sharpe and Paul Bogle, rebelled against the white establishment, standing up for their rights at the risk of their lives. Bedward too was arrested three times for his subversive activities.[28] Thus Bedward led his followers directly into Garveyism and could be best described in terms of the biblical character Aaron, who accompanied Moses (Marcus Garvey) in leading the black masses out of exile.[29]

Scholars of Garveyism and Rastafari concur with the views of Satchell and Chevannes and view Bedward as a prophet who helped to prepare the way for Rastafari.[30] Garveyite scholar Rupert Lewis, for example, believes that Bedward ought to be seen as a socioreligious nationalist, as the restless, frustrated, downtrodden and displaced peasant masses, who looked to God for salvation, saw in Bedward their anticolonial hero. Bedward's identification with Paul Bogle of Morant Bay and his proclivity to quote Bible passages, such as Psalms 68:31, "Ethiopia shall stretch out her hand unto God", further attracted the black masses to him. With such a following and influence, Bedwardism was an ominous threat to the colonial way of life and Bedward, the masses' hero, had to pay the price, as another Morant Bay Rebellion could not occur. In addition, Bedward and Robert Love were two most important influences on the development of Marcus Garvey, one of the country's national heroes.[31]

Yoshiko Nagashima, an anthropologist who interviewed numerous Bedwardites in 1980, is also of the view that Bedward's alleged insanity was "created" by the colonial government as the most convenient means to crush a largely unemployed grassroots proletarian movement. The Bedwardites believed their prophet was a rational individual who shared with them the revelation that he too had to suffer, as did Jesus, the Christ. Bedward could have freed himself but knew that he was destined to remain in the asylum until the calling came to him. This is one of the reasons why his followers, though discouraged, were confident in and faithful to him even unto death. Thus a number of African religious leaders with a similar grassroots appeal, such as Leonard Howell and the Reverend Claudius Henry, passed through the same persecution.[32]

Roxanne Watson, in her article on Bedward, is also of the view that Bedward and his Native Baptist Church were targeted by the colonial government, since they sought to improve the conditions of the black masses. Bedward's sentence to an asylum for insanity must be seen in the context of the fear of the privileged classes, who saw that the Native Baptist Church was becoming a social force in Jamaica and that such a situation would lead to an uprising by the lower classes in an attempt to change the status quo.[33]

Patrick Bryan also lays to rest the idea that Bedwardism was just a spontaneous outburst of religious revival. He argues that the movement was a well-organized one. It was also a legitimate Christian movement. In every sense of the word, Bedwardism was a formal church with a well-developed theology, and not a cultic movement, as some would believe. Its understanding of the Trinity seemed quite orthodox when compared with other churches, and it had a strong consciousness of New Testament theology. In addition, the Bedwardites' emphasis on the spiritual discipline of fasting was not that dissimilar from that of Orthodox Christianity, although their rituals surrounding fasting would be more in line with those of other Revivalist groups in the island.[34]

Even literary fiction has also sought to revise the initial story of Bedward's insanity. The late Louis Marriott, the renowned actor, director and playwright, shares a similar analysis of the various colonial organs of the state's contriving the insanity of Bedward. Marriott, in the 1960s, revised the work of Bedward in a play in two acts and argues strongly that up to 1921, when Bedward was committed to Bellevue, the only humorous stories surrounding him came through the healing he did from the healing stream. Marriott emphasized that there were no stories of Bedward literally attempting to fly to heaven. Bedward, who stated that he could fly, postponed his ascension each time, ahead of time, until the people of his generation developed the jingle, "Bedward say him would fly, but him put it off till July." Marriott blamed the *Daily Gleaner*, which was antagonistic to Bedward, for editorializing and propagating the view that Bedward literally attempted to fly. This narrative was to ensure that Bedward's legacy became one of insanity.[35]

Kei Miller, the celebrated novelist and poet, in his brilliant novel *Augustown*, interprets the story of Bedward's desire to fly as a metaphor for doing the impossible and the improbable and actually achieving them, but Bedward is literally dragged back to earth from flying by the colonial authorities. Since Bedward taught his followers the importance of black power and believing in themselves as black people and in their motherland,

Africa, their home, to which they would all literally fly back, he had to pay the price.³⁶

While post-colonial scholars are reinterpreting Bedwardism, with perspectives ranging from proto-nationalism to a Rastafari prophet, to date, there has not been a detailed study of Bedwardism covering the genesis of his ministry on 10 October 1891 to his death in 1930. Much of the literature on Bedwardism culminates with his first trial in 1898, when he was charged with sedition, but freed. Garvey and Rastafari scholars, on the other hand, highlight Bedward's Revivalism as an important stream in the development of both sociopolitical movements. But even in those studies, Alexander Bedward is not the focus, and thus he is minimally covered. Therefore, scholars who write on the labour riots of the 1930s also mention Bedward and his contribution as part of the vanguard of resistance leading to the 1930s. But again, Bedward is minimally covered.³⁷ Satchell's articles and the monograph by Brian Moore and Michelle Johnson are good sources which provide a satisfactory analysis of his impact.³⁸ Unfortunately, Bedward is not the focus in Moore and Johnson, and their analysis of him is brief. Satchell, whose focus is Bedward, discusses him in more detail by comparison, but even then, his articles were limited, since they were written for journals.

This study therefore attempts to fill the gap in the literature by providing a more detailed study of Bedward's life from 1891 to 1930. Secondly, it attempts to show that Bedwardism was the most significant national movement of social defiance from the latter nineteenth century to the early twentieth century. In the face of a colonial culture hostile to African-led movements, Bedwardism triumphed. It was a major bridge of colonial resistance in Jamaica from the Morant Bay War in 1865 to the return of Marcus Garvey in 1927 and the birth of Rastafari in the 1930s. For thirty years, from 1891 to 1921, Alexander Bedward fought the colonial system successfully and was a shining light and an inspiration to thousands of Jamaicans, especially from poor black working-class communities.

Thirdly, Bedwardism was an important social force which shaped the sociopolitical history of Jamaica from the late nineteenth to the early twentieth centuries. Bedwardism was like a tick in the backside of the Jamaican colonial state, as witnessed in the direct and indirect legislation passed to neutralize him and his fellow Revivalists across the country. Thus Bedwardism covers a most important period in Jamaica's history, as it was the most self-sustaining resistance movement, which excelled despite colonial attempts to crush it.

Fourthly, Bedwardism was the largest organized black-led sociopolitical movement in Jamaica nurturing the seeds of Ethiopianism and black nationalism and forging a black identity among its members. Bedwardism, being a fruit of the 1865 Great Religious Revival in Jamaica, watered the seed of colonial resistance and, although declining post-1930, inspired other African-led movements, such as Garveyism, Rastafari and the 1930s labour rebellions.

Fifthly, Alexander Bedward, as leader of a resistance movement, ought to be redeemed from the colonial crusade which categorized him as insane. Bedward must be celebrated as one of Jamaica's premier social leaders and placed on a similar platform to leaders such as Paul Bogle, Samuel Sharpe and Marcus Garvey. Despite being formally illiterate and wrongly diagnosed with serious mental challenges, he rose above the stigma and built a national and international movement of socioreligious resistance. Bedward identified with the black Christ and saw his mission as one given by his father to save his black brothers and sisters from colonial oppression. With such a divine identity, Bedward further placed himself within the black prophetic/radical tradition and realized that he was continuing the work of former black Baptist heroes, such as Sharpe and Bogle. One of the important qualities of Bedward's leadership is his spirit of boldness, a daringness, a figurative badness or even madness, as he was willing to sacrifice his life for his beliefs.

Black nationalist leaders such as Bedward figuratively had to be "insane" to take on the colonial forces and its various auxiliaries. He had to be "insane" to create a viable alternative perspective to the colonial view that deemed black people culturally inferior and uncivilized. British colonialists in Jamaica, as in other colonized territories, sought to socially re-engineer the sociocultural norms of its black inhabitants, to fit colonial values. Alexander Bedward and the Bedwardites experienced the brutal hand of the state, character assassination and had their mental capacity questioned. Bedward did not allow the colonial state to dangle over his head the contrived stories of his insanity to keep him in check. He remained fixed on his purpose despite the engineered narrative of his insanity.

The colonial perspective of Bedward's insanity, however, has been so culturally imprinted and repeated ad nauseam to succeeding Jamaican generations that it has become the major narrative. Just the very mention of his name in social spaces today in Jamaica still evokes laughter and cynicism, rather than respect and admiration for his anticolonial resistance. Despite revisionist attempts at retelling the story of Alexander Bedward, the version of insanity has been so historically and culturally etched in our memory that even current historians still in some ways perpetuate the myth. Philip Sherlock, for example, who wrote a detailed history of Jamaica, praises Robert Love for his approach to black nationalism but categorizes Bedward as confrontational. Without dismissing or relegating the important role Love played in building a national agenda on the issue of race, Bedward should not be contrasted with Love and viewed as "confrontational".[39] This reinforces the narrative of his insanity and gives the impression that Bedwardism was an uncontrolled and sporadic movement without an intelligent centre. Alexander Bedward was a smart, strategic leader who planned and organized a national movement of sociocultural resistance. Bedward knew when it was time to focus on institutional strengthening, and when to become assertive in protecting and preserving the rights and freedoms of African Jamaicans to live and worship as they desired. The colonial state did not have the right to command non-Europeans to practise colonial culture.

Bedward's resistance resonated with his followers and was critical, as it made his movement successful. Although Bedwardism had members from the middle classes, the working-class blacks in particular saw in him a leader who fought for them against the oppressive colonial system.

Any legitimate interpretation of Bedward must consider colonial violence and that the behaviour of resistance leaders is very much in response to colonial dictates. Colonial states are not only predatory but also violent. Jürgen Osterhammel, in his book on colonialism, makes it clear that colonialism is not only a process of territorial acquisition but sociopolitical, economic and ideological systems of domination.[40] Frantz Fanon concluded decades ago that European colonialism was not as benign as some would want us to believe, but was rooted in a level of violence done to non-Europeans.[41] The Jamaican colonial state was no exception. Its narrative of Bedward's insanity was just one of the many ways to keep colonialism intact. Such psychological destruction of an individual, and by extension the demise of a movement for the safety of the colonial state, has to be seen in similar terms – as violent. It is in this context of a colonial state which would resort to anything to destroy its resistors that Bedward and his movement must be analysed.

It is this social defiance of the colonized world which Bedward carved out for himself and his followers which made his movement so attractive to the black working class nationally and internationally. It is in this context that Bedward ought to be seen not just as a proto-nationalist but as a legitimate nationalist leader. It is in this context of social defiance that Bedward could also be seen as insane, as he created an alternative world where African culture and practice could be fleshed out without any care for the consequences. At times, he deliberately took on the white colonial establishment through planned protest marches, and the only apparent logical conclusion was that he had to be insane to confront British colonial power both indirectly and directly. Whether Bedward saw himself as a nationalist is not the germane issue; the poor black masses saw him as their leader, providing an alternative to the colonial way of life, and they looked to him for leadership.

Despite the current claim of insanity attached to Bedward, the average black Jamaican of the 1920s saw Bedward as a prophet. As late as 1966, one visitor to Jamaica recorded an inscription he saw on a wall at the end of Duke Street in the Kingston Harbour as he walked from his vessel. It read:

> During 1920, Jamaica knew two prophets
> One called Bedward attempted to fly. He was
> tried and placed in asylum. The other rank by far
> The most important prophet. He was Marcus Garvey
> Who founded the Universal Negro Improvement
> Association in the USA. Proclaimed Black nationalism and preached
> Africa for Africans at far land abroad. One God, one aim, one destiny.[42]

Whoever wrote the inscription, although highlighting Garvey as more successful, does acknowledge the prominence of Bedward in Jamaica's history of radical thinkers. The colonial myth of Bedward's attempted flight ought to be interpreted figuratively. What is quite clear is that Bedward's nationalism is embedded in folk culture and is symbolic of the masses' opinion of him. Bedward was their prophet and he attempted to fly.

Chapter 1

Revivalism and the Birth of Bedwardism, 1860s–90s

The Great Revival in Jamaica, which started in 1860, is less documented by scholars than is the Morant Bay War of 1865. Yet the former had a significant impact on the latter. This Revival, which allegedly started in September 1860 at a Moravian chapel in St Elizabeth, spread across the entire island, affecting every religious denomination.

The journal of missionary Theodor Sonderman of the American Missionary Society provides fascinating details of this revival. Sonderman notes, in one of his regular community visits in 1861, that he met a large group of African Jamaicans, some of whom were weeping because of the tremendous joy they were experiencing. Others were weeping because of the strong conviction of sin that was pressing down upon them. Then there were others who were perplexed at what they were witnessing. Sonderman attempted to calm the emotions that were being expressed, but as he began praying, he himself was overcome and cautiously stepped back, deciding to "leave them to the direction of the Holy Spirit".[1]

In his own church a few days after, on Friday, 28 September 1860, a meeting which began with a hymn and an opening prayer got out of control. In rapid succession, people were spontaneously praying, one after the other. Children also participated in public prayers, and as one young boy was pouring out his soul, the power of God descended upon everyone present, causing their bodies to tremble. Everywhere, people were crying out for mercy, and some uttering deep groans as God exposed the true conditions of their hearts. While one young girl was praying with deep passion and fluency, the Holy Spirit came "like a rushing mighty wind". At the same time grown men were seen bowing on their knees, trembling, as if shaken by an invisible power. The meeting that day continued until midnight, but those who were under severe conviction of sin left the church and reassembled at the school building to receive counsel from Sonderman. In just 4 weeks after the outbreak of the Revival, he had counselled 315 people who were desperately seeking relief from the overwhelming conviction of their sins.

Other missionaries also shared similar experiences of the Great Revival. In early November 1860, one of the Jamaican missionaries wrote that he travelled to Montego Bay to preach at a Sunday morning service. Upon his arrival he found that God was already at work. His church members, along with other seekers, had already arrived for worship from 5 p.m. on Saturday, and there was a continual flow of people coming to the church seeking salvation. An overwhelming God-consciousness had settled upon the town. God was the subject of every conversation, whether it was in the home, the fields, along the ocean front or in the marketplace. The town was filled with an unusual awareness of the presence of God.[2]

Another missionary noted that after a Sunday service in Bethel Town, Westmoreland, a mission colleague proposed a prayer meeting to be held early the next morning. At dawn on Monday, five hundred people gathered for prayer, which was very unusual. An announcement was later given that a service would be held that evening by the church's local leader. When that evening service was about to end, the Holy Spirit was poured out, and a powerful Revival commenced. The presence of God was so real during the service that no one wanted to leave. The missionary was notified as to what had happened and immediately hurried back on Wednesday evening, when he witnessed some "unforgettable scenes". One involved no fewer than a hundred sinners simultaneously being overcome by the presence of God and, having lost all bodily strength to stand, lying prostrate on the ground. Another astounding occurrence was the announcement by dozens of couples who were "living in concubinage relationships" that they were applying to be married.[3]

At the Mount Carey Baptist church chapel in St James, where the service was presided over by a justice of the peace, an unusual crowd of twelve hundred had gathered by 11 a.m., with many standing outside the church looking in through the windows. Tremendous excitement was created when seven people were overcome by the power of God and were prostrated on the ground. In the three previously mentioned locations, Montego Bay, Bethel Town and Mount Carey, there were an estimated three thousand conversions.[4]

The Great Revival was not only limited to western Jamaica, where it allegedly started. Bigelow Penfield, from the American Missionary Society, wrote in a letter that the Revival, which had been spreading through a great portion of the island gradually, had now reached eastern Jamaica, near Kingston, where he was located. He wrote: "We have had glorious times at Providence since the commencement of the Revival. Our church there has just about doubled its numbers already and next Sabbath we are to receive twelve more, eight on profession of their faith and four by letter. The church as a whole has been greatly blessed and quickened in the divine course, and several of the backsliders have been reclaimed."[5]

Another missionary, Foote, from the Methodist church in Portland, reported that the Revival also reached Port Antonio and Manchioneal, where he was stationed, in April 1861.[6] Noted Baptist missionary Mursell Phillippo also highlights the impact of the Revival on the Baptist churches in Jamaica. He notes that the returns at the close of the year from 59 out of the 61 churches of the Baptist Union state that 3,757 people were baptized, while there were restored to fellowship from a backsliding state no fewer than 1,570. The net increase to the churches exhibited a total of 4,422, bringing up the membership to 20,026 people of all ages. The classes of inquirers were also largely filled and numbered 6,058 individuals.[7]

Evaluating the Great Revival

Caribbean historians generally agree that the 1840s was a period when many African Jamaicans supported the mission-led churches, as the European missionaries kept in close and friendly contact with them.[8] The missionaries helped some of the former enslaved Africans in their quest to buy land in the early emancipation period and followed them into the hills, where they assisted them to found free villages.[9] As a result, some of the mission-led churches, particularly the Baptists, grew significantly, as shown by William Gardner. He writes that within three years after emancipation, eleven thousand people were baptized by the Baptist movement. The membership of the Baptist churches had increased from about 10,000 members to 33,658, the chapels from 15 to 50, and the congregations comprised 80,000 people, of whom nearly 15,000 were inquirers.[10]

The increase of African Jamaicans in the Baptist church would not have been strange, since the Baptist church was started by the formerly enslaved African George Leile (or Liele), who had migrated to Jamaica as a loyalist, given the events after the American War of Independence in 1783. Leile and his fellow black pastors (Moses Baker, George Lewis, George Gibbs and Nicholas Swiegle) built a vibrant indigenous movement among the black population.

A significant reason for the rise of Africans in the Baptist church in the post-emancipation period was their continued use of their ticket-leader system. It was designed by the black pastors, such as Leile, and the white British missionaries continued the practice of allowing the members to choose their own cell/group leaders in the various villages. These Baptist cell/group leaders on the respective plantations gave tickets to fellow Africans who, in their view, were ready for baptism and church membership of the church. This meant that the criteria used in approving such members depended on their understanding of Christianity and not the understanding of the white Baptist missionaries. The ability of inquirers into the Baptist church to have visions and dreams was one such criterion of these cell/group leaders, and it meant that the white Baptist missionaries were not in control of the theology of many of its black members.

So while the Baptists were growing numerically, the beliefs and practices of its members were really being shaped by African group leaders. As the largest Christian denomination in the island, they were heavily criticized by other denominations for letting their congregations grow beyond the personal supervision of the white ministers. The African group leaders were accused of selling tickets for a veneration as a charm and requiring special dreams and seizure by the spirit as a criterion for baptism. Furthermore, baptism by immersion had become a superstitious rite. More important, given the Baptist church's many African adherents, they were influencing fellow Africans in other missionary-led churches. The Baptist movement led by white English missionaries had become similar to the black-led Native Baptists and the independent Baptist groups, in the criteria for baptism and church membership. Fellow European missionaries concluded that superstition and ignorance abounded among the Africans in the Baptist movement.[11]

To the shock of the missionaries, the Great Revival, which they thought would eliminate Africanism in the church, spread outside the missionary chapels along the roadways and into people's homes. Here elements other than demonstrative penitence and prostration entered in, as obeahmen and myalists now participated in the Revival on their own terms.[12] Thus missionary fervour about the Revival soon faded, it became clear to them that they had misread the Revival. It was predominantly African, as African Jamaicans were authenticating their own religion with their own rituals and doctrines. The missionaries, in their disappointment, accused the Africans of practising obeah and myalism and bringing the church into disrepute. Missionary historian William Gardner, for example, writes that the Revival, which was initially clear and transparent, became foul and repulsive. In many of the central districts of Jamaica there was much wild extravagance and almost blasphemous fanaticism. This was especially the case where the Native Baptists had any considerable influence. Among these were the manifestations occasioned by the influence of myalism.[13]

Gardner, a Presbyterian missionary, acknowledged that the African population had always been overwhelmed by practices of myalism and obeah since their enslavement. The missionaries had always fought to remove this plague from their lives, especially after the Emancipation Act of 1838, which provided them more opportunities to work more closely with the African population. Gardner writes:

> Old superstitions were struggling to regain their former ascendency over the minds of Christian communicants in Jamaica. In 1842, several negroes residing on an estate near Montego Bay gave themselves out to be Myalmen; and in St James, Westmoreland, and Trelawny, thousands of deluded people became their followers. They were accustomed to meet together after nightfall, generally beneath the shadow of a cotton tree. Fowls were sacrificed, and wild songs sung, in the chorus of which the multitude joined. Dancing then began, becoming more and more weirdlike in character, until one and another fell exhausted to the ground, when their incoherent utterances were listened to as divine revelations. Half-demented creatures sat among the branches, or in the hollow trunks of trees, singing; while others, with their heads bound in a fantastic fashion, ran about with arms outstretched and declared that they were flying. It became necessary at last to swear in several hundreds of special constables, and to punish numbers of these deluded people for disturbing the peace.[14]

The missionaries thought they were winning the fight, as in 1848, a myal practitioner named Dr Taylor gave much trouble in the parishes of Manchester and Clarendon, drawing great crowds after him. He was sent to the penitentiary, where he was accidentally killed. Things quieted down for a while. Then, in 1852, the delusion again appeared, as some now gave themselves out to be prophets, and saw visions, but the firmness of the missionaries, petitioning the colonial state to intervene and stop the madness, brought it to an end.[15] But it was now clear that the African practices went underground and had now resurfaced.

The colonial missionaries had a patronizing and exalted view of themselves and their colonizing mission, not understanding that the African Jamaican population were highly intelligent and could make rational decisions on their own. The missionaries did not understand that during African enslavement many of the Christian converts chose Christianity on the basis of convenience. Christianity provided the enslaved Christian leaders in particular with a legitimate organization through which they worked. It also provided them with missionary protection, as they were known on many plantations to be in charge of Christian cell groups. These Christian enslaved leaders were the ones who taught fellow enslaved Africans the catechisms, which would later be recited before the missionaries.[16]

From as early as enslavement on many sugar plantations in Jamaica, these Christian enslaved Africans were already developing an indigenous form of Christianity, which was predominantly African, fused with European Christianity. Many of the African elements of their brand of Christianity would be masked before the missionaries, although at times the missionaries were dissatisfied that what they were witnessing was Christianity. Seeing that African traditional religion was flexible in contrast to Christianity, in adding new spirits to their already wide pantheon of gods, enslaved Africans could easily create a new brand of religion which was partly Christian and partly African.

It was not only in the Caribbean that African converts to Christianity created an Afro-Christian religion but also on the African continent. Africans of traditional religion, when faced with Christianity, made one of three choices: acceptance, rejection or adaptation.[17] Rejection meant that they stayed away from Christianity and continued their African traditional practices or a modification of African religions. Those who accepted European Christianity remained loyal to missionary Christianity, but it was not necessarily an indication that convenience was not still a driving force. Having their children attend missionary schools or acquiring the social status of attending a mission-led church were reasons some Africans accepted missionary Christianity. Those who adapted fused missionary Christianity with traditional African traditions, creating a new indigenous religion.

For such Africans, whether in West Africa or Jamaica, fusing Christianity with African traditions was the most pragmatic choice. They realized that for Christianity to be useful in the Jamaican context it had to be blended. European Christianity had to become Jamaican and Africans as Christian practitioners had an African religious tradition to draw on. More important, they recognized that missionary Christianity had a major flaw in that it separated the sacred or spiritual life from secular affairs such as politics and economics. Thus the same missionaries who fed their souls spiritually on Sundays were the same ones who encouraged obedience to the colonial economic and political system during the rest of the week, as they supported colonialism. Missionary Christianity was indeed the social arm of the Jamaican colonial state. The Africans had a fundamental problem with this colonial paradigm, as their African concept of religion could not be divorced from secular affairs. For Africans, religion was the philosophical basis of all aspects of life. True religion could not be separated from sociopolitical and socioeconomic realities.

The African scholar John S. Mbiti argues that African religion is foundational to the Africans' understanding of culture, and as such, provides ammunition against and a counter to European forms of culture.[18] In African religion and its evolution in the Americas, the sacred is not separated from the secular, and religion provides the foundation for politics, society and economics. An African Jamaican religion, such as Revivalism, would ultimately provide a better paradigm for community development, political agitation and sociocultural affirmation.

Maria Robinson-Smith highlights the importance of African Jamaicans creating their own Revivalist religion. She writes:

> Revivalism, like its forerunner Myalism, is focused on keeping alive the links with the ancestral spirits through rituals and ceremony. Revivalism created a space where African Jamaicans could practise their religion to fulfil their spiritual needs. It offered its followers healing and protection from harm and provided individual and community security, as well as a feeling of well-being. All of these were important to a people dispossessed and broken by the harsh realities of slavery and poverty. Revivalism has its strongest and most loyal support among people from the poorest class of society and, by extension, those who are also predominantly black.[19]

Another African scholar, K. Asare Opoku, shows that the rise of black independent indigenous churches in colonial West Africa from the 1880s to the 1930s was a result of the Africans developing their own religion to make sense of their colonial context. He writes:

> In these churches forms of worship are provided to satisfy the spiritual and emotional needs of members, thereby enabling Christianity, like traditional religion, to cover every area of human life and fulfil all human needs. Included in these is the concern for healing, whose centrality in both traditional religion and indigenous Christianity cannot be over-emphasized. In addition to healing, the religious needs of divining, prophesying and visioning are also fulfilled, for there is the firm belief that God reveals the future and the causes of misfortune through visions.[20]

Clinton Hutton makes a similar observation with regard to African Jamaicans in the 1860s creating their own Revival religions. The Great Revival of the early 1860s was a good example of the ways in which people of African descent sought to modernize older forms of African Jamaican spirituality. By begetting Revival Zion and Poco Revival, they were in a better position to engage ancestral episteme, ontology and culture in recreating their existential pathways in post-slavery. Their creation of Revival Zion and Poco Revival had trans-parish/national appeal.[21] It was not only Revival Sixty and Sixty-One that the African Jamaican populace created. Other movements, such as the Isaiah movement, Kumina and a host of other independent Revivalist movements emerged all over Jamaica. It is this stream of Revival religion which will later produce an Alexander Bedward of August Town by the 1890s.[22]

Even the new indentured labourers brought to Jamaica from Central Africa expressed a preference for the Native Baptist religion, as new converts had to be baptized in various rivers. This emphasis on water rituals was a sign of closeness to the river gods who had protected them in the past and would protect them in the future. In addition, in the Native Baptist tradition, the Holy Spirit, the third person in the Christian Trinity, had become venerated as a supremely special spirit, in contrast to God the father and Jesus Christ the son. African Jamaicans, in their interpretation of Christianity generally, had moved closer in their doctrine to the myalists. The Holy Spirit, being more important than Jesus himself, would give them all the protection they needed and all the necessary guidance.[23] The crises of the 1850s eventually pushed many Africans into a new Revivalist stream of religion.

The Crises of the 1850s

The 1850s witnessed numerous crises culminating in the Great Revival. During the cholera epidemic of 1850 some forty thousand people died, most of whom were from the vulnerable black poor masses. The impact in the 1850s of the Sugar Duties Act of 1846 was another significant event. The act, which equalized the duties on non-British sugar to those in the British colonies, had a severe effect on those colonies, such as Jamaica. The Jamaican Assembly complained bitterly in 1850 that a survey in 1849 showed 144 sugar estates and 465 coffee plantations were ruined and abandoned.[24] While the majority of African Jamaicans were peasants on their own land, they were nevertheless directly affected, as they still depended on the plantations to supplement their income.[25]

High taxation had become the Jamaican political state's response, both to garner more income for its coffers and to force many of the black peasants to work for the remaining planters. The Africans were taxed on their salt, their bread, their lucifers, their clothes and everything else they used.[26] Between 1840 and 1865, the import tax on herring rose 166 per cent; on saltfish, 366 per cent; on mackerel, 433 per cent. All of these were staples of the African masses.[27]

Under the Jamaican government's Main Roads Law, to rebuild the island's infrastructure in the 1850s, the burden of toll-road taxes fell more on the African masses than on the planters. On three successive nights in February 1859, 500–600 small settlers, frustrated by the official indifference to their complaints, tore down the tollgates and tollhouses.[28] Six months later came the "Trelawny Riots". These grew out of land-tenure disputes at Florence Hall Pen in Trelawny, which, according to reports, led to rioting. Further trouble broke out when all but one of those apprehended in connection with the Florence Hall Pen incident were freed by "a large number of men and women", who set upon the police and two magistrates entrusted with taking the prisoners to the Falmouth gaol.[29]

The crowd proceeded to attack the police station and the houses of Bourke, Justices Lindo and Nunes with "stones and other missiles". The crowd retreated when a prominent member of the planter and merchant class, Castle, read the Riot Act. The rebels returned, however, and resumed stoning the police station, and the police opened fire on them, killing three. Present at the police station while it was under attack were prominent members of the Trelawny planter and merchant classes – Kitchen, Castle, Salmon, Abraham, Lindo, Bliss, M.A. Nunes and Fowles. After the shooting incident, at least two fires were started in the town. The roof of "one of the buildings connected with the Druggist Store of Mr Charles Delgado" was in bright flame. Another fire gutted "one of the stores on the Trelawny Wharf". That wharf was operated by George Delisser and Son.[30]

In addition, the poor vulnerable black masses were also victimized by the estates and pens, whose cattle often trampled their provision crops. In 1858, a revised law to address the issue favoured the planter class, as suing for damages had to be done in the Petty Debt Court for small amounts – less than forty shillings – and in the Superior Court for larger amounts. This meant delay and expense that often could not be recouped by these African small freeholders and renters.[31]

It is in such a context of severe socioeconomic hardships that African Jamaicans clung to their source – their religion. The Great Revival was not from Revivals in Europe, as suggested by Curtin.[32] The Revival was strongly African and its beginning was in the mission churches, but its scope and extent far surpassed these mission-led churches and swept the entire island.

The Morant Bay War of 1865 was also a product of the Africans' spirituality. Kofi Barima and Clinton Hutton have ably highlighted the Native Baptist influence in the war and the importance of the African rituals of rum and gunpowder that were used by African Jamaicans, as they sought the intervention of the spirits to war with the colonial state.[33] That imagery of the Africans led by Paul Bogle going to war to fight the Jamaican colonial system became a fundamental pillar of later Revivalists such as Bedward.

African Jamaicans in the 1860s exhibited sociopolitical maturity. It was a time of renewed confidence in their ability (black power). This was a time when the majority of them no longer looked to white missionary assistance and clung faithfully to their black religion as their hope, to guide them in their socioeconomic and political hardships. They believed that once they conducted their religious rituals correctly, they would be divinely guided. That is the reason the praxis emerging from their rituals led to the Morant Bay War of 1865. It also explains the proliferation of Revivalist bands all over the country towards the end of the nineteenth century and their continued attempt at creating new forms of Revival religion, leading to Bedwardism.

The Health Crisis in Jamaica, 1860s–90s

In 1861, the year of the Great Revival, there were only fifty qualified doctors in Jamaica, compared to two hundred in 1833. By 1890, there was only 1 doctor to 7,185 people islandwide; Kingston was better served, with 23 doctors to every 2,109 people. However, Kingston's healthcare system was no better than the countryside's. Healthcare in the island was poor, especially for the majority of African Jamaicans, despite the installation of district medical officers (DMOs) across the island from 1868. This initiative of Governor Sir John Grant in dividing the island into medical districts was a good idea, but it did not solve the health crisis, given the shortage of trained European doctors. These DMOs had an onerous job description. They were responsible for all health issues within their region, such as placing paupers on a parochial list, assisting the hospital, providing healthcare to the poorhouses and prisons, attending to the constabulary, controlling and supervising the dispensaries, providing vaccination and advising the parochial boards.

Given the decline in sugar production in the island and the very low prices being offered by the plantations, finding money to pay for healthcare for many African Jamaicans was most difficult. Those seeking advice and medicines at a DMO's consultation as physician or surgeon were to pay twenty-one shillings. If the individual visited the DMO's residence or private facility or the government dispensary, the charge was four shillings. For each subsequent visit in the same case, the charge was two shillings. For each visit to the DMO in town between the hours of 6 a.m. and 7 p.m., within a radius of a mile from the centre of the town, the cost was six shillings.

For each visit by the DMO in a rural area within a radius of a mile from the DMO's residence, the cost was six shillings. Mileage in addition to the fee for the visit for any distance between one and five miles from the DMO's residence was at the rate of two shillings per mile or part of a mile. Mileage between five and twelve cost two shillings and sixpence per mile or part of a mile; while mileage over twelve was three shillings per mile. The above charges for ordinary medicines and mileage to be charged were only in one direction and not in both directions.[34]

Night visits from 7 p.m. to 6 a.m. incurred one half-fee and half-mileage extra. If the DMO was asked to stay for a day and night and he consented, the fee was twenty-one shillings – at the above rate. Every subsequent consultation on the same case as above was ten shillings and sixpence. Consultation by letter and medicine supplied if necessary was six shillings. To obtain a medical certificate cost twenty-one shillings. For midwifery and for attendance at delivery, the cost was two pounds and two shillings, along with the cost of mileage. For minor surgery the cost was ten shillings and sixpence, while for fractures of upper and lower extremities, the cost was twenty-one shillings.[35]

Despite the colonial government's increase in funding healthcare from the 1850s, its initiatives were not radical enough in meeting the serious health crisis in the island, particularly among the black population. The government's expenditure on health for the latter half of the nineteenth century shows its incremental approach despite some years of massive increases. Healthcare rose from £2,300 in 1852 to £11,325 in 1870–71, and to £31,924 ten years later. In 1889–90 expenditure declined to £29,890; in 1894–95 it increased to £34,087 and to £35,202 in 1897–98. In 1898–99 it decreased to £31,390. After almost tripling between 1870 and 1880, perhaps a result of capital expenditure, there were only marginal increases between 1880 and the end of the nineteenth century. Bed space in the hospitals increased only marginally between 1880 and 1900, from 945 beds in 1880–81 to 1,117 in 1893–94 and 1,171 in 1899–1900.[36]

The Jamaican government's failure in not investing heavily in assisting both permanent and temporary paupers, on a longer-term basis, resulted in their mortality and morbidity rates increasing significantly. This situation was especially so for the vulnerable blacks across the island. In 1895, taking into account the thirteen parishes other than Kingston, 80 per cent of deaths were uncertified. That is, deaths occurred without medical aid being obtained in the last illness. Under Jamaican law, when a person dies, the registered medical practitioner who attended to them before death must sign and indicate to the Registrar General's Department information concerning the death. The problem, however, was that many poor people were not visiting these medical practitioners frequently enough for the doctors to certify the causes of death, and this resulted in a high rate of uncertified deaths. The Registrar General's Department even admitted to an increase in uncertified deaths and wrote to the doctors, since these deaths indicated a serious medical crisis in the island.[37] The deaths in 1906–07 of forty out of forty-five people from enteric fever were attributed to the unavailability of medical treatment for the poor.

In 1890, citizens from the leeward districts of Hanover, representing some eight thousand people, noted that medical attention was available to them only once a week and that medical fees were exorbitant. The petition was signed by a justice of the peace, a minister of religion and over eighty others. In the same year, the residents of Porus in Manchester delivered a similar petition, noting that for medical assistance they either had to travel over the hills for ten miles to Mandeville, or to May Pen, which was fifteen miles away.

In 1883, the Maroons complained of the expense of medical attention. "It is no use," wrote the Reverend Stuart to the colonial secretary, "talking to maroons about receiving medical attendance, poor relief and roads, when one visit of a doctor would cost more than one of them could earn in six months."[38] However much independence the small settler could achieve by cultivating his own plot, the proceeds of which assisted in feeding himself and family, his cash income was limited. Taxes and medical expenses had to be paid in cash, not in bananas or in ginger. Stuart noted with respect to the Maroons of Accompong (and the same situation applied to other isolated peasant communities) that "one person can on average carry only one shilling and sixpence worth of breadkind to market – which was twenty to twenty-four miles distant . . . they have but small return for their labour".

In 1885–86, the collector-general, citing the poor health of the inhabitants of St James parish, explained that small settlers had felt and were still feeling keenly the tax on their slender resources to provide medical aid, medicines and so on. Scarcity of money was also a reality for estate labourers, when estate crops were poor. Good crops of ground provisions glutted the market and depressed prices and therefore cash income. In 1897, the Reverend W. Webb cited figures of up to three pounds and three shillings for medical attention and associated transportation costs.[39]

E.H.B. Stafford, a practising physician in the parish of St Elizabeth, in a letter to the *Daily Gleaner*, also chastised the Jamaican government for its short-sightedness as the core reason for the shortage of trained doctors in the island. Foolishly, the Jamaican law only recognized trained doctors from the London or Edinburgh licensing boards in the United Kingdom, on the basis of the private prejudices of the medical council in Jamaica, aided by the Jamaican government. He therefore recommended recruiting doctors from Canada specifically and having them placed on the same footing as those from London and Edinburgh. Ironically, four universities in Canada were recognized by the licensing board in England, but not in Jamaica. Furthermore, Canada was expanding materially and becoming an economic powerhouse and Jamaica could benefit from this relationship with Canada.[40]

Where Stafford is incorrect and short-sighted is in his critique of traditional medicine practised by the predominant black population of the island. He writes:

> The bulk of the Jamaica rural population consists of the peasant class who are unfamiliar with the general laws of hygiene and undisciplined by habits of thrift. The government has out of their humanitarian concern sent them public medical officers but clearly are limited in the number of doctors they can employ. As such, the only alternatives for many are the untrained dispensers or worse still the ignorant bush doctors and vicious obeah men and the sorcerer.[41]

Richard Sheridan and other Caribbean historians have highlighted the important contribution made by black and coloured doctresses during the period of slavery in looking after the ill in the hospitals and hothouses. On many plantations they were the core healers and were even recognized by many plantation managers and employed in slave hospitals.[42] The majority of the colonial elites would not accept that reality and affirm their contribution to the healthcare system. Recognizing and valuing African forms of healing would destroy the colonial myth of black inferiority and the need to civilize, retrain and resocialize the African population in a European world view.

Given the general poverty among the former enslaved Africans after slavery, the majority of the impoverished population continued to rely on folk medicine passed on to them by their enslaved, Maroon and free black ancestors. From the very interaction of Europeans and Africans in the Caribbean, scholars have identified two parallel but distinct healthcare systems in Jamaica: European (or biomedicine) and folk medicine (here used interchangeably with "traditional medicine").[43] Jamaican folk medicine was robust enough and had become creolized from the fusion of indigenous (Taíno), African, European and Asian immigrants. Despite its creolization, the African influence predominated.[44]

One of the interesting features of this form of traditional healing was the clear link between West African folk medicine and religion, although folk medicine has been negatively characterized by the colonial society and described as obeah, black magic, witchcraft and evil. The Maroons, along with many other spiritual practitioners in the black community, while not discarding European medicine, still took pride in retaining many aspects of their African religious practices. Obeah, for example, represented the positive and the noble application of African spiritual knowledge, used for healing, spiritual protection and addressing the problems of daily life.[45]

When resolution of a particular health problem was not achieved, or they were unable to visit a European doctor, most blacks resorted to their traditional practitioner. So three significant divisions of traditional practitioners were distinguished in Jamaica as early as the nineteenth century. First, natural practitioners, such as bush doctors (herbalists) and lay midwives. Secondly, spiritual healers, such as church healers, psychic mothers, revealers and balm-yard healers; and third, obeah practitioners.[46]

Revivalism and Healing

The large majority of poor and working-class blacks continued to depend on their traditional doctors in all three categories in the late nineteenth and the early twentieth century. What became characteristic by the 1880s was the clear link between Revivalist preachers and their healing ability. In the late 1870s and early 1880s the "Haddo Doctor", a black man named Stewart who claimed that Christ had endowed him with the ability to heal, was acknowledged as one of the most popular Revivalists on the island. He dispensed herbal tea as part of his prescription. At Haddo, in the highlands of western Jamaica, he established a balm or healing encampment. During the period of his greatest success, thousands of people reportedly visited the place, week after week. In mid-career, however, for unknown reasons, he gave up his calling and spent many years of penance in a tent. He subsequently settled on a site called Mount Grace near Mackfield. There his balm yard consisted of a score or more of small low-roofed thatched huts built very close to one another, from a distance resembling an aviary. At nights, he held Revival meetings where participants danced in a ring, singing Salvation Army choruses. When he died, over a thousand people, including many East Indians, marched in his funeral cortege.[47]

J.J. Williams was another famous Revivalist preacher and herbalist who had an encampment at Cameron Hill in St Elizabeth parish. His nightly Revivalist meetings were held, in a booth covered with coconut boughs, to the music of drums and cymbals, with much singing and dancing as members occasionally became prostrate and spoke in an unknown tongue. More importantly, Williams did not pick his herbs from around him, as some others did. He purchased herbs from a doctor's shop in Black River.

Williams also trained several young girls as herbal missionaries who went around the parish as publicity agents. In promoting himself as an authentic Revivalist preacher and healer, Williams highlighted his call:

> Poor people, for many years have been sick and suffering from all kinds of excruciating pains, bed-ridden, barreness, halt, and man-sufferings of all description, have been cured by the inspiration and influence of God's Spirit by the spiritual doctor. How I got my doctoring trade. I went to sleep one night in 1896, and after I fell into a short nap, I was troubled and jumped out of sleep finding myself on my two knees: there I prayed for about an hour, and after the manner I was stolen away by a subitaneous sleep quite subside. Then in my vision I saw a large white man who called me by name J. J. W. and I replied "Here I am sir," and the man said, "I have something for you and whatsoever I shall give unto thee this day let not man prohibit thee, and take away. For what I have give it is given, and what I take it has taken." And he took me away in the spirit and showed me an immense number of long sick-suffering people who have been boxed down for many years under the hands of their viperous and inhuman fellowmen. And I was asked by the man what I can do to these people; and I answered and said, whatsoever thou would'st. The man gave me a weed and many other lots of herbal and in a loud voice said, "go into all the world heal and cure the sick, as much as will accept you, and believing in the Lord Jesus Christ who died on the cross for sinners redemption." I am raised up by Jesus own self not to be a doctor only but also a prophet. Tell it out far and wide that the Lord has elicit a herbalist and put him in the midst of the sufferers in this island.[48]

Religious healers who worked in balm yards had become so prominent by the latter nineteenth century that they were targeted by the state as obeah workers and prosecuted as such. For example, in 1899, Samuel Reid, also known as Dr Reid, from Clarendon, faced intense persecution from the state. As part of his religious work, Reid kept a regular dispensary and hospital with a matron and other assistants. In one of his famous cases, in the treatment of one Sarah Fraser, he diagnosed her as having three duppies inside her which caused her illness. Fraser stayed at his hospital for three days, receiving treatment that involved taking medicine. In order to expel the ghosts, it is alleged that Reid threw Fraser on the ground and walked several times up and down on her body. He also squeezed and kneaded her stomach with his hands for the same purpose. He then flogged her with a supplejack and afterwards his assistants formed a ring around Reid also sprinkled her with some kind of medicine, which he said would cut the duppies' eyes "fine as linen". He also sold a cure-all draught described as "a decoction of boiled weeds", the recipe for which he had received by revelation, for one shilling per bottle.

The medicine was said to be popular with great numbers of the peasantry of northwest Clarendon and the adjoining districts of Manchester.[49]

By the 1890s, a new form of Revivalism had emerged in which black practitioners set themselves up as "convinced doctors".[50] They claimed that they were able to cure diseases with a draught of blessed water, interpret all mysteries and counter the work of obeah. Their message was that God had raised them as prophets and doctors to heal the oppressed blacks and to deliver them from the slavery of the white doctors and parsons.[51] W.F. Elkins argues that given the increasing rate of illnesses in the 1890s, it was not surprising that many such blacks clung to this form of Revivalism.[52]

Given the high rate of uncertified deaths, as much as 90 per cent in some rural districts, it is understandable why many Afro-Jamaicans clung to these Revivalist doctors for healing. Even the *Daily Gleaner* highlighted the poor state of healthcare and commented on the way many poor blacks "died like beasts in the fields".[53] The hospitals were sometimes so overcrowded that many of the sick were turned away. In 1912, the Kingston hospitals refused entry to more than four thousand patients, a member of the Legislative Council revealed in a letter to a British journal.[54]

There was clearly a relationship between the high rate of material poverty and the growth of such a Revival movement, given the demand of many poor Jamaicans for healing from their ailments. Smith's Lane in western Kingston is a good example, as it was one of the most densely populated areas where blacks lived and where material poverty was overwhelming. It also boasted a large concentration of Revivalist churches in the late nineteenth and early twentieth centuries. George Eaton Simpson posits that some sixty to eighty various Revivalist movements, ranging in size from twenty-five to two hundred members, were located in West Kingston within the period. These Revivalist groups rose and declined, given their fortunes, from month to month, and as leaders moved from one neighbourhood to another or increased or decreased in popularity.[55]

Among these later Revivalists, in contrast to the earlier Revivalists of the 1860s, it is striking that their gift of healing was more associated with water rituals. "Healing streams" became the literal source of health for the sick, and many individuals who became famous as Revivalist leaders relied on the healing waters of streams or springs in their neighbourhood. One Mother Knott, who started her Revivalist work at Corn Hill, St Mary, and later established herself at Black Hill in Portland, had water brought from a little stream at Corn Hill to fill the tank where she practised healing. This practice coincided with the rise of the greatest Revivalist healer of them all, Alexander Bedward, and his baptism in the healing stream of the Mona River.[56]

The Birth and Development of Bedwardism

As John the Baptist of the Bible is regarded as the forerunner to Jesus the "Christ", so too is Prophet Harrison E.S. Woods, otherwise known as Shakespeare, viewed as the forerunner to Alexander Bedward. The Jamaica Native Baptist Free Church in August Town, St Andrew, known as the Bedwardite church, was actually founded in approximately 1879 by Harrison Woods.[57] Shakespeare was one of the many black North Americans who voluntarily migrated to Jamaica. He lived in Spanish Town, and sources claimed he was called by God to live in the parish of St Andrew around 1876. Shakespeare followed the practices of an ascetic religious individual, who bonded with nature and lived a very simple life void of material pleasures. His home was either in a stone hole or a cave in the wilderness, from whence he habitually went on preaching missions, prophesying to various communities.

The Jamaica Native Baptist Free Church was born from one of those prophetic ministries in August Town. In June 1879, Shakespeare visited Dallas Castle, St Andrew, and prophesied destruction by flood, which some people claimed to have occurred on 11 October. It entirely destroyed a Wesleyan chapel and many other buildings and property, along with several lives. In December 1888, Shakespeare visited the village of August Town with a message, saying,

> Thus saith the Lord behold the sins of August Town have come up before me, and I will destroy the place as I did Dallas Castle, except the people repent. If they will come together, take their white cups, and hold to Me a fast, I will not destroy them. But if they will not repent and obey Me, I will sink the valley and make the two hills meet.[58]

During his visit to August Town, Shakespeare lodged during the day with his hosts, but in the evenings, in accordance with his prophetic lifestyle, he departed to the woods to spend the night in solitude and prayer.

He later gave notice of a general meeting of the three existing church denominations in August Town – the Anglicans, the Baptists and the Wesleyans – to hold a solemn fast unto the Lord, saying, "Thus saith the Lord, if the people will only observe the Fast and do as I command them, I will abundantly help them temporally and spiritually. But if they refuse to obey Me, I will sink the valley of Augustown, and close the hills." The people, chiefly Baptists and Wesleyans, obeyed and a goodly number assembled on 19 April 1889 in Papine. A very solemn and impressive meeting was held. The residents broke their fast at about 3 p.m that day. A few minutes before,

Shakespeare was reported to have said, "The Lord is coming and will soon be here."[59] Then there was the sound of a strong wind, followed by a light drizzling rain, and then a remarkable and general prostration. All were filled with the Spirit. After this, Shakespeare withdrew into an apartment where there was a large jar of water from the Mona River. Upon the jar, a Bible was placed, and he called in by name twelve men, and then twelve women, constituting them twenty-four elders. Each one in turn laid his or her hand on the Bible, while expressing the solemn vow to be faithfully devoted to the service of God even unto death.

On that occasion, Shakespeare made other very remarkable and prophetic utterances. Looking on the elders, he said, "There is one among you who shall succeed me, and be the leader of a great Religious Movement, which shall be centered right here in Augustown, and it shall be a blessing to millions. As yet however, I know not who he, my successor is." Shakespeare further prophesied that "Fruits would so abound in Augustown, that from various parts of the world, people would come to enjoy them."[60] At that time not even Shakespeare himself knew the nature of those fruits and that it referred to Bedward and Bedwardism. Also, "that a fountain would be opened in Augustown, but the man to rule it was not yet ready".[61] To many, that latter prophecy was ridiculous, given the natural sterility of August Town. Shakespeare returned to Spanish Town in 1889, but paid occasional visits to August Town, to see how the work prospered.[62]

When Alexander Bedward became the leader of the Jamaica Native Baptist Free Church, on 10 October 1891, it did not seem to many that he would be the great one to whom Shakespeare referred. Bedward shirked, refused and begged to be excused from the task, given his lack of education and his impediment in speech. But becoming convinced that it was his father's will, he acquiesced, trusting in the goodness of God to guide him by way of divine revelation.[63]

Bedward, who was born into an impoverished family of rural labourers in 1859, was the only son of his parents, with two sisters.[64] He seems to have been raised in Barbican, St Andrew, and became a labourer on the Mona Estate. Some accounts describe him as a cowherd and later a cooper there. He was also a renowned gambler and an adulterer, resulting in various problems in his marriage. Brooks describes Bedward's moral and ethical life as one of vice and folly.[65] Bedward even admitted in an interview that his moral and ethical life before accepting God's call as a shepherd was extremely awful. He had committed every sin possible except for that of murder.[66] Like many Jamaicans, however, his parents sent him to a

Christian church, the Providence Methodist Church, which is still adjacent to Matilda's Corner, Kingston, and later a church in Papine.[67]

One of the severe physical difficulties he experienced in his early adult life was poor health, along with a speech impediment.[68] This illness would later shape his ministry as shepherd of his church, as many poor Jamaicans like himself also suffered from health complications and needed miraculous healing. Bedward was afflicted with an unknown disease for thirteen years and woke up each morning with a high fever, his broad forehead drenched with sweat, and his insides feeling as if they were being turned inside out. The pain was so unbearable that one novelist, using contemporary language, writes that on such mornings Bedward would hold his head and bawl out, with much profanity, "Oh lawd! Oh lawd! Why de raasclawt dis here sickness won't leave me be?"[69] The doctors could find no cure, resulting in one of the possible reasons Bedward decided that a change of climate might best help him. He migrated to Colón, Panama, in 1883, suddenly, leaving his wife, alleged girlfriends and his seven children.[70]

Bedward's experience of racial discrimination in Panama seems to have contributed to his formation of a black racial identity. He worked on the construction of the Panama Canal, an exhausting and traumatizing experience. Along with hundreds of other labourers from the Caribbean, he worked long, arduous days in immensely hazardous conditions, before being boarded up at night like cattle in shoddy, disease-ridden shacks.

It was a humiliation that seemed to have left a permanent mark, as did the realization that while white workers from the United States and Europe were paid in gold, their black counterparts were paid in silver for the same work.[71] As many of the overseers were Southern whites, still smarting from the Civil War, it was perhaps inevitable that race relations would be strained, even bitter. This was a learning experience for migrants such as Bedward, who were also learning of the fragility of the political regime in Cuba and Central America and the possibility of competing strategies for social change. This Central American experience seems to have aided in the politicization of a number of Jamaicans who later became leaders fighting for social change. Such leaders apart from Bedward were Marcus Garvey and Rastafari founders Leonard Howell, Joseph Nathaniel Hibbert and Archibald Dunkley.[72]

By all these experiences, Bedward was being prepared for the mighty task which his father had called him to undertake. It underscored Shakespeare's prophecy that God was preparing a man for the task ahead of him. For thirteen years, Bedward was medically afflicted in Jamaica, but the moment he went to Colón, he started enjoying good health. Brooks opines that God must have orchestrated such a plan to get Bedward's attention.[73] Bedward stayed for two years in Colón in good health, but on his return to Jamaica in August 1885 he was immediately seized with the old disease.

Novelist Kei Miller describes humorously his return to Jamaica after two years in Colón:

> Bedward visited Jamaica with a thick gold chain around his neck. He walked into Augustown with two packed suitcases in his calloused hands, but before he reached home he leaned the luggage against the door of a rum-bar and there he sat, well into the night, buying quart after quart of white rum so that everyone was drunk from his charity and by the end of the night he had spent a good deal of his money he had brought back for his wife, his girlfriends and his seven children. He stumbled home at last, stinking of rum, climbed into bed beside his wife and before she could raise her voice against him, he put his hand against her mouth and pushed himself into her; that the next morning he woke up and felt a sickness that was more than just a hangover – it was the old sickness come back.[74]

Bedward left Jamaica days later, returning to Colón, leaving wife, children and all, with the express intention of never returning. In Colón, he resumed his former employment, but on this occasion his health was very bad, and for the first three or four days he went to work only to fall so severely ill that he was forced back to his bed. On the sixth night after his arrival in Colón, Bedward had two very remarkable visions. He saw a man who stood before him and said, "Go back to Jamaica. If you stay here, you will die and lose your soul, but if you go back to Jamaica, you will save your soul and be the means of saving many others."[75] Bedward retorted, "But, I cannot go, for having recently come here, I have no money to pay my passage."[76] "I will provide the means,"[77] he was answered. "Go to John Renford, Jos. Waters, Wm. Waters, and Robert Law, and ask them for the help you need."[78]

Bedward saw another vision, in which he found himself in Jamaica, going up the Constant Spring Road. When he arrived at a certain place there was a wide gate ajar, but a man passing in just before him hindered his getting through before the gate was shut. The gatekeeper was on the other side and asked Bedward for his passport. He showed what he thought was his passport, upon which the gatekeeper said, in an impressive tone, "But you are lost."[79] This so confounded Bedward with mortifying grief and anguish of soul that, with his hand upon his head, he turned back, crying at the top of his voice, "I am lost. I am lost."[80] He soon met another man standing by the roadside, who said to him, "Come here, did I not send you to Augustown?"[81]

"To Augustown?"[82] said Bedward. "Why, that is the place I am fleeing from."[83]

The man stamped his foot upon the ground so that the earth shook dreadfully, and with an authority which was awe-inspiring, said, "Go to Augustown, submit yourself to Mr Raderford (one of the leading elders at Shakespeare's Church) for instruction, with fastings on Mondays, Wednesdays and Fridays. Then be baptized, for I have a special work for you to do."[84] Bedward awoke to find it was a dream, and that he was still in Colón.

During the evening of the following day, Bedward and several others were sitting outside in the open air, when he saw a man in white approaching him, who in great anger said, "Did not I send you to those men for money to return to Jamaica? Why have you not obeyed?"[85] Bedward replied, "Yes, but I know they are not going to help me, therefore I did not ask them."[86] Then the man produced a whip with which he inflicted so severe a chastisement on Bedward that he was in agony. Those standing by observed with extreme astonishment as they heard Bedward's agony and heard him speaking to someone but did not see anyone else. This seems to have been a turning point for Bedward, who learnt through those visions that God was directing him to return to Jamaica and that he had to learn to be obedient. He left Colón and arrived in Jamaica on 10 August 1885, immediately commenced the formal preparations for baptism under Mr Raderford and was baptized by him on the second Sunday in January 1886.[87]

Bedward then worked on the Mona Estate and later became an elder at the Jamaica Native Baptist Free Church. As a fulfilment of Shakespeare's prophecies, Bedward was already receiving phantasmal visitation from the spirit of God. W.F. Elkins describes one such occasion:

> The evangelist awakened one night to a loud "pam", "pam", "pam" on the bedroom door of his house, the Mission House in August Town. "Who's there", Alexander Bedward called out. A voice came through the darkness ordering him to live apart from his wife. The "pams" then alarmingly transferred from the door to Bedward's ribs. Searching and finding no one, he went berserk. Neighbours tried to tie him up, but he fought furiously. Finally, someone hit him on the head with a stick. . . . In most of the occurrences a spirit appeared in the form of a man, a being Bedward came to identify as the Son of God. The spirit usually gave Bedward instructions.[88]

Bedward, after much internal struggle, accepted the mantle of shepherd of the congregation and was ordained on 10 October 1891. Either before or after his ordination, in one of his visitations he was instructed that water from the Hope River, an independent stream flowing out of a huge rock in what is today known as "Berry" in August Town (appendix 1), could be turned into medicine. For a week Bedward fasted. Then from the river he got a large jar of water, took it to his house and walked around it, praying, for several hours. He gave doses of the water to a woman who had been sick for years. She improved and became healthy. The story of the cure spread and sufferers of all sorts came to Bedward, the crippled and deformed, asthmatics and blind people, lepers and consumptives. The jar had to be refilled many times a day, as Bedward administered the water without charge. In another of his visitations, Bedward received further instructions to convert the whole of the river into a healing stream and to commence his public ministry. He should also maintain a public fast and pray three times a week.[89] So began his public ministry, on 22 December 1891. Bedward made his first public appearance at the Mona River, dispensing the water as medicine and baptizing people.[90]

Two hundred of his followers along with others gathered at the river that day to witness his initial public ministry. The crowd had gathered as a result of his healing successes, which were already known in the community of August Town and beyond.[91] On that occasion there were many sick people, but only seven would take the water as medicine, and it is alleged that they were immediately cured. The news of the potency of the water from the Mona River once Bedward blessed it travelled like wildfire all over the country, and all kinds of afflicted people with all kinds of diseases started coming to Bedward's healing stream.

The more reports circulated about Bedward's healing, the more people came from all over the country and packed into August Town to be healed by Bedward or to obtain bottles of healing water, which he sold. To add to his healing repertoire, Bedward was even alleged to have called an old bush doctor by the name of Allen to follow Jesus and to assist him in making traditional African medicine to help others in need. Allen seems to have significantly aided Bedward's ministry, as the possibility of complete healing further drew the crowd to August Town.[92]

Allen died subsequently, but the importance of providing traditional forms of medicine became embedded in Bedward's ministry. One Bedwardite recalls that her entry into the movement was the result of her severe illness and her parents' inability to pay for traditional healthcare. Her parents travelled all the way from the parish of Portland to bring her to Bedward when she was two years old, as she was very ill. Bedward told her mother to get a particular bush medicine and put it out in the sun and make a sign of ten over it and to keep bathing her with it. Bedward then encouraged her mother to persevere with the medicine. Her mother did and the child recovered, resulting in both her parents and herself becoming Bedwardites.[93]

Following Bedward's first public ministry in December 1891, every Wednesday morning he walked to the river with his followers. It is estimated that on some days as many as twelve thousand people attended. The audience consisted of barefooted peasants with bottles to receive Bedward's holy water, others with calabashes and other water containers. There were also buggies, wagons, mules, donkeys and pedestrians all over the August Town roads. Higglers sold their wares, with booths for coffee, tea, chocolate, pudding, beer, bread, fish and beer. Bedward wisely used the occasion to deliver a sermon to the multitude, standing on a huge rock overlooking the river (appendix 2). He then blessed the waters, inviting the people to bathe, drink and be cured. Singing hymns, the crowd would enter the river, using white cups to dip up the water.[94]

His healing stream in August Town, Kingston, which emerged from the Hope River, had become the most popular of all such streams in the island. Thousands of people from all over Jamaica and even from overseas flocked weekly to it for healing and restoration, and he gathered a large number of converts to his movement. Roman Henry, Bedward's secretary and treasurer, provides a vivid description of the healing stream and its sacredness:

> The stream is the same Hope River that supplies Kingston. The head of it is up Gordon Town and comes over Newcastle. A de same Hope River but it is only two hours in de days of Bedward that it turn into medicine, from 7:00–9:00. Bedward leave him the church yard at 4:00 clock and march down with the crowd of people to the riverside, singing all the while, Jesus, the water of life is giving freely, freely, freely. And as the sun come over the hill it call to Bedward and him look up wid the staff in is hand. And every sick, the medicine mix from in the sun to suit you. And Bedward fold him hand like dat – dat fe show you dat im touch anything. Him don't ask you what do you. The sun call to him as it come over the hill. Every-body singing until the flag wave. Any time the medicine complete to suit every affliction, the flag begin to wave. Jesus the water of life is giving freely, freely freely . . . but just wey de crowd is. Just where de crowd is . . . because the rest a people who don't believe, dem tek below dat, dem tek water for dem don't business with it. Some of them must have come to get water to sell. Some man try it, for a three rum shop was here and man say is pure water for it dem drinking the whole year. So man tek it, and throw rum on top of it . . . to drink. After him swallow it done, him tongue come out a him head about six inches. Him have to know that is something different.[95]

Another Bedwardite made the following observation on the nature of Bedward's miracles at the healing stream.

> Some have lame feet, some have big pregnant belly, can't have no baby and all these kind of things. And Bedward would . . . stood on a stone down the river there and pray and after he prayed people went in the water, drank a little, have their bath and when they come out they deliver a baby; bullfrog, bungle of hair and all kinds of things and get better. I understand that snake come out of some of them sore foot and the foot heal up after that. After him pray the water . . . and everybody just go in and bathe. People come down pon . . . carry down pon hammock. And after him come and dem go in the water and bathe, bathe done, him get up and walk, go home from August Town ya, go straight a country, walk on him foot.[96]

Revivalists in Jamaica were well known to rely on water as one of their sources of healing. Thus, Bedward was no different. Bedward differentiated himself, however, with the claim that God revealed to him by special revelation that the Hope River was particularly blessed for healing the affliction of the suffering masses. This was indeed a masterstroke which got the attention of the largely sick populace. To have people testifying to the river's healing properties when Bedward blessed the water differentiated him as a special man of God and authenticated him as a true prophet sent by God. Bedward recalled the specific role given to him by God through revelation. He said in an interview that the Lord told him, "Once I made water wine. Behold, now I make water medicine. And you have I ordained my Dispenser, Watchman, Shepherd and Trumpeter."[97]

Residents of August Town who moved into the community in the post-1930 period remember growing up with legendary stories they were told as children that the water which supplied Bedward's healing stream was independent of the two known rivers but flowed into them.[98] One older resident who knew Bedward as a child remembers that the Bedwardites placed a huge barrel on the bank of the stream under the rock to ensure that the water could be better contained. That is the reason the independent stream always had enough water for baptism and for bottling for the purpose of healing.[99]

Another resident even remembers the story that a goldfish, or a river maid, lived in the independent special stream of the rock.[100] That fish was the divine source behind the healing properties of the water, and it lived in the fountainhead of the independent stream. This was strongly believed by Africans and reinforces Bedward's strong affinity and link to African culture and cosmology.[101]

No wonder the Bedwardites were convinced that the independent stream from the rock, which was the source of the healing stream, was divinely given by God and was a sacred place. Roman Henry recalls how he tried to source water from the same rock for agricultural purposes by digging a well on the other side of the river. He was just about to acquire some dynamite to blast open a section of the huge rock, when he had a dream from the river maid not to proceed. He was warned that if he did, she would flood the whole of August Town. She was the one who walked through a little hole in the rock and travelled every night up the river head and guarded it.

By the next morning, another Bedwardite sister from Gordon Town told him that the river maid had appeared to her and told her that if he proceeded, he would lose one of his children. In the evening, another female Bedwardite from Jones Town told him a similar tale about the river maid. It was a clear sign to them that the healing stream was indeed a sacred site that, if tampered with, could lead to one's downfall.

The excitement of the Jamaican public surrounding the potency of the Hope River when blessed by Bedward resulted in some members of the medical profession lobbying the government chemist to take samples of the water to prevent a public health crisis. They were certain that the water the Jamaican masses were being given as medicinal water was contaminated. The common view of the masses, however, was that the government recognized that the water contained every medicinal quality, excepting those of castor oil; but the government could not acknowledge Bedward's claim that God had used him to make water into medicine as He had used Jesus to turn water into wine. No wonder Bedward was becoming a national treasure as the masses looked to him for healing.

It was not only the poor blacks who sought healing from Bedward; whites were also seen requesting healing, along with people from the "traditional" churches. One former Bedwardite, Sister Dixon, recalls:

> And the doctors could not get the people, for him mostly attract the people there. For some Catholic people did went there and them acolyte did get better by the water. It was a Father go there which the wife of a friend, and dat friend tell another friend working at the white people that him have a boy who was a acolyte in the Catholic path, and this boy get cripple, sick, and Father was tending to him but him can't get better. And this woman now tell him about this man in August Town. And the white woman bring him son up there.[102]

Brooks also records the testimonies of other Christians from traditional churches who claimed that they were healed by Bedward. He writes:

> I was for many years a member of the Church of England and felt quite satisfied with my formal profession of Christianity. In the year 1901, after having heard

of the Bedwardites, and made certain remarks against them, saying, "I would be the last one to go to Augustown," I had a vision in the night. In my sleep, I saw a white cup presented to me, and I received a powerful conviction with instruction in favour of fasting. I awoke with a very peculiar sense of joy and happiness, so that early in the morning I asked a certain lady to kindly buy me a pair of white cup and saucer. She answered, "Yes, I know what you want the cup for, and I will buy you the proper kind. I am a Bedwardite too you know." And so, I commenced the observance of fasting. Then, I began to continually see myself on the way to Augustown. Whether I slept at night or day I dreamed I was going to Augustown. Then I had a vision and saw a man in very white apparel stand before me and he said, "Go and be baptised." When, in my dream, I found myself on the bank of the river in Augustown with the same man, who baptised me and departed, leaving my underclothes in a bundle in which was a pure white dress which I did not know. Awaking, I felt that I was indeed baptised by the Spirit, and resolved to be baptised in Augustown, which I did soon after. Since that time, how wonderful has God been in His Providences in my behalf I can only say, Tis more than tongue can tell.[103]

Numerous other factors converged to herald Bedward into further national and international prominence. First, reports circulated among the general populace that Bedward had been blessed by God with the unusual power to stare directly at the sun for a long time without blinking or injury to his eyes.[104] Sun-gazing had roots in the wider context of Revival ideology. The sun is regarded as the giver and generator of life, a symbol of male strength and sexuality, just as the moon, receiver of the light of the sun, is the symbol of female fertility. This practice was not an isolated one, as several Revivalists were known to have performed this art.[105] Nevertheless, among many admirers of Bedward his ability to engage nature was attractive.

Secondly, people who knew of Shakespeare's prophecies concerning the future greatness of August Town were repeating to others and highlighting Bedward as the chosen one, saying the prophecy was being fulfilled. Doubts about the legitimacy of Bedward as a genuine prophet were now being cast aside. Under Bedward's leadership, August Town was becoming a fruitful centre and a spiritual blessing to the many sick flooding the community to be healed.

To further underscore Bedward's authenticity as a mighty prophet, people were recalling the story that he had predicted the terrible earthquake of 14 January 1907, which destroyed large sections of the city of Kingston. Almost every building was damaged. The subsequent fires, which lasted for three hours before any efforts could be made to check them, culminated in the death of eight hundred to a thousand people and left approximately ten thousand people homeless and $25 million in material damage. To complicate matters, shortly after, a tsunami was reported on the north coast of Jamaica, with waves of about two metres, or six to eight feet.[106]

Given Bedward's prophecy of the impending doom, around nine hundred people ran to him to be baptized, believing the world was coming to an end.[107] Bedward was said to have baptized as many as 750 people on another occasion, with the help of his twenty-four elders. These massive baptisms, which were frequent, would occur over two days.[108]

Third and most important was Bedward's identification with blacks and the oppression they faced under white British colonial rule. Bedward stirred up painful memories of the 1865 Morant Bay Rebellion and offered social and political criticism of the white power structure and its dealings with the poor masses. Although he practised baptism by immersion, as the native and traditional Baptists did, he legitimized African rituals by adding African ideas of the spiritual properties of water to this Christian rite. Using as a prototype Jesus's forty-day fast before facing his spiritual battle and trial, Bedward required his followers to fast and pray in preparation for war with spiritual and political forces in Jamaica.[109]

With Bedward's popularity soaring, thousands of people were coming not just for healing but for him to baptize them so that they could join his church and start other branches all across the island.[110] The Native Baptist Free Church had become so successful that it was able to build a massive house of worship in 1903, Union Chapel, which became the headquarters of the movement (appendix 3). The structure, which was not far from the Mona River, was built with stones drawn from the river and cut by masons. The building was an imposing structure, ninety-one feet long, sixty-one feet wide and twenty-four feet high. When finished, it was to house two floors or storeys, with galleries on three sides.[111] The land on which the church was built was in total around an acre and could accommodate many more buildings. For the Bedwardites, who were predominantly poor, to be building such an impressive sanctuary, so large, on such a large portion of land, was a monumental statement of their sociopolitical presence.

The Bedwardites cooperated voluntarily in building their chapel. Five carpenters who were Bedwardites, along with masons from the movement, all worked together on it, in addition to members who brought stones from the river. White lime, which they processed in a kiln, was used as the cement to hold the stones together. The bell for the church, along with hymnals, was ordered from overseas, however.[112] Even a non-Bedwardite donated £5 to the building of the church, as he claimed that Bedward had healed him, and he was not able to show his gratitude at that time. The

Bedwardites acknowledged that this generous giver held on to the £5 for a long period, until the appropriate time.[113]

The 1951 hurricane destroyed sections of the building. Despite the damage, the chapel was so impressive that residents of August Town and people who knew the building still refer to its monumental significance.[114] Historian Edward White remarks that this confirmation of a building cast in stone was a testament to the continued role of the 1860s Great Revival. It had produced a genuine competitor in Bedwardism to stand up against the traditional centres of community power.[115]

Given Bedward's popularity as a preacher, healer and leader, conversations about him were on the tongues of nearly all Jamaicans. It naturally aroused the hostility of many in the ruling echelons of the colonial class and its sympathizers in the media, the church and civil society. The newspapers, particularly the *Daily Gleaner*, sent more reporters to cover Bedward's public meetings; the police force sent both undercover and uniformed policemen to provide reports; ministers of religion, doctors and many other professional bodies all became interested in Bedward's messages and in his healing to see how they could trap him.

It was not surprising that a confidential medical report by colonial doctors was released to the public. It questioned Bedward's capacity for leadership, claiming he was dangerously insane and suffered from religious monomania. In short, the report made it clear that Bedward should be confined to Bellevue, the country's hospital for the insane. Since Bedward's family was too poor to follow the process of hospitalization with treatment, Dr Bronstorph had recommended that Bedward be let loose on the streets of Kingston for the police to naturally detain him and send him to Bellevue. Bronstorph claimed that some two or three women had brought Bedward to him for examination in 1892 at his office on Harbour Street. These women believed that Bedward was mad, as he had threatened to kill his wife and children. "He had gone on in the most extravagant manner, said he was a man sent from God, that God had appeared to him in a dream and that he possessed miraculous powers."[116] Another doctor, Cargill, also claimed, at Bedward's trial in 1895, that he too had examined Bedward and had also declared him a lunatic.[117]

With such comments circulating on Bedward's alleged insanity, the *Daily Gleaner* newspaper revelled in the controversy. Its various publications on Bedward supported the view that he was really insane. For example, it published a story about a woman who was too physically ill to reach August Town to attend Bedward's healing service. She commissioned a relative to go for the healing bottled water. On the return journey, the relative told some strangers of the miracles he had seen the water work. Someone offered to buy the "shut pan" of blessed water their informant was carrying. He sold it all at a good price and went his way until he came to a spring, where he filled the pan, which he then took to his sick relative, who eagerly swallowed a cupful and leaped from her bed, shouting, "Glory, I is now free."[118]

Overnight, Bedward's healing stream in August Town had catapulted him into national and international prominence. By 1895, Bedward's name was on the tongue of every Jamaican. Stories of his healing powers circulated to the point where he had become a figure of love, admiration and hope for the sick but was also immensely criticized and hated for his work. Poor blacks with their sickness and ailments flocked to his healing stream, while the colonial whites and their advocates, shocked at his sway over the black populace, started plotting ways to bring him down. Alexander Bedward and Bedwardism had become a genuine movement of resistance to colonial culture in the 1890s and would remain so for the next thirty years.

Chapter 2

The Fundamental Pillars of the Jamaica Native Baptist Free Church

The first fundamental pillar of the movement is its complete dependence on divine revelation. Bedward made it clear to his followers that God, via angels, had given him specific instructions or an order which had to be followed literally. Thus services at Union Temple had to start and end at a specific time, and if they went over, Bedward blew his whistle for all to know that they had to stop, so as not to offend the spirit who guided them. For night services, the lamp had to be lit specifically at 6 p.m. and service started promptly at 7 p.m. and ended at 9 p.m. They could continue up to 10 or 11 p.m only if it was a members' meeting or a very special event. At 9 p.m. the whistle was blown for service to end so that the angel who guided them would be pleased, as things had to be done decently and in an orderly way. Furthermore, at some night services, not more than nine people were to pray, so that the service ended at 9 p.m. These rules were embedded in their code of conduct and had to be strictly adhered to.[1]

Even the details of their litanies had to be literally followed. Only certain ordained leaders were entitled to lead services. Thus Deacon Allen, one of the first people Bedward ordained in that office, had a specific function outlined by an angel, as he oversaw preparing bush medicine for fasting. Only Allen could go into the medicine room and prepare the medicine for fasting, as that angel only knew Allen and would inform him of the specific bushes to pick and how to boil them.[2] Furthermore, in the assigned duties of the church, it was made clear that the deacons were fully responsible for collecting funds and leading the services, as they were so divinely ordained. The angels who kept guard over the services knew these deacons only, and hence other members could not lead.[3] It was clear that the Bedwardites believed that they had to follow specific instructions and could not depart from them.

The Bedwardites shared with fellow Revivalists this literal dependence on an angelic guide and angelic orders. Where the Bedwardites differed was in their understanding of their orders. They were to become a movement of restoration – to set things right and to do things correctly so that they could access maximum spiritual power.[4]

The Bedwardites also differed from fellow Revivalists in the manifestation of the Holy Spirit, the third person in the Christian Trinity. The Holy Spirit was far more important operationally for Revivalists and Bedwardites than the historical Jesus. The Holy Spirit was also more important than the Bible and its ethical appeals. These Revivalists and Bedwardites saw themselves as living in the demonstrable age of the Holy Spirit, who guided them through visions and dreams. The Spirit's role was sufficient ammunition in the Revivalist tradition and a clear rejection of missionary theology.

But although the Bedwardites depended on the role and work of the Holy Spirit to guide them through angelic orders, nevertheless, they were uncomfortable in accommodating various manifestations of the spirit, as Revivalists are accustomed to. "Getting into the spirit" by way of dancing and singing and drumming, as practised by fellow Revivalists, was forbidden for Bedwardites. They argued that their guiding angel should guide the believers without the use of the drum. Hence rule thirteen in their report of 1920, as seen in appendix 7, is as follows:

> The Society strictly prohibits what is commonly called Revival of shaking the head and tramping the ground and wallowing on the earth and saying: "It is the Spirit." Such are not Spirit that the Lord teach us to pray for those are the Spirit that works in the children of disobedience. God want is the Revival of the heart, a Revival from sin to grace, and a surrendering of the heart to God, that the Spirit of truth and grace may reign therein.

The second core pillar of the Bedwardites is the concept of an inward cleansing or a purification of the soul. This could only be accomplished first through baptism, which took place quarterly, followed by much fasting and prayer. These quarterly baptisms seem to have been spectacular, as they were usually attended by hundreds of people. One August Town resident who remembers Bedward as a child recalls that preparations started from Saturday night in Union Chapel, with their singing and their banners. It had become such a festival that people lined the road selling fried fish, jerk pork, bread and bammies. They sang all of Saturday night in the camp to prepare for baptism and left early in the mornings for the river, with Bedward as head and Dawson as his pastor.[5]

The sacrament of baptism in the Jamaica Native Baptist Free Church had not just religious but also political significance. Being baptized in the living stream (running water) meant much more than washing away sins and transforming the sinner into a child and elect of God. Baptism into Bedwardism meant that the baptized, in solidarity with other baptized members, vowed to fight societal and spiritual evils. It came to encompass the fight of the black lower classes against the evils of socioeconomic and racial oppression. At each baptismal service, Bedward instructed the newly baptized and reminded other members of the congregation that through baptism they were transformed into the elect of God, with a mission to bring an end to oppression forced on them by the government and the whites.[6]

Fasting and prayer for achieving inward cleansing were also fundamental to the movement. Bedward highlighted this important point with Beckwith that the candle and the tri-weekly fasts are fundamental in accomplishing this inward purification. All Bedwardites were expected to observe the fasting tri-weekly services (Mondays, Wednesdays and Fridays). Just as clothes are washed in the secular life, so the fasts are expected to cleanse the inner clothes. The three separate days were so ordained specifically, "a day for washing, a day for drying and starching, a day for ironing"; so the heart is made clean by the fasts. The candle was a symbol of the Christian Trinity. The tallow in the candle is like God; the wick is like Christ in the bosom of the Father; the flame is the Holy Ghost who came from the Father and the Son.[7]

It is important to emphasize that this preparation by the Bedwardites to be inwardly pure was not just for personal spiritual growth but to ensure that they were readily available to be used by God for battle, as they were being prepared for spiritual and political warfare. This political battle was for the purpose of breaking the power of British colonialism and its hold over black people. Roman Henry explains the importance of Bedwardite fasting:

> Bedward's task was to take away the ism from England; the sceptre and crown because it must return to Africa where it came from. To do that they had to use the weapon of fasting. They start from Tuesday evening 6 o'clock and not break until Friday 12 o'clock and eat and drink nothing. Seven hundred and fifty of them do that four times yearly to bound the dragon as Bedward reinforced the point that the father tell him to carry on the fasting to take away the power from England and send it back to the black man. So the work of August Town is to take away the power from the white man and hand it back to the black man because all the power that the white man have is black man him get it from.[8]

The Bedwardites further argued that as a result of the fasting the sceptre was now in August Town. Bedward had empowered the black race, as he had broken the power of the white race to rule the black race. That is the reason Ras Tafari could be crowned as "Haile Selassie, the conquering lion of the tribe of Judah". The black race must now appropriate their power and live it.⁹ To achieve more power and to live in that power the Bedwardites had to continue their fasting and steadfastness so that the glory and the symbol of God were not removed from August Town.

Barry Chevannes, in underscoring the importance of fasting for the Bedwardites, argues that "the prototype of this spiritual battle was obviously Jesus' fasting for forty days".¹⁰ Bedward's mission, as given by divine revelation, was not only that of a shepherd dispensing healing water but also that of a "watchman and a trumpeter". He and his disciples had to be inwardly pure to receive God's revelation, as they were called to be the prophets among the nations and to sound the alarm, the trumpet. This concept of being a "watchman and a trumpeter" seems to be an element of myalism in Revivalism. Such a watchman and trumpeter, going around the city preaching and warning of impending danger, has always been a common feature in Jamaican towns and villages. Chevannes notes:

> This figure has not entirely disappeared from the religious life of the people. Occasionally in Kingston one may still see the warner, usually female, enrobed, head wrapped in a turban, armed with a Bible and a palm frond, going out among the "highways and byways" and warning the people to avert imminent danger by turning from evil. In respect to this warning against evil the tradition shows affinity to Myal. The role of warner therefore had two aspects to it: that of prophesying the future and that of calling society to account for its corrupt violation of God's moral laws. Both aspects were integrated, in that the failure of men to lead upright lives merited the retributive justice of God, administered in catastrophes such as natural disasters.¹¹

Even the appropriate colour, given by divine revelation, had to be worn to these fasting services, for spiritual success in warfare. The requirements surrounding the tri-weekly fasts on Mondays, Wednesdays and Fridays were also important. Abstinence for those fasting services started around midnight. The day began with a public prayer meeting from 5 a.m. and lasted for about an hour. The notice bell rang at 11 a.m. and the table was then spread. At noon, the Fast or Duty Service commenced and continued for about an hour. The form of this service was remarkable. Long rows of tables were covered with white cloths, upon which each Bedwardite placed his or her cup and saucer in a row, on each side of the table. At the head were placed the elements, bread and the medicinal water. The tables were occupied by people clad only in white. Those who were clad otherwise sat elsewhere. All, however, partook alike and the minister at the head presided. The service was opened by singing a hymn, followed by reading of the Word of God with exhortation. Another hymn was sung, and prayer was offered.¹²

On rising from their knees, each Bedwardite turned up his or her cup while standing and the minister pronounced the blessing. The congregation was then seated while the elements were served. Then all stood with their cups in hand when the minister asked, "Are all in peace?" Only when the affirmation was given that all members were in peace with each other and with others would the prayer of grace be said, and each one lifted his or her cup and broke the fast. When all had partaken of the elements freely, the rows of cups and saucers were drawn to the centre of the tables and the cloths turned over them. A hymn was sung while the offering was taken up. Another prayer followed, after which the cups were again uncovered and drawn to their former places. The grace "We Bless Thee Lord" was sung, and the meeting closed with the New Testament benediction.[13]

The special three-day fast, which was three continuous days of fasting, was even more detailed, as, historically, it was the weapon Bedward used to maintain maximum spiritual power. The story is told that at Bedward's first baptism, when he baptized seven people, badmen surrounded the river and told Bedward that he would not have any baptism there. After singing for a while he decided to postpone the baptism. The boys went up the hill to the main road. Bedward then started the baptism while the badmen were gone. When they realized and returned to end the baptism, Bedward was already finished. God then instructed him that before the next baptism, he was to fast for three continuous days, from 6 p.m. on Tuesday until Friday at noon. Only then would he have power over his enemies. When he commenced this special three-day fast no one dared disturb their baptism or dared to bother him or make him fearful.[14]

This three-day fast was observed quarterly and immediately preceded the baptism of new Bedwardites, as they had to be immersed with this kind of power. These three days of fasting served the special function of invoking God's blessing on the baptism, and particularly on behalf of the new candidates to be baptized. On the Tuesday preceding the second Sunday in each quarter, at about 5 p.m., the fast began. Each one who entered it received a ticket, and all were admonished by the Shepherd to be true, and that if anyone felt that he or she could not hold out, and would break the fast before the scheduled time, they should not do so falsely. The three-day fast would thus begin.

Each morning at 5 and 6:30, there was a public prayer meeting. No one was expected to leave Union Camp before the fast was broken at about 3 p.m. on Friday. About noon on Friday, the service was moved to the open yard, where large jars of water were placed, and the shepherd, pastor and the two chief elders stood by them, while the people, all in white apparel, stood around. A very peculiar form of service was then begun by singing and praying, followed by the reading of the Bible and exhortation. Then the audience marched around, backward and forward, while their cups were filled from the jars. Then, at a given signal from the shepherd, each threw the water up in the air. They then marched around into the church, delivering their tickets at the door.[15]

Bedwardite Dixon recalls the seriousness of the three days of continuous fasting to empower new initiates into Bedwardism. Although her version differs slightly from that of Brooks, she states:

> And dem keep this June meeting, this three-day fasting. Some of the people tek up the fasting 12 in the day to 6 in the evening and some tek it 6 in the morning to 12, and break it. And some tek it 2 in the day and break it 6 in the evening. Is so the band of people dem march and go up dere and baptize. And who want to keep it up three days them go under a tree by themselves. And they have a nurse to get their mouth wash, bring basin and wash their mouth. You have to have your mouth cleansed, for dem don't eat nothing, no drink, nothing. And dem break it in three days; in the evening dem go pon de parade and break it 6 o'clock. The three-day people call it June meeting. And the people dem that break the fast baptize. All baby and all baptize in the river.[16]

Millenarianism

A third core pillar of the Bedwardites is the millennial view that the Bible makes specific reference to Alexander Bedward, who will culminate history with his Second Coming to the earth. With Bedward's return as Christ, the righteous will reign with him and the unrighteous will be judged.[17] Such a view is found in the book of Revelation, and the Bedwardites claim that the Bible points specifically to them and the end of time. The books of Genesis to Malachi were interpreted as the Father's Age; the books of Matthew to Jude as the Gospel Age; and the final book, of Revelation, Bedward's Age.[18] Chapter 7 of Revelation is even more important, as the Bedwardites view themselves as the specially chosen twelve tribes of Israel. What is more noteworthy is the view that the Bedwardites were the ones who have been saved and sealed by God as distinct. More important, they were the righteous remnant who were all dressed in white robes, as Rev. 7:9 states, "After this I beheld, and, lo, a great multitude, which no man could number, of all nations, and kindreds, and people, and tongues, stood before the throne, and before the Lamb, clothed with white robes, and palms in their hands."

This is the reason the colour white was so important to the Bedwardites, as it highlighted the Bedwardite era and his significance for the end of time. This also explains the white cups and saucers and white tablecloths. All the women had to wear full white, from shoes to head-ties, in attending their services. The men were not exempted from wearing white either. As Roman Henry stressed, "It must be full white, as the Book of Revelation shows the 144,000 in the Bible have on the father's seal out of the twelve tribes of Israel."[19]

It is in this millenarial context that Bedward identified with the historical Jesus and saw himself as the Second Coming. This allowed him to speak authoritatively, as his sermons were harsh and stinging. They were based on the Bible, but his application was critical of the colonial system and its auxiliaries. Bedward criticized particularly the established white preachers of the day and their black allies as supporting colonial values. Together, they kept the poor black masses in bondage rather than liberating them. These preachers, Bedward argued, would not preach without being rewarded handsomely by the poor, and the doctors would also not attend to the poor black masses without first being paid.

As stated categorically by one of the police sergeants, Nelson, who covered Bedward's meetings over a three-year span, the masses were flocking to Bedward's healing stream because he did not charge a fee for his services, unlike colonial doctors and other preachers.[20] The perception by the poor black masses that Bedward was their prophet and healer, and the mere fact that the colonial establishment was highly critical of him, further endeared him to the Jamaican masses.

Edward White comments on one of Bedward's sermons in 1895:

> Bedward delivered what was then the most radical sermon ever preached on Jamaican soil, injecting the tart invective of racial politics into the Baptist message of spiritual rebirth. He denounced the white establishment as "the Anti-Christ" sent to plague "the true people," and spoke of Jamaican society in terms of "a white wall" and "a black wall," two solid, monolithic structures, immovable and irreducible. "The Government passes laws which oppress the black people," the *Gleaner* reported Bedward as saying. "They take their money out of their pockets, they rob them of their bread and they do nothing for it." He also warned "the white wall" to "remember the Morant War," an ominous reference to an event in 1865 when the government massacred hundreds of black people who had taken to the streets in protest against poverty and racial discrimination.[21]

Bedward's distinct black wall and white wall, with the black wall positioning itself to tear down the white wall of oppression and victimization, was a call to fellow blacks to become more racially conscious and to appropriate the gains which Bedward made. Bedward was making it quite clear that colonial Jamaica was built on the racial premise that whites were entitled to political and socioeconomic privileges, and that was the significant reason for black oppression. More important, blacks had to take the issue of racial identity seriously and work to build black institutions, like his, which would be powerful enough to destroy white oppression. With the rise and influence of Bedwardism, they had already started to tear down the white wall, as Bedwardism had become a viable alternative to white traditional Christianity. Bedward's preaching had serious sociopolitical and economic implications, as Bedwardism carried the torch of black racial consciousness.

Marxist historian Ken Post shares the view that the racial nature of some of Bedward's sermons was in fact a call to his audience to take the issue of race seriously. He views Bedwardism as a religion with racial philosophical ideas. These ideas were planted in the minds of his members and would eventually be passed on to other suffering, poor blacks, thus preparing the ground for future peasant revolts such as the 1938 rebellions.[22] As Bedward challenged established white authority, both ecclesiastical and secular, and by making reference to the Morant Bay Rebellion, he was in reality setting off a political tsunami, which would later find political expressions in movements of national resistance. Speeches such as the following had to find political outlet: "The government passes laws which oppress the black people. They take their money out of their pockets; they rob them of their bread, and they do nothing for it. Let them remember the Morant War."[23]

While I agree that Bedward's sermon on the black wall tearing down the white wall fanned the flame of black nationalism, I disagree with some historians that it was a call to armed insurrection. Bedward's reference to the Morant Bay Rebellion was not an invitation to arms or violent protest.[24] While it has to be admitted that the reference to a black wall destroying the white wall was politically inflammable, Bedward's goal was to teach blacks that his movement was the alternative. He was the black wall and he was indeed tearing down the white wall in the present with his work and ministry. Bedward's black wall destroying the white wall is consistent with what theologians view as inaugurated eschatology – the here but not yet. Judgement on colonialism has already been started by Bedward's divine presence and ministry. Such tearing down of the white wall will continue in the present but will not be finally concluded until the last days. Black people will not have to wait for salvation in the future, since Bedwardism has already started. Bedward's kingdom is literally here and inaugurated but will not be fully consummated until the end of time.

Identity

The Bedwardites' self-identity was another important pillar of the movement. Such self-identification occurred in two domains: first in the form of representation and secondly with reference to itself as a movement. As stated previously, the colour white was significant to the movement, since its members saw themselves as the pure, righteous remnant – exemplified by white. Apart from the various liturgies for which members wore full white apparel, the colour white had far more relevance.

Fellow Revivalists utilized various elaborate multi-coloured robes and crowns for ritual purposes, their three primary colours being white, red and blue.[25] Other colours were also used, such as pink, green and yellow. The Bedwardites stuck with one primary colour – white. Revivalists relied on various colours for varying occasions. A white gown is used primarily for a secret working in purity, for healing someone who is physically or mentally ill. The white gown is even used by the Revivalist Shepherds when they desire divine insight in understanding a complex problem.[26]

Revivalists wear a red gown or cloth to express the blood of Christ and the love of Christ. Red will also be worn as a sign of sacrifice and surrender and for calling on the spirit of Jesus, the Christ, for cutting, clearing and driving away evil forces. The colour blue is primarily worn for invoking all the individual spirits and for a general conference with all the various spirits for greater understanding and insight. Pink is used for happiness, joy and peace, and green for understanding.[27]

Other African-led religious movements, such as Kumina, also utilized various colours for ritual purposes, such as green, blue, white, red, black and yellow. They used white for peace, purity and forgiveness. Oftentimes, they combined colours, such as green and blue for peace, love and thanksgiving; blue and white or green and white for peace and love. Devotees of Kumina relied on red for aggression, and combined black and another colour for danger, evil or punishment.[28]

The Bedwardites were preoccupied with their one colour – white. By adhering to one colour, the Bedwardites were distancing themselves from fellow Revivalists and from an overdependence on spirit manifestation. Although the Bedwardites stressed that they too were guided by a heavenly spiritual order and were highly spiritual people, it was clear from their regulations that they were firmly against entertaining too many spirits and their manifestation. As mentioned earlier, rule thirteen of their regulations encouraged moderation, decency and order.

Article seventeen was even more specific. Candle march, balm yards and the spreading of the so-called mourning tables entertained by fellow Revivalists were strictly prohibited for Bedwardites. Candles were only to be used in their vowing ceremonies or any other special matter approved by the society of the Bedwardites.[29] There was even an Order of Divine Service clearly given in article eighteen to ensure that Bedwardites didn't become too carried away with spirit possession.[30] It is clear that the Bedwardites wanted to be identified as a movement of holiness and purity, a movement which represented God's holy remnant, providing holistic healing of both mind and body of the poor and oppressed of Jamaica and the world. Hence white was the only colour that mattered, as it distinguished the purity they sought and their humility in approaching the God who guided them. It further explains their need for so many fasting and purification ceremonies, as previously explained.

The fixation on the colour white was so characteristic of the Bedwardites that Governor Probyn of Jamaica requested Dr D.J. Williams, the medical superintendent of the Kingston Lunatic Asylum, to comment. Williams assured the governor that the feature was satisfactory, as white represented their trademark of purity.[31] This further explains the reason full white regalia was worn in all their public engagements, such as their planned manifestation to Kingston in 1921, as seen in appendix 8.

Bedward's obsession with white is clearly misunderstood by Barry Chevannes. He argues that Bedward's comments to North American anthropologist Martha Beckwith, that in heaven his skin will be transformed to white like hers, revealed his affinity and accommodation to the status quo.[32] Chevannes is of the view that Bedward's affinity with whiteness represented missionary influence on him. This is not necessarily the case, as the colour white symbolizing purity predates European and North American Christianity in the Caribbean and the Americas.

In traditional African religion, colours, rituals, equipment, rhythm and songs were carefully chosen, prepared and practised. The primary colours seem to have been conceived from the human body and its secretions and were thus red, white and black. Red stood for human blood, white for a mother's milk and a man's semen, and black was for dirt, a person's shadow and the grave in which the body is laid. Thus white symbolized fertility, manliness, health and life and stood for joy. Nothing secret or dangerous was hidden behind the colour white. So it stood for honesty and visibility and had the character of revelation. The colour white, then, was the colour of the African ancestors, who possessed greater powers than the living.[33]

It is most probable that Bedward's comment to Beckwith was misunderstood. Bedward could have been alluding to the African concept of the spirit world, which was different from the Western understanding of heaven. For Africans, there was no literal heaven or hell where one goes after death, as believed by Europeans. When Africans die, they enter the spirit world, where the individual is ushered into the presence of the ancestors, who are usually adorned in white. For Bedward, not only were the garments of the ancestors white, but the ancestors themselves have become white.

This distinct symbolism of the colour white as representing purity and sacredness was common among a number of precolonial societies in Eastern Africa, such as the Abaluyia, the Baganda, the Watembatu and the Gofa. Those cultures use only white animals or birds for their religious rites, since white is their sacred colour. It is interesting to note that although white was a predominant colour, some traditional precolonial African societies used black as their sacred colour. The Bavenda, the Luo and the Nandi, all of Eastern Africa, and the Ndebele and Shona of Southern Africa sacrifice black animals to their gods, as black represents purity.[34]

It must also be noted that white represented innocence and rejoicing among the Ashanti of West Africa. Given the significant Ashanti presence in Jamaica, the point must be made that with missionary influence, the colour white for purity resonated with the former enslaved Africans, since it had religious significance in both African and European culture. As Steeve Buckridge noted, during African enslavement, the wearing of white dresses enabled some women to move freely and undetected between the established churches and the Afro-Jamaican religions.[35]

The second aspect of their identity was their fluidity as a movement. In reality, Bedwardism was an organization with a fixed membership with clear rules and procedures. On the other hand, it was also a flexible movement with a floating membership. A Bedwardite was not only a member worshipping at Union Temple, their headquarters, or in one of their chapters across the island. Bedwardites included people baptized by Bedward or one of his many pastors across the island but worshipping in other religious groups or attending other churches. The Bedwardites baptized anyone who believed in adult baptism and wanted to be baptized. It did not matter if you remained in your denomination or religious group and would not be seeking formal membership as a Bedwardite. Hence Bedward baptized many Anglicans and others from other traditional churches.[36] This was a brilliant strategy, as Bedward viewed everyone he baptized as his children. He was building a national movement which permeated other groups, churches and religions.

That is the reason it is difficult to verify the Bedwardites' claim of a membership of thirty-six thousand.[37] Satchell argues that although the census figures for 1911 and 1921 never recorded more than 1,135 and 1,309 members, in its heyday the movement attracted over seven thousand people.[38] Satchell further claims that the low recorded figures in the census resulted from the dual membership of many working-class Jamaicans, who would not publicly acknowledge that they were members of African-derived religious movements, given the colonial rejection of African values and ideas. Instead, they would highlight their membership in traditional religious movements which were accepted by the colonial society.[39]

Bedwardism also had international appeal, as indicated by members coming to Jamaica towards the end of 1920, to be among the faithful believers to witness Bedward's final manifestation. Such members descended on August Town from Cuba and as far as Colón in Panama.[40] Other Bedwardite stations were also believed to exist in other countries of Central America, outside of Panama. This would not be difficult to imagine, given the migration of working-class Jamaicans overseas for employment. The Bedwardites had organized effective cells overseas. Rosco Pierson has even argued that, given the large number of Bedwardites who migrated to Puerto Limón, Costa Rica, a missionary from Jamaica was chosen to minister and work among the Bedwardites who had migrated.[41] The extent to which Bedwardism had become international is seen in the British magazine *Britannia and Eve*, which devoted almost an entire issue to Bedward and Bedwardism.[42] This proves the influence of the Bedwardites numerically and sociopolitically.

The Bedwardites also claimed 125 local stations or chapters. This too is difficult to prove.[43] What can be confirmed is its seventy-three stations in eight of the fourteen parishes of Jamaica in 1920, as seen in appendix 4. The point must be made, however, that the 125 stations with the 36,000 members recorded by secretary treasurer Roman Henry are possible, given the movement's polity and practices. The Bedwardites allowed Revivalist bands to claim formal membership as a new Bedwardite station or chapter, on the one hand. But on the other hand, stations or chapters could also disassociate themselves from or even be expelled by the Bedwardites, as seen in their Rules and Report of 1920 in appendix 7.

If Henry counted everyone baptized by the movement, then his tally of thirty-six thousand was possible. If he also counted all bands which at one point were associated with them, the 125 stations are also possible.

Of the seventy-three confirmed Bedwardite stations in 1920, the parishes without a station were Manchester and the four Western parishes of St Elizabeth, Westmoreland, St James and Trelawny. Bedwardite stations were scattered all over the island, which highlight the national scope of Bedwardism. Kingston had the most stations, with twenty, and the parish of St Catherine had sixteen. Overall, the movement was listed in 1920 as having approximately 2,498 members. Although 63 of the 73 stations had a listed membership of under 50, there were stations like Beulah in the parish of St Mary with a membership of 213; Trinity Vale in Portland with 122 members; Bethalla in Portland with 100; Mount Nebo in St Catherine with over 100; Little Zion in St Andrew had 128; and Bedward's station at Union Camp had 465 members.

It is quite clear that Bedwardism was a powerful national movement. What is even more interesting is that the Bedwardites viewed their identity as a "republic". Their 1920 report stated clearly that owing to circumstances, their international churches could not send a report to be included in the annual booklet. Bedwardism, then, was both a national and an international movement. As one elderly gentleman told North American anthropologist Martha Beckwith, he lived in the 1860s and remembered vividly the Morant Bay Rebellion and the Great Revival which followed. Those events were most influential, as they consumed the entire world. "Today, the whole world is taken up with Mr Bedward."[44]

Chapter 3

The Arrest and Trial of Alexander Bedward

It was quite clear to the colonial authorities that Alexander Bedward, with his massive following numbering in the thousands, had to be silenced in the interest of colonial culture. The city of Kingston and towns all across the island were riddled with all kinds of Revivalist preachers like Bedward. While a number of them were flagged by the colonial government as dangerous, none was a more viable threat than Bedward.

Bedward was not seen as a violent individual, although his messages were race-based and his use of language and symbolism had a great impact. The viable threat was his influence on the thinking and behaviour of his large following. The colonial government feared Bedward's power over those whom they considered "as the ignorant and excitable masses", who were capable of creating widespread disturbance.[1] It is in that context that Bedward was considered dangerous, and he knew that he was being monitored and could be arrested at any time.

On Monday, 21 January 1895, around 7 p.m., Bedward was reported to have said, "They are coming for me tonight."[2] A few hours later, during the stillness of the night, a company of about thirty-one men with side arms and rifles surrounded Bedward's house in Union Camp, August Town. Bedward meekly said, "You take me like a thief in the night.[3] Why so many of you have come for me? If you had sent a child for me, I would have come."[4] Consequently, they placed him in a carriage between two officers. On either side of the carriage rode a horseman. Bedward was arrested on the charge of sedition.

On the following day, a Jamaican lawyer of Jewish descent who had studied overseas, Philip Stern, offered himself for Bedward's defence. Stern, who had not been practising long in Jamaica, was one of the few Jamaican lawyers who could practise both as a solicitor and a barrister. He was therefore adequately prepared. Bedward initially declined his offer but later accepted.[5] Bedward spent four months in the Spanish Town prison awaiting his trial. It was obvious that the charges were unsubstantiated, but Bedward had to be silenced, as he could not be allowed to succeed. He had to be humbled. While members of the colonial elite were happy that he was to face the court, Bedward's faithful disciples registered their disgust at the arrest of their prophet and stated clearly that the charges were absolutely false and groundless.[6] When the transcript of the trial is examined the Bedwardites were correct to argue that their leader was innocent and unfairly targeted.

Trial of Alexander Bedward

The trial began in the Circuit Court on 24 April 1895, before the chief justice, Sir Henry Burford Hancock. The prisoner was driven down Sutton Street from the station shortly after 9 a.m. in a bus, a small crowd of people running alongside. Over six hundred of Bedward's followers vigorously demonstrated outside the courthouse, some throwing stones at the mounted orderlies. However, they were soon dispelled by the authorities.[7] At the courthouse more excitement continued as numerous people gathered in the hope of catching a glimpse of the "Prophet".[8]

Bedward was dressed in white and this time appeared without his Bible. He was in good health, apparently, and had not suffered in that respect from his confinement. He took a sort of careless interest in the proceedings and occasionally looked up from his reverie and sent short messages to his counsel.

The specific charges of sedition against Bedward read as follows:

> He told them after baptism they had undertaken to throw off the oppression cast upon them by the white people and the Government. He spoke in a most insulting way of the Governor, the Government and the Clergy, designating the latter as vagabonds, thieves, robbers and liars, saying that they had filled our hospitals, alms-houses and prisons, that they were blasphemers and scoundrels who were worshipping Anti Christ, that he and Shakespeare (his assistant at the river) were the only servants of the true Christ and that they had been sent to stop all the tricks of the parsons and the Government, that he knew the police and the detectives were watching him but they could go and tell those who sent them that he defied them to touch him as he was right, that the Governor had refused to interfere with him. He called upon the people to drive out the white population who were oppressing them, holding out to them the fires of hell as their doom if they neglected to do it and reminding them of the Morant Bay Rebellion. He referred to the black population as the "black wall" and the white as the "white wall" saying that the white wall had long enough oppressed the black wall and that the time had now arrived when the black wall must knock down and oppress the white.[9]

The Prosecution's Case

Mr Oughton, in addressing the jury, said that the accused, Alexander Bedward, was charged with the crime of sedition – using seditious language. Before addressing them on the facts of the case, he would make one preliminary observation. It is pretentious to assume that any person of intelligence in the island who took an interest in what was going on here was ignorant of the existence of the prisoner or in a general way of the circumstances which gave rise to the prosecution. He had to remind them, in considering the case, that it would be their duty to consider the case dispassionately, calmly, having no regard to anything that they might have heard at any other time, or in any other place, but to return a verdict according to the evidence given there, and to do it fearlessly and truly.

The prisoner lived near the banks of the Hope River at Mona in St Andrew. A little more than three years ago, he commenced holding services of a certain description there, and that went on until on 16 January of this year, when he made the seditious address. On Wednesday mornings, he always had a special gathering when he blessed the Hope River, which would then possess certain curative properties. On 16 January a reporter of the *Daily Gleaner*, Mr Lanigan, was there at the bank, and Sub-Inspector Calder, and a crowd of about a thousand. Bedward came down from his dwelling at the head of the procession and eventually mounted a big boulder by the side of the river and addressed the crowd. Counsel, having read portions of the address, said they were taken by Mr Lanigan in shorthand at the time and contributed to the first two counts of the indictment. Inspector Calder's statement contributed to the other two counts.[10]

Mr Oughton then sought to define sedition for the jury. It is a comprehensive term covering all practices, whether by word, deed or writing, which are calculated to disturb the tranquillity of the state and lead ignorant persons to endeavour to subvert the government and the laws of the empire.

> Sedition could also be defined as containing all behaviour, whether by word or deed, to excite discontent or dissatisfaction, to create public disturbance or to lead to civil war. It could also be defined as action leading to hatred or contempt of our sovereign leaders, or the Government, the laws, or constitution of the kingdom, and generally, all endeavours to promote public disorder. Sedition, then is high misdemeanour, punishable with fines and imprisonment.

Oughton submitted that sedition was embedded in Bedward's address to the crowd. In using such language as "Hell will be your portion if you don't rise and crush the white wall", "The white wall has been oppressing you", "Remember Morant Bay War", Oughton wondered whether the whole character of the address was not calculated to excite discontent and dissatisfaction. He would humbly submit that Bedward's address was intended to lead the crowd into such a state and condition that they would be persuaded possibly to try and emulate the proceedings of the Morant Bay Rebellion of 1865.[11]

Evidence of Mr Lanigan

The prosecution then called John Lanigan, subeditor and reporter of the *Daily Gleaner*, to first provide evidence. Lanigan stated that he knew the accused. On Wednesday, 16 January last, he went to Hope River, St Andrew, about 6 or 7 a.m., to a place called the Mona water. When he got there, several people were lying about on the banks of the river, some washing themselves in the river and evidently waiting for something. The number increased until about 8 a.m., when the prisoner, accompanied by two hundred to three hundred persons, came down to the riverside in a procession. The prisoner and one or two others, so far as he recollects, carried banners heading to the crowd. On arriving at the riverside, the prisoner and some others who appeared to be leaders mounted a large boulder; hymns were sung, and prayers were delivered, and the prisoner commenced to address the crowd. He took down the greater portion of the address in shorthand, which was handed to the clerk at the preliminary hearing. About one thousand persons were present. The great majority were black men.[12]

Bedward gave out a text from Matthew 16. It commenced about the Pharisees and the Sadducees. Lanigan took shorthand notes at the time. On his notes are these words: "The Pharisees and the Saducees came and tempting." Then the accused spoke as follows: "Brethren, the Bible is difficult to understand. Thanks to Jesus, I am able to understand it. Thanks to Jesus and blessed be his holy name; I can understand it and I the servant of Jesus will tell you. The Pharisees and the Sadducees are the white men. We are the true people. The white men are hypocrites, robbers and thieves. They are all liars."

The prisoner then read the second and third verses. The words are: "And in the morning, it will be lowering to the words 'signs of the times.'" He then spoke as follows.

> Yes, brethren, it will be foul weather. Can ye not discern the signs of the times? The white men are hypocrites. I can discern the signs of the times. Look over there at the top of the hill, you see white things which you call clouds. I tell you they are not clouds, they are angels, and the angels are telling me what I am

telling you now. The ministers are thieves and liars and worship the Antichrist. I am the true servant of the true Christ.[13]

He then referred to Revelation 11 and read the words, "And I will give power . . ." He then said, "Bedward and Shakespeare are the two witnesses. Shakespeare is a man with whom I had spoken and who took a part of the service." The prisoner read again, "And they shall prophesy, one thousand two hundred and sixty days." He expressed it as 1,203 score. The accused then addressed the people again, saying: "I have been prophesying to you for three years and I tell you the time is near at hand. They have tried to stop me, but they could not do it"; and he read again: "If any man will hurt them, fire proceeded out of their mouth and devoureth their enemies, and if any man will hurt them, he must in this manner be killed."

Bedward also said:

> See, here are constables, corporals and inspectors. I defy them to arrest me. They may kill the body, but they cannot kill the soul. Let them come up here and arrest me. They cannot do it. I defy them. Brethren, hell will be your portion if you do not rise up and crush the white man. The time is coming. I tell you the time is coming. There is a white wall and a black wall and the white wall has been closing around the black wall, but now the black wall is becoming bigger than the white, and they must knock the white wall down. The white wall has oppressed us for years. Now we must oppress the white wall. The Government passes laws that oppress the black people. They take their money out of their pockets. They rob them of their bread, and they do nothing for them. Let them remember the Morant War. I tell you that the Government are thieves and liars, and the head of the Government and the Governor is a scoundrel and a robber. I defy them to arrest me. What I say is true for Alexander Bedward is the true prophet of Jesus. The ministers of religion look after the money. They are thieves and liars, and they only want your money. They are blasphemers. I say so. They do wrong that good may come and they worship the Anti-Christ. The constables and inspectors are scoundrels, and I laugh at them and defy them. The ministers can do nothing for you. The only thing that can save you is the August Town healing stream, and Alexander Bedward is the prophet of Jesus and can save you.[14]

There were about one thousand people present. He made a note at the time. In referring to the white wall and the black wall, he understood Bedward to speak of the white people and the black people of this country. The crowd he was addressing was composed as follows: a little over half were women, and the remainder men and youths. They were Jamaicans, he believes. In using the words "Brethren, hell will be your portion if you do not rise up and crush the white", the "you" here referred to those whom he was then addressing. These were principally black people.

When he used the expression "The Government are thieves and liars", he understood him to mean the Government of Jamaica, and any person who took part in the government, the governor and any or all of his council. The words "The Government passes laws to oppress the black people. They take their money out of their pockets, they rob them of their bread and they do nothing for them. Let them remember the Morant War" he understood were meant to be used as a threat to the white people and the government of Jamaica. He understood by the "Morant War" an insurrection which occurred at Morant Bay in 1865. During his evidence Mr Lanigan repeated a remark of the prisoner that he and Shakespeare were the witnesses to Christ.

Asked by Mr Oughton what exactly Bedward meant by the "black wall and the white wall", Lanigan stated categorically that it referred to the black people and the white people of Jamaica. Mr Oughton further enquired what Bedward meant by the phrase "Hell will be your portion if you do not rise up and crush the white wall". Again, Lanigan stated that his understanding was that the black people were being oppressed and they were to rebel. He understood Bedward's reference to "remember Morant Bay" to refer to the insurrection at Morant Bay about thirty years earlier. By his reference to the government as thieves and robbers, he took him to mean the government that was administering the country.[15]

Inspector Calder's Testimony

The second witness called by the prosecution was Sub-Inspector of Police William Jameson Calder. He testified that in January last, he started acting for the inspector for St Andrew. He knew the accused, Alexander Bedward, and he saw him on 16 January last, at the side of the Hope River in the parish of St Andrew. He was talking to a crowd of six or seven hundred people and using quotations from the Bible. Bedward was standing on a large stone, and he, Calder, was two or three yards away. He categorically heard Bedward say among other things that the white people were hypocrites, liars and thieves; the ministers of religion were rogues and vagabonds; that there was a white wall and a black wall; that the white wall had been closing round the black wall, but now the black wall was stronger than the white wall and that the black wall must now crush the white wall; that the Pharisees and the Sadducees were among us today; they are the true people; the white men are liars, the governor is a scoundrel and a robber. The governor and the council pass laws to oppress the black people, take their money from their pockets, deprive them of their bread and do nothing for it.

Calder further testified that Bedward said the following:

> Tell your ministers, I say they are scoundrels, that they fill your almshouses, hospitals and your prisons. I have a sign that the black people must rise. Remember the Morant War. The fires of hell will be your portion if you do not rise and crush the white people. The only thing to heal all diseases is this Hope River water for it was blessed by me, the true prophet of Christ. The Governor can't stop me, and the police are here, and I defy them to arrest me.[16]

Bedward then referred to the clouds passing overhead as angels. With reference to the white wall and the black wall, he understood Bedward to mean specifically the black people and the white people. When Bedward referred to the governor, he understood him to mean the governor of Jamaica, the Privy Council and the Legislative Council. When Bedward said the fires of hell, he understood him to mean that if the people did not rise against the white people, create a rebellion or something of the sort, they would be punished severely hereafter. When Bedward referenced the Morant War, he understood him to refer to the rebellion of 1865 in Morant Bay. In clarifying the notes he took on his shirtsleeves, he emphasized that the original notes had been washed out. Nevertheless, he had transcribed them from his shirtsleeve in a report the same day. That report was immediately sent to the governor of the island.[17]

James Rainford Taylor's Testimony

The third witness called by the prosecution was a rural policeman by the name of James Rainford Taylor. Taylor testified that on 16 January, he was at the Hope River and heard the prisoner address the crowd: "I am Alexander Bedward, listen to me. There is many Sadducees and Pharisees here now, but they can't do me nothing. There is a white wall and a black wall. The white wall is keeping down the black wall for a long time, but now the time is come when the black wall to put down the white wall."[18] Bedward's statement was clear to him, that there should be no confusion between the white people and the black people. Bedward said emphatically that all the ministers, from the bishop and everyone else, were thieves and robbers. The governor himself will have to come to him, Bedward, because he was the head. They can do as they please, but they could not arrest him because he was safe. The black people were the true people, and the white people were hypocrites. Having heard that, he left while Bedward was still on the stone pulpit preaching.

But Taylor, when cross-examined by Mr Stern, proved to be a pawn of Inspector Calder. It was clear that Taylor abhorred Bedward and saw him as a fraud, a trickster and a false prophet. Taylor admitted that he was a Christian preacher with both local and international experience and he was not pleased with Bedward's attacking the ministers of religion. He disagreed with much of Bedward's teachings and thought that Bedward should have been arrested a long time ago for heresy. It was clear to him that Bedward had not been trained to expound the scriptures.[19] When asked by Mr Stern if jealousy was not the reason he was so averse to Bedward, Taylor admitted to the court that he was ordered there by Inspector Calder, who did not know that he was a catechist. Furthermore, he was not jealous of Bedward, as members of his church had not joined the Bedwardites, as had been the case with other traditional churches.

Daniel Wilson's Testimony

Wilson was the fourth person called to support the prosecution. He lived at August Town and was on his own premises at the riverside on 16 January. He was about seven or eight steps from Bedward, who was standing on a stone. He heard him say, "We are the true people. The white folks are trying to keep down the black folks. They are thieves and liars. They are robbing the poor black. The Governor was a thief, he is actually taking the money out of the poor black people's pockets. He is a scoundrel. He would have the Governor and the Queen under his foot-bottom."[20] He moved off thereafter and did not pay proper attention to what he said afterwards.

Stern, in his cross-examination of Wilson, argued that he was a rival of Bedward, and thus an unreliable witness. Although he was an engineer by trade, he was a small pedlar who sold items of little consequence four or five days of the week. He too had a spring in his yard but could not compete commercially or spiritually with Bedward. His spring was adjacent to where Bedward gathered his congregants. Wilson, although downplaying the impact of Bedward's operations on his spring, however, highlighted the damage it did to his spring, as it deteriorated, given the hundreds of people following Bedward. He noted that "people come down there and break their demijohns and throw them among my cresses, which are cut out and damaged. . . . They could come as much as they liked once they did not damage his place. When they damage it, he would like it to be stopped."[21]

The Case for the Defence

Mr Stern's first concern was the special jury, which seemed to have been specifically constituted to judge Bedward. Mr Stern argued that he did not desire to have the jury which had been empanelled, as they were collected from the wrong list and their empowerment was illegal. His Honour the judge decided that no objection could be made to the special jury.[22] Despite repeated pleas from Mr Stern, the judge remained unmoved and ordered Mr Stern to sit down and be quiet, as he stated firmly, "I won't hear you any further upon the point." Mr Stern sat down, and the case proceeded.[23]

In his opening statement before the jury, Mr Stern argued that this was one of those cases which ought to have been laughed out of court. A poor half-witted creature, Lanigan, a reporter wishing to make a nice, interesting and pretty article for his paper, without knowing at the time that any charge was to come out of it, or that he would have to go subsequently into the witness box and swear to it, started making a fancy sketch, here and there, undoubtedly, prescribing words attributed to Bedward that he did not say.

That was the beginning of the story. Lanigan took it for granted that he need not tell his audience that the grand language which appeared in the *Daily Gleaner* newspaper, and which Mr Lanigan had given to them, never fell from the lips of Bedward. Indeed, as Mr Lanigan told the court, he could not capture verbatim Bedward's words, since they were in Jamaican dialect. Translation was a very dangerous thing in relation to specific charges surrounding the issue of words. There could be no doctrine sounder in relation to that of slander. In indictments for sedition, or anything whereby a man was imperilled by the use of words, the *ipsissima verba*, the very words themselves, must be placed before him and not the florid, free translations of a clever reporter.

That was the basis of the whole thing. Subject to the correction of the learned judge, they would agree with him that Lanigan's flawed report of Bedward's sermon was really the lynchpin behind the charge of sedition. A reporter wished to write an article. The language in his notebook did not represent the exact literal words as they were said, and therefore it was not a shorthand report. It must be as clear as noonday that Bedward could not speak the English language so fluently as had been ascribed to him by Lanigan. It was impossible for them to believe that Bedward delivered that really clever, but very wicked, speech with the connection and a flowing language of a practised orator. He would prefer to believe the two non-educated witnesses.

Bedward was far from being an orator and could merely string together a few disjointed sentences. Look at the connection of the whole thing, Stern remarked. In Lanigan's report, the language and the logical sequence were that of a practised orator. He had listened to many clergymen and he had not often heard anything better. It was a good sermon, of which no one would complain of the length, the manner and the flow and diction. That was not the language of Bedward, a man who could not write and who could only read the Bible in a halting fashion.

Lanigan was the author of all that, Stern stressed. He had ascribed to his memory what had been the result of his imagination and dressed up a beautiful sermon. He supposed they knew that many divines in London got their sermons from journalists. Most likely, Lanigan had done the work, for the sermon was the work of a man who had done it before. If that was not a sample of educated intelligence, he was a fool.[24]

Mr Stern then addressed Inspector Calder's evidence, as that of a junior officer who was hankering for promotion. Policemen Nelson and Hall, who were down as witnesses, were never called at the preliminary hearing, but immediately after the hearing they were sent away to other parishes – a very strange coincidence. Wilson and Taylor were simply rivals of Bedward, and there was no placing any dependence upon their evidence. He contended that preachers such as Bedward did a great deal of good and referred to the work of the Salvation Army as an illustration. For three years Bedward had been at Mona, and they had never heard of sedition before. On the contrary, from first to last, one of his injunctions to the people was to be peaceable.[25]

He hoped the jury would not give in to the stereotype that a white jury would automatically convict a black man. It certainly was a curious circumstance that a special jury had been called in the case. If they believed that the evidence was true that Bedward was not aware of the importance of the language or had no guilty intent, they could not find him guilty. If they thought that Bedward was not a responsible man, they must hold that he could not feel the consequences of this act and that would be a very happy solution to a very grave matter.

The country had already been besmirched with the taint of sedition, and they were only getting over it. The people of Jamaica were not a seditious people and were fond of the law. He wished earnestly that the special jury of white gentlemen, considering the charge of sedition in the statement, that the black wall would close round the white, would find it inconsistent with the evidence produced – and find Bedward not guilty. They had a great chance of doing "poetic justice" to themselves and the country.[26]

Regarding the specific accusation against Bedward, Mr Stern then highlighted the serious problems with the case and why Bedward ought to be acquitted. First, the official police report and the method by which information was collected, stored and transmitted were highly questionable. John Lanigan was a zealous *Daily Gleaner* reporter whose report was not a verbatim account of what Bedward said. It could not be used as the primary source to prosecute Bedward.[27] How could the court be sure that what was attributed to Bedward as verbatim words were correct, when he communicated in a Jamaican dialect, which had peculiarities that Lanigan, as a foreigner, could not easily understand?[28]

Stern's argument seems quite logical, as Lanigan, under cross-examination from Stern, acknowledged that his report was in the interest of the *Daily Gleaner*. Lanigan claimed:

> Up to a certain point I took a verbatim report, and afterwards stray notes. I did not take the whole speech from beginning to end. I remained there until the end. I use my own judgment as to what I took down and what I don't in the interests of my paper. What I did not take would not have spoiled a fair and impartial report. I wasn't taking notes for the purpose of giving evidence, but for the paper. A reporter would be very lax in his work if he did not always take notes with a full sense of responsibility.[29]

Lanigan further admitted under intense cross-examination from Stern that stories about Bedward brought more profitability and visibility to the *Daily Gleaner*. The general public believed that Bedward was crazy and the public would be most interested in his activities at August Town. Lanigan then admitted: "When I saw him first, I certainly should have said he could have done with a little more sense – that he was not rational occasionally. . . . I believe I wrote an interview with him in which I said he was scarcely responsible for what he said or something to that effect." Stern then reinforced his point to the jury that Lanigan's admission of Bedward's alleged insanity affected his sensationalization of Bedward's sermon. Lanigan's goal was to sell more copies of the *Daily Gleaner*. Thus, the accuracy and the authenticity of Lanigan's report were secondary, and that was what made his report highly suspicious.

On his second major point, Stern also questioned Inspector Calder's assertion that he initially wrote notes on his shirtsleeve. Stern asked the jurors rhetorically how Inspector Calder's statement could be taken seriously, that he had taken verbatim notes on his shirtsleeve before transcribing them. He then asked Inspector Calder, "Did you keep a copy of those notes?"

"I did," replied Inspector Calder.

The judge, however, interrupted Stern by pronouncing "that a copy of the original notes would not be taken into evidence". Despite Mr Stern's objection and protest that Inspector Calder could be subpoenaed to produce it as evidence, the judge made it clear that he would not tolerate that line of questioning and that he should get on with the case.[30]

Calder seemed to have lied to Stern that he had a copy of the transcribed notes. Stern asked Lanigan under cross-examination if he saw the notes on Calder's shirtsleeve when both men had breakfast that very morning. Lanigan replied. "I had breakfast with him. I did not compare notes with him. I did not see notes on his cuffs. I am not intimate enough with him to know about his laundry. It would require long sleeves to take down that speech. I did not see notes. Inspector Calder told me he had taken notes; he saw me taking notes. I never compared notes with the Inspector."[31]

Stern then argued that there had to have been collaboration by Calder and Lanigan the very day Bedward was arrested, in creating a single narrative. They seemed to have shared notes, as their reports were similar. More important, they met together for breakfast on the day of the arrest, which was too much of a serious coincidence. Stern's argument about collaboration is most relevant. Lanigan claimed that he had travelled to August Town to hear Bedward's sermons on several occasions with his own transport, and on those occasions Bedward did not preach sedition.

It is rather strange that the first time Lanigan was transported to August Town by Inspector Calder was the very day Bedward preached a seditious sermon. Why would they travel together that morning – the very morning Bedward allegedly preached sedition – if it was not planned by Calder and Lanigan? Was it also impossible to believe that Calder and Lanigan did not share notes while they had breakfast together, having heard Bedward preach an alleged seditious sermon? Furthermore, they had breakfast at Inspector Calder's house, and the two men never met again for any other social engagement. Why would Lanigan meet Calder at his house that very morning?

Calder, in attempting to argue they had not collaborated, noted "that they drove down together arriving home at about one in the afternoon and that he was the one who invited Lanigan to breakfast. They only talked generally about Bedward's proceedings but did not compare notes. Although Lanigan stayed about an hour, they did not talk particularly about the speech."[32] The collaboration between the two men seems undeniable.

The Evidence of Sergeant Nelson

The most important revelation in Stern's defence, however, was the conspiracy of Inspector Calder to suppress the truth in regard to Bedward's sermon on 16 January. Stern claimed that police sergeant Robert Nelson's interpretation of Bedward's seditious sermon differed from that of his inspector. Nelson was a twenty-seven-year veteran of the police force, who had spent the last twenty-one years stationed at the Half Way Tree police station. He was immediately transferred to another police post after he refused to support the inspector's interpretation of the sermon.[33] Nelson had been specially sent by the previous inspector of the Half Way Tree police station three years ago to visit August Town weekly and record all of Bedward's sermons. Over the three-year span he had been carefully watching and listening to Bedward and had never found any of his sermons seditious.

Nelson's first and second reports of Bedward's alleged seditious sermon were both refused by Inspector Calder, who insisted that they were insufficient and not fulsome.[34] After Calder ordered Nelson to correct his second submission and realized that he would not, Nelson was transferred to a police station in Port Maria in the parish of St Mary, on 1 February 1895. Another police corporal, Hall, whose testimony Inspector Calder disagreed with was also transferred from the Half Way Tree station and was also not called at the preliminary investigation.

In court, Nelson made it clear that the sudden transfer was not a promotion, as was the seeming tradition for such quick transfers. He was also not transferred for any misconduct, as he would have been aptly reprimanded before the transfer, and he was not. Nelson had no idea why he was being transferred and frankly did not like the transfer.[35] Nelson further stated the following after he gave Inspector Calder his second report:

> He asked me if I had seen the warrant and I said no. He told me then to come to Half Way Tree and he would show it to me. I did so; he read the warrant to me containing the words charged. He asked me if I heard any of the words charged in the warrant and I said, "No." He got annoyed and said I must write my statement. I did so and gave it to him. This occurred on the Saturday after the 16th January. At the police examination, my name and that of Constables Hall and Foster were given in for the prosecution. We turned out to court but were not called. Corporal Hall was transferred to St Thomas-in-the East at the same time as I was transferred.[36]

Nelson's report raises critical questions in the government's case that Bedward had been guilty of sedition. The government argued that Bedward's analogy of the black wall crushing the white wall was an admission that Bedward was calling on blacks to take up arms. Nelson, while admitting that Bedward used the analogy of the black wall and the white wall, argued that his understanding was different. The white wall was a reference to the white doctors who were charging high prices for medicine, but not healing the people. That was the reason Bedward's healing services were in demand. Second, the white preachers and black ones who supported them were also at fault, as they propagated certain ideologies which kept the masses in bondage. Thus, Bedward had made no verbal assault on the governor nor the ministers of state. His attack was constantly on doctors and pastors who conspired against him and his movement.

Nelson stated categorically that Bedward gave a stinging rebuke against "the preachers who won't preach without money and the doctors who won't see you without money, and that is why the people went to the stream without money".[37] Nelson further emphasized that Bedward did not say that "all white men are hypocrites, liars and thieves", as such a statement would have been clearly remembered. What was clear to him was that the whole sermon was against doctors and colonial pastors.

Nelson further clarified the reference to Morant Bay as a symbolic reminder of the judgement of the people against the corrupt doctors and preachers. Nelson stated, "It is not true that he told the people to remember the Morant Bay War of 1865. He said the ministers and doctors went to the Governor to arrest him and the Governor told them, no! They must remember the Morant Bay War." Nelson also refuted the claim that Bedward accused the governor of Jamaica of being a scoundrel and a robber. Nelson noted that if he had said so he would have personally arrested him. Nelson was quick to add that he heard Bedward abuse one of the doctors, Cargill, and he, Nelson, told the doctor immediately. He concluded that Bedward used no seditious language nor said anything which would excite the people to rebel.[38]

Under cross-examination by Mr Oughton, Nelson emphasized that he had never had a bath at August Town and shared no allegiance to Alexander Bedward. His testimony was authentic, as he remembered vividly the morning of 16 January. The first thing Bedward did was to wave his hat to the people and say, "Good morning". Then he prayed and sang a hymn. He had his Bible in his hand. He took a passage from Matthew 16. "He said, 'The Pharisees and the Sadducees are here. They come to arrest me, but arrest me if you can. The devil sergeant, the devil and all of them is here. You come to arrest me, but arrest me if you can.' There was no other sergeant but me and I was the devil sergeant."

Bedward then said:

> Every minister and every doctor is a thief and a liar. When the Governor go to do something for the poor people the ministers go in the Council and tell them not and they assist to oppress the people. Your forefathers come from over yonder and bring pothooks and handcuffs and put them on my grandfather's and grandmother's necks. Thanks be to God we have shake it off now, and you will all have to come under me at this river side and bathe. I am the rock and I will

trample you. There is a white wall and a black wall and the black wall will have to fall on the white wall and crush them.³⁹

Inspector James, the inspector of police for St Andrew who had initially sent Nelson to watch Bedward, even provided a character reference on Nelson's behalf. In addressing the court, James remarked:

> I performed my duties up to the sixth of August. I know Sergeant Nelson who is an efficient officer and I have always found him a straight forward and a truthful man. I was in St Andrews before prisoner commenced to sermonize. I have attended some of his meetings. If he had abused the Governor or the Queen I would have taken steps against him. I have heard him make out to the people that he was under divine influence and if they drank the water after he had blessed it, it would do them good. He spoke disparagingly of the ministers, doctors and police. There was a collection supposed to be for a Temple which they now call a Union Camp.⁴⁰

Bedward was being watched and targeted by the colonial state for years before his eventual arrest. Nelson was ordered by the previous inspector, James, to go to August Town every Wednesday over the three years to listen to Bedward and to carry a detective and a few constables. He was usually dressed in plain clothes and had never carried any damaging report to Inspector James. Bedward was never seditious in his sermons, although he was critical of certain colonial institutions.

On 16 January 1895, Nelson was specifically summoned by Calder to go and to carry a notebook and a pencil, but not to use them at the riverside when recording Bedward's speech. After the speech Nelson waited until he was around three chains from the river before he recorded notes in his book and sent in his report the following day. The other policemen with him that day were Corporals Hall and Foster. Both men agreed with Nelson's interpretation, in contrast to that of Inspector Calder.

The arrest of Bedward on 21 January 1895 on the unsubstantiated charges of sedition has to be interpreted as a deliberate attempt to silence Bedward.⁴¹

The Evidence of Corporal Steele

Another policeman who was called in defence of Bedward was Corporal Alfred Steele, who was on his third visit to hear Bedward and who also recorded what he heard. He too noted that Bedward's sermon on 16 January was primarily aimed at colonial pastors and doctors. Bedward told his audience "to be careful as the Pharisees and Sadducees are here. They come to take me, but they can't. All the ministers and doctors are thieves and robbers. The ministers go to the Council to make laws to oppress the poor people. They will take the last halfpenny out of their pockets."[42] Steele further emphasized that Bedward was not dismissive of the governor, as the prosecution claimed. It was the ministers and doctors who had reported Bedward to the governor, and it was the governor who told them not to interfere. It was in that context that Morant Bay was mentioned. Bedward then retorted, "You that are not among them come away from them. When the governor might have done some good for the people, they told him no." On the issue of the black wall destroying the white wall, Steele claimed that he could not remember the exact word Bedward used. It was either "crush" or "close"; that is, the black wall crushing the white wall or the black wall closing around the white wall.[43]

Interestingly, Inspector Calder was not pleased with Steele's first report and he was asked to write a second report of Bedward's sermon on 16 January. Calder claimed that Steele's first report was blotted and his signature was indistinct.[44]

Most of the policemen who gave evidence concur that before 16 January, Bedward did not use seditious language against the governor or the queen. They admitted that Bedward was, however, very critical of ministers of religion, doctors and the police. Wollaston, a police detective who was also covering Bedward's activities in August Town, even stated:

> I have attended meetings addressed by prisoner. I have never heard him use seditious language. I went there to hear what was going on and to make a report if anything wrong went on. Beyond his religious doctrines I saw no harm in him. I heard him say unless they were peaceable and law-abiding the water would do them no good. I have heard him abuse ministers and doctors. I was not there on the 16.[45]

The testimonies of Sergeant Nelson and Corporal Steele strongly support Stern's claim that Bedward made no seditious statement in his sermon on 16 January 1895. His outrage was against fellow preachers and doctors, and their unfair treatment of the poor black masses. Inspector Calder's testimony in court, under cross-examination by Stern, revealed that he was determined to send Bedward to prison, as he was only interested in statements which agreed with his. He noted in court:

> I described at the preliminary investigation that Bedward was a fanatic. I had charge of the case, but I don't know why Hall and Nelson were not called. I ordered Nelson to make a statement which I disapproved of. I asked for another statement which I also disapproved of. A little while afterwards he was transferred to another parish. Hall made a statement which I did not approve of. My idea of those not being called is that their evidence was not full enough.[46]

While Calder dismissed the evidence of Nelson and Steele, he quickly found policeman Taylor, who was strongly against Bedward's religion, to corroborate his statement. When Stern asked how he got Taylor to give evidence, Calder remarked that it was Taylor who approached him and volunteered himself. Calder also claimed that other people who also gave evidence for the crown, such as a pedlar by the name of Wilson, also volunteered himself.

Mr Stern's Address to the Jury

Stern, in addressing the jury, made the point that it must be apparent to them that he could have flooded the box with witnesses from the congregation to show that the prisoner never said anything that was ascribed to him. He preferred to point out discrepancies in the evidence for the prosecution and to refer to the evidence of Sergeant Nelson, who stood in front of Bedward, in contrast to Lanigan, who stood behind. Stern stressed that it was not surprising that the reporter (Lanigan), while transcribing his notes, availed himself of the power of imagination possessed by writers of fiction. A lame attempt had been made to show that Sergeant Nelson would not tell the truth, but his testimony had been unshaken. In great newspapers, every precaution was taken by employing the highest and the best men and paying them handsomely. In no institution was it more necessary to keep a rein upon the imagination than in writing for the press.[47]

In addition, Mr Lanigan had the disadvantage of not altogether understanding the lingo of the people. "Writing notes was a dangerous thing to rely on, and he need not impress on them the truth of evil creeping in as an abuse out of good things. Bunyan said, there was a bypath to hell even through the gates of paradise." The jury had a great function to perform, and he hoped they would not be niggardly in their award of a generous construction on the prisoner's actions and words. One great thing Bedward had done is that he had taught the people to wash (laughter), and he had not the slightest doubt that many of their sufferings could be alleviated by a constant course of cold water. The cold-water cure was no doctrine, and in his humble way, the man had done no harm and was entitled to some consideration from them.

His reference to the Morant Bay War might have had a different construction from that placed upon it by the prosecution and was uttered only as a warning to the people. Bedward had used cheeky but not seditious language. He therefore should be acquitted.

"Amongst other things," Stern continued, "I do not like the unlikeable coincidence of the meeting between the inspector and the reporter." Half a lie was the most difficult to be met and the narrative of the reporter Lanigan, who might have reported two or three words correctly, was far from being the whole truth.

He did not know whether there was any sinister motive in bringing such a jury from their business, instead of summoning a jury in the ordinary way. Mr Stern went on to deal with political signs of the times in Jamaica. There were gradually becoming but two classes in Jamaica. After a while, this country would become nothing but black people and officials. They should make allowance for the extravagant language of an ignorant man.[48]

The three points that he specially relied on were, first, that the notes of Mr Lanigan were not reliable for the purposes of convicting a man for sedition. Secondly, that Sergeant Nelson was not called for the prosecution, as he was the most reliable witness, and as such, his testimony should be taken seriously. Third, that there was no malicious intent on the part of the prisoner, even admitting that he used the words attributed to him.

They had a body of evidence indicating that malice could not be brought home to him. It was not consistent with law, common sense or justice that he should be punished to prevent him from doing worse. The English law held that it was not prudent to act in that way, and Stern asked the jury to view the case as it was and not allow their minds to be led away by any ideas that had been promulgated elsewhere. The point they had to decide was whether he used the words with the malicious intent to stir up rebellion among the black people. There was a serious doubt in the case. Furthermore, he did not like the idea of Lanigan and Sub-Inspector Calder "cottoning" together on 16 January. It might have been a curious coincidence, but he did not care for it. It was easy to make mistakes in transcribing shorthand notes. A newspaper must not be allowed to run a country.

They must rise above selfishness and resent despotism and cruelty, even to a dog or a Negro.[49] Justice was for all persons, and always its principles were eternal and immutable – guided by those principles of justice which he believed existed in the hearts of every one of them. He left the prisoner in their hands, asking them to remember they were judges of the fact. They had a solemn duty to perform. They had more than Bedward's case in their hands; they had the reputation of Jamaica; therefore, as gentlemen, they had to stand up for justice and resentment to all kinds of cruelty.[50]

The Prosecution's Closing Speech

Mr Oughton, in his submission to the jury, said he concurred with his learned friend in his reference to the impersonal character of justice, and he regretted that anything had been said about differences of colour. There was no suggestion in the case that the people in the country were ready for sedition. There was nothing to warrant such a suggestion, and the verdict would not imply it, whether it was given one way or the other. The invitation of Inspector Calder to Mr Lanigan to breakfast with him was a most reasonable thing, and the former would have been lacking in hospitality if he had not done so. Mr Lanigan was a reporter of experience and accuracy, and his notes could be relied on.

Sergeant Nelson corroborated Steele's evidence on the important point of what the prisoner said about the black wall crushing the white wall. He could not think that his learned friend, in speaking of the diction and connectivity of Mr Lanigan's report, was suggesting that it should not be taken seriously. He would admit that Lanigan's report was most disconnected. If Bedward's sermon was calculated to excite discontent, dissatisfaction and rebellion among the people, they would have to bring in a verdict against the prisoner. At first, Bedward was a spiritual and bodily healer, then he abused doctors and ministers, and in process of his evolution arrived at the stage of using seditious language.[51]

In using language professedly inspired, such as was deposed to, there could be no doubt about the consequences. Rebutting the contention that the prisoner was a half-witted man, Mr Oughton said they had to decide whether Bedward knew the difference between right and wrong. From the surrounding circumstances, he thought they would have no hesitation in deciding that Bedward was responsible for his actions. They had three questions to decide. Did the prisoner use the language charged, were the words likely to excite discontent and was Bedward sane or insane?

The Judge's Charge

The judge, in his summary, remarked that he was sorry to detain them much longer, but he would be as succinct as possible, because the case had been so exhaustively dealt with by counsel on both sides. His goal was to put them on the right track and leave them to form their own conclusions. The backbone of the prosecution might be taken to be the report by Mr Lanigan. That report was taken by an experienced shorthand writer, who was on the spot and at a distance from the utterer of the words sufficient for him to hear the words thoroughly. They were taken without any ulterior object, merely as a newspaper report, and therefore, he suggested, must be at all events fairly accurate. No question as to collusion between Mr Lanigan and Inspector Calder would trouble them. Nothing could be more natural than the explanation which had been given of the occurrences of the day, which was given both by Inspector Calder and Mr Lanigan; and in the mere fact of the former extending his hospitality towards a man who had been kept from his ordinary meal until one in the afternoon. He did not think Inspector Calder transgressed the old traditions of Jamaica. The notes which were taken by Mr Lanigan were very full, and he had sworn that his verbatim notes represented what was said in his hearing during the meeting.[52]

Some questions had been raised by the learned counsel for the defence, and very properly so, as to certain expressions used by Mr Lanigan in his evidence, in which he said that he did not reproduce the exact language used by the accused; that is to say, he did not reproduce Bedward's dialect and pronunciation. It was perhaps necessary for him, as the judge, to tell them that in replicating the language, mere mistakes, spelling and grammatical errors were not necessarily reproduced in a verbatim report. Half the reports of speeches in Parliament, which he supposed were the best reported ones, were not exactly verbatim. The statements were corrected as to grammar and pronunciation by the reporters; and no one would ever venture to question the veracity of Hansard's reports, which were made up in that manner and were accepted as evidence in every court of law throughout the United Kingdom.

Therefore, the mere statement of Mr Lanigan that he did not reproduce the peculiar pronunciation and grammatical errors indulged in by Bedward at the meeting was not worthy of their consideration. Of course, they would put their own construction upon Mr Lanigan's report and would attach to it the value that they thought right. Lanigan's evidence appeared to be perfectly correct and was unshaken in cross-examination. His Honour then reviewed at length the evidence of the witnesses in the case, reading the more important statements.[53]

Having shared his views with the jurors, the judge encouraged them to rule upon the evidence given and not upon their preferred outcome as sensible and reasonable persons. He stated:

> You are entitled in putting the construction upon it to take into consideration the characters of the persons to whom the language was addressed, in connection with the effect that that language was likely to have upon them.

The question that you must decide is, first of all, did the defendant speak the words with which he is charged? Secondly, are those words seditious in the acceptance I have given you of the word? Thirdly, whether they were uttered with a seditious intent or whether they were such words as would entitle you, from their probable effect, to assume that intent. Those are the questions you have to solve.⁵⁴

The judge then reminded the jury that if they considered that those words were actually uttered by Bedward, that when he expressed those words, he had the intention in his mind of sedition, or that those words, whatever might have been his intention, were such as to excite people to sedition, then they must find him guilty. If, on the other hand, they had a reasonable doubt on any of those points, they must give him the benefit of it and acquit him; and if they were of the opinion from the evidence they had heard that at the time of uttering these words, his mind was in such a state as to hinder him from knowing the difference between right and wrong, that these words were uttered as words of a machine, when he was incapable of knowing that he was erring in using them, then they would acquit him on the ground of insanity; but if they acquitted him on that ground, they must be sure at the time these words were used, he was absolutely incapable of deciding between right and wrong. "I am perfectly certain I need do no more now than ask you to devote your best attention to the questions before you and to consider your verdict."

The jury retired to consider their verdict, and after a twenty-minute absence, a message was sent to the judge relating to a question. On returning to the courtroom, they asked whether the verdict had to be unanimous. His Honour replied in the affirmative and the gentlemen again retired. Another quarter of an hour elapsed; it was announced that a verdict had been arrived at. The jury again returned, and his Honour asked if they had agreed upon a verdict.⁵⁵

The foreman of the jury replied, "We have."

The registrar of the court then asked the foreman, "Do you find the prisoner at the bar guilty or not guilty?"

The foreman replied, "We are satisfied that the accused did make use of the seditious language with which he has been charged, but our verdict is not guilty on the ground of insanity."

Mr Stern spontaneously exclaimed, "On that I would claim two things from your Honour."

The judge replied firmly, "There is nothing further to be said, Mr Stern."

Mr Stern insisted, "Unless your Honour allows me to put what I mean . . ."

The judge responded, "I will allow you to state what you wish."

Mr Stern stated, "I don't pretend I am wholly pleased with the result, but what I want to ask your Honour before your Honour passes sentence . . ."

The judge: "I cannot pass sentence, Mr Stern."

Mr Stern continued, "I ask the opportunity of bringing before your Honour in the Supreme Court the question as to jury. I wish to argue it in the Supreme Court. I would like your Honour to reserve doing anything. I claim the verdict to be a general verdict of not guilty. I never formally pleaded insanity."

The judge sarcastically concluded, "That doesn't matter, it is perfectly immaterial."

But Mr Stern insisted, "Will your Honour give me an opportunity of coming before your Honour on the first question?"

The judge firmly responded, "No."

Mr Stern disappointedly responded, "Then I will sit down."

The judge, in affirming the decision of the jury, concluded, "The jury having found the defendant not guilty on the ground of insanity, he must therefore be detained awaiting Her Majesty's pleasure." Then he stated, "I have much pleasure in discharging you, with the thanks of the community for your services. You have had an arduous three days and I think the conclusion you have come to is most satisfactory."

Bedward's guilty verdict seemed to have shocked even the court reporter, as she wrote, "The verdict created a slight sensation in the body of the court for many persons believed that the verdict of the jury would entitle Bedward to a discharge. Indeed, this was the opinion which gained currency among the streets."[56]

Bedward remained in the same attitude as he had done throughout the trial, completely impassive to what was transpiring and with his hands tightly clasped. After the order was announced to the onlookers, two or three sympathizers came up to him and patted him on the back and bade him to be of good cheer.[57]

Alexander Bedward's Vindication

The judge erred in his attempt to persuade the jury to have Bedward detained for lunacy. Rather than admonishing the jury to find Bedward either guilty or innocent, he provided a third option, of finding him guilty of sedition but linking his sedition to insanity. It was not surprising that within thirty-five minutes, the jury chose that third option as the penalty. Even stranger was the attitude of the very experienced chief justice, who, having thanked the jury for their three days of service, proceeded to congratulate them on arriving at a "most satisfactory" decision. The chief justice thought that sending Bedward to a lunatic asylum was surely one way of silencing him.

Luckily for Bedward, the judge's error opened the door for Mr Stern to lodge an appeal for a writ of habeas corpus in the Supreme Court for illegally detaining Bedward, as the Jamaican law does not give the judge that power. Stern, having received the habeas corpus, went quietly to the head of the lunatic asylum, Dr Plaxton, and handed it to him, demanding Bedward's immediate release from the asylum.

A confused Plaxton stared at Stern, amused, and said, "Stern, I refuse to surrender Bedward to you."[58]

"Now look here, Plaxton," said Mr Stern, "you and I are friends, but I want you to understand that if you do not let me have Bedward, I will take a suit against you for unlawfully detaining in an asylum a freeborn subject of the crown."

Plaxton replied, "Mr Stern, you forget that it was the judge who committed this man to the asylum."

"And he had no right to do so," retorted Mr Stern. "If he had the right I would not be armed at the moment with a writ of habeas corpus. And it is this writ which you will have to obey, not what the judge may have said or done in court."

"I do not understand all this," Dr Plaxton replied, getting red with anger.

"I don't suppose you do," said Stern. "I will tell you this: Bedward was brought before the court for sedition and the charge failed. He was not charged with lunacy. He has not been examined for lunacy by any doctor and you yourself know that no man can be committed to the asylum unless he is certified as insane by qualified medical men. The chief justice blundered when he thought he could send Bedward to you, and now I have come to you for Bedward. Do I get him, or do I take a suit against you?"

Dr Plaxton thought for a moment and then nodded. "I suppose you are right." And he handed over Bedward to Stern.

The release of Bedward from a colonial Jamaican court of law, when he was found guilty by a jury, significantly increased his popularity among the masses and his followers. His followers seemed to be more convinced now than ever that this man was indeed God's prophet and no colonial power or other forces could stop the black wall from rising and crushing the white wall. A *Daily Gleaner* reporter who summarized the feelings of the Bedwardites wrote, "No earthly power could keep a holy prophet like Bedward in such an unholy place, such as an asylum."[59] Even Mr Stern, Bedward's lawyer, became a legal celebrity and would later use his fame to enter Jamaican politics and to become the mayor of Kingston, a member of the Jamaican legislature and also clerk of the Executive Council.[60]

Bedward chose not to pursue the recommendation of his attorney to file for damages for illegal imprisonment. With increasing pressure to sue the state, Bedward said clearly that God told him, "See thou do it not, I am thy reward."[61] The persecution of Bedward, instead of weakening the movement, promoted his work and made Bedward immortal in the eyes of the persecuted Jamaican masses. The state, however, embarrassed and disappointed, would make the next move.

Chapter 4

Bedwardism, Revivalism and the Jamaican State

The alleged weaknesses in the existing law, "The Lunatic Asylum Law", were one of the major reasons cited by many in the judiciary for the failure to have Bedward incarcerated in a lunatic asylum. The larger problem was not necessarily the law but the rush to have Bedward convicted of lunacy. Thus, both the judge and the attorney general erred legally in not following the existing laws or in using outdated lunacy laws. The judge in particular must have been thinking of section 13 of the 1861 Lunatic Law, which allowed for those charged with a felony in the courts to be sent to a lunatic asylum. Sedition, of which Bedward was found guilty, is a felony, but based on law 29 of 1885, a medical superintendent had to have examined him before the trial to confirm that he was indeed insane. The judge had no right to give the jury the option that Bedward could be found guilty but on the ground of insanity.

What the judge could have done, if he had not been that anxious to send Bedward to the asylum, was to leave the jury to decide on Bedward's guilt or innocence. The jury having declared Bedward guilty, the judge would have him sentenced to prison and later have a medical superintendent examine him in prison for lunacy. Sections 1–4 of the Jamaican lunacy law of 1861 made it clear that any prisoner who was medically examined by the appropriate individuals and declared insane would be removed to the lunatic asylum. The attorney general should have seen the judge's error and had Bedward released immediately, rather than sending him to the asylum.

The embarrassment of having a court finding Bedward guilty of sedition and sending him to the asylum, and yet Bedward was able to walk free because he had been illegally detained, must have been a hard blow to the colonial authorities. They comforted themselves with the narrative of the inadequacies of the Lunatic Law. It was a clear intent of the colonial state to strengthen the Lunatic Law as best as it could, and it had the law so strongly amended that people like Bedward could no longer escape the dragnet. Bedward's release from the asylum was to become a defining moment for the Jamaican colonial state, to stop playing around with "lunatics" and to ensure that the full weight of the law could be applied to Bedwardites, Revivalists and all others who resisted colonial culture.

The Jamaican government decided it had to use the heavy weight of the Lunatic Law better to convict as well the hundreds of Revival groups spread all over the island. It was also an imperative to revise other, related legislation, such as the Obeah Act, the Vagrancy Act and the Medical Act, to eliminate all forms of Africanism. These laws would hopefully deter copycats from seeking to emulate the success of Alexander Bedward.

Sir Henry Arthur Blake, who had been serving as governor of the island for the last nine years, in explaining to the Colonial Office Bedward's release, stated that the Chief Justice was of the mistaken view that the Jamaican law surrounding insanity was the same as the law of England. Steps would be taken to amend the Jamaican law so that it was similar to British law and to address the acquittal of cases on the ground of insanity.[1]

The governor further noted that if the state did not act quickly to neutralize his power, Bedward's influence would become much more cemented. The country had hundreds of similar preachers who were copying Bedward's style of leadership. He inspired numerous Jamaicans, and the unpredictable masses could be politically stimulated to rebel. The laws had to be immediately amended for the safety of the Jamaican colonial state. This admission by the governor speaks volumes of the impact of Alexander Bedward. He wrote:

> This release of Bedward is accepted by his followers as a miracle and will in all probability greatly increase his power. Under our lunacy laws we cannot deal with him and we can only continue to observe his sect carefully and re-arrest him in the event of him preaching sedition. I do not apprehend danger from himself, but he may be used by others for the benefit of creating disturbance among people so excitable and ignorant as our population. I therefore think it well to inform your Lordship of the circumstances.[2]

By the following year (1896), the Jamaican Lunatic Law was indeed updated, with two separate amendments. Law 5 of 1896, the Trial of Lunatics Act, gave the court the power to form a special verdict against those charged with an offence committed by reason of insanity. Secondly, whenever the court delivered a special verdict, it had the right to keep the insane person in custody as a "criminal lunatic" until the governor decided the insane person's fate.[3] This amended law 5 of 1896 replaced law 5 of 1890, which only gave the resident magistrate's court special and exclusive jurisdiction over the petty debts courts in handling issues of lunacy.[4]

The revised law was a direct reaction to Bedward's freedom. Under this revised law, if Bedward was again found guilty by the courts on the ground of insanity, he would be legally deemed a criminal lunatic. He could then be legitimately sent to prison to await the governor's directive, and the governor had the legal right to send him to the asylum.

The second significant amendment was the Lunatic Asylum Laws Amendment Law 1896 (law 16 of 1896), and it replaced other previous laws, such as 30 of 1873, 29 of 1885 and 5 of 1890, with seventeen different provisions.[5] Acting Attorney General T. Bancroft Oughton highlighted the importance of this revised law for the safety and advancement of the Jamaican colonial state from the "insane" Bedwardites scattered all over the country. He emphasized that the passing of this revised law was extremely important, given the "miscarriage of justice" which occurred when Bedward was acquitted of sedition on the ground of insanity but could not be detained.[6] This revised lunacy law now equipped the Jamaican state with far greater powers and provided the flexibility for detention and incarceration of people like Bedward. The essence of the revised law was: Section 1 (Power to arrest persons of unsound mind without warrant) empowered any police constable to arrest any person who in his estimation was "wandering at large or roaming about". Such an individual could be charged as a dangerous lunatic and be brought to a justice of the peace; section 2 (Power to issue warrant on information for arrest of person of unsound mind) gave the justice of the peace the right to have such an individual arrested if he was convinced by the evidence that the person in question was a lunatic.

Under section 3 (Examination of Lunatic and order for detention in a lunatic asylum) the justices of the peace could examine the individual and hold the person up to ten days for medical observation. Sections 4–6 addressed people on board ships and so on, who were lunatics, but could not be prosecuted, since they were not wandering the streets. Section 7 (Suspension of Order of detention and care of lunatic) gave a justice of the peace the right to suspend the order to have the lunatic travel for fourteen days. This provision gave the medical superintendent at the asylum more time and would not tie his hand with due process of days.

Section 8 (Care of lunatic by relative or friend) gave the relatives and friends of the person in question the chance to prove that they could take care of the lunatic and that the person could be removed from their care. Section 9 (Order for detention in the lunatic asylum) carried the forms to be used in detaining the lunatic, while sections 11–13 discussed how their expenses would be financed. Section 16 (Definition of lunatic asylum) gave the governor the right to declare any space a lunatic asylum.[7]

The goal of the legislation was to strengthen the Lunatic Laws so that criminal charges could be easily brought against Bedwardites, Revivalists and others of similar persuasion. Before this new legislation, there were generally two kinds of lunatics. First, lunatics sent from homes to the asylum and, secondly, those sent to the asylum by way of the state's agencies (poorhouses and the courts) and ships carrying mentally challenged individuals. Under this revised law, there was now a new category, "criminal lunatics". Sections 1 and 2 of the act were particularly designed to give the police and the justices of the peace more powers to clamp down on suspected Bedwardites or Revivalists. A criminal lunatic was left fully to their discretion and all that was now required was a medical confirmation. Even if the medical diagnosis disagreed that the individual was insane, the state would already have incarcerated and harassed the individual for days without facing any legal penalty for illegal arrest.

A close examination of the Revised Lunatic Law, especially section 1, highlights the fluidity with which lunacy was to be used as an important tool of colonial control for Bedwardites and others resisting colonial control. The Revised Lunatic Laws in Jamaica did not hinder the continued growth of the Bedwardite movement or retard the Revivalist influence on the island. However, they empowered the various parish boards to send to the asylum any Jamaican, especially an African Jamaican, whom they deemed a financial or a social burden. The result was a dramatic increase in annual admissions to the asylum on the ground of insanity, as seen in both table 1 and figure 1. The situation was similar in Barbados, Trinidad and British Guiana, where the lunacy laws were strengthened to enforce colonial values.

In Barbados, the lunatic asylum contained forty-three patients in 1851. It was enlarged during that year by taking over adjoining buildings that had been intended as a lazaretto (leper asylum). In 1872, there were 114 patients in the asylum, and by 1905, its patient population had increased to more than 100 per cent, to 370. In Trinidad, the asylum at Belmont, which had opened in 1858, survived for more than forty years, with a growth in patient numbers from 48 in 1860 to 93 in 1870, 242 in 1880, 360 in 1890 and nearly 500 in 1899. The new lunatic asylum in Trinidad was finally opened in 1900 in St Ann's, with patient numbers that year reaching 524.

In British Guiana, the construction of a replacement for the unsatisfactory Demerara asylum had begun by 1864. It was situated in an old army barracks in a remote location near the sea, a mile away from New Amsterdam, in the sparsely populated province of Berbice. Once opened in 1867, patient numbers at Fort Canje grew rapidly, as in the other colonies. By 1876, there

Table 1. Admission of Persons to the Jamaica Lunatic Asylum, 1885/86–1925/26

Year	Admitted	Patients	Recovery (%)	Prisoners
1885–86	136	531	33	
1895–86	174	795	45.95	
1905–06	230	1,264	48.2	
1906–07	234	1,291	64.52	
1907–08	279	1,292	42.65	
1908–09	237	1,269	35.86	
1909–10	262	1,320	37.02	
1910–11	324	1,400	44.14	
1911–12	268	1,439	53.89	1,114
1912–13	349	1,544	38.94	1,217
1913–14	318	1,632	49.82	1,440
1914–15	329	1,670	47.27	1,266
1915–16	333	1,733	42.25	1,510
1916–17	285	1,730	57.54	1,575
1917–18	310	1,637	50.64	1,890
1918–19	372	1,727	40.32	2,218
1919–20	333	1,745	65.16	2,282
1920–21	362	1,747	34.8	
1921–22	394	1,595	46.62	1,521
1922–23	375	1,650	54.28	
1923–24	346	1,684		1,616
1924–25	386	1,846		1,668
1925–26	362			

were 182 patients, and the number had risen to 333 by 1800, and increased by over 100 per cent by 1900, to 680 inmates.[8]

The Revised Lunatic Law passed in Jamaica, the year after Bedward's release from the asylum, must have accounted for this significant increase in the number of detainees after 1895. Before the 1890s, the increase in admissions to the Jamaican lunatic asylum was minimal. Between 1905 and 1906, roughly 10 years after the law was revised, the annual intake of inmates jumped from 174 to 230. It continued to increase so drastically that by the 1920s, the annual intake was as high as 394 in 1921–22.

Most of these new detainees were not necessarily Bedwardites or Revivalists but people sent from the gaols across the country as criminal

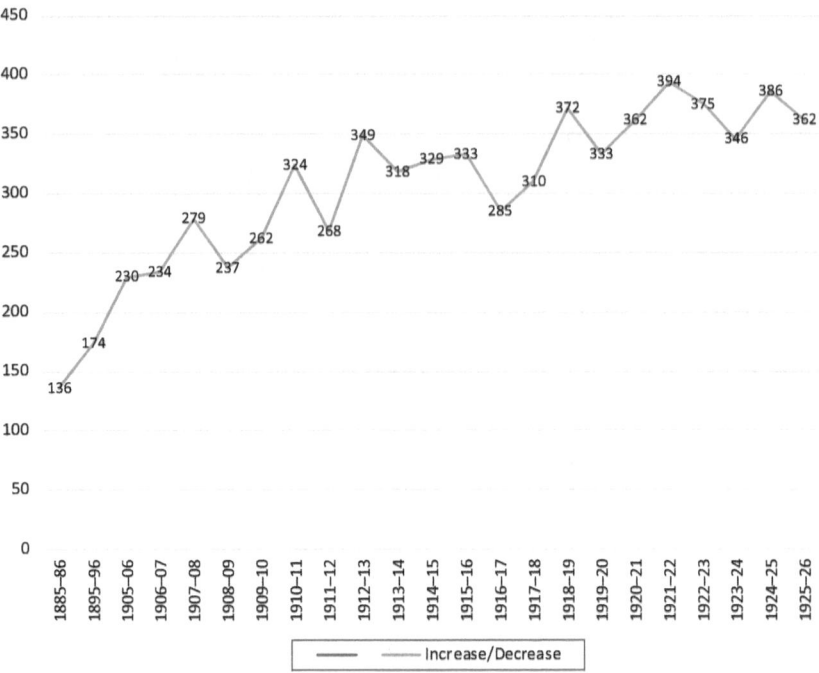

Figure 1. Increase/decrease in people sent to Bellevue, 1885/86–1925/26.

lunatics. African Jamaicans were the predominant ethnic group taken from these gaols to the lunatic asylum (Bellevue) as a means of detention. For example, from 1 April 1898 to 31 March 1900, of the 189 people sent there, blacks constituted 138 (65 males and 73 females) in contrast to the 39 described as brown, the 7 described as coolies and the 5 described as whites.[9] Similarly, between 1901 and 1902, of the 182 people sent to the asylum, 113 were listed as black (59 men and 54 women), 51 brown, 7 white and 1 Chinese.[10] The targeting of African Jamaicans continued throughout the period.

Even women were not spared being dragged away to the asylum, as seen in the period from April 1895 to March 1896. Of the 174 admissions that year, 151 (74 males and 77 females) were sent there by the courts and the majority were females.[11] Females outnumbering males was not a strange phenomenon, as the Bedwardites and Revivalist groups had a larger concentration of women than men.[12] More significantly, women have always constituted the backbone of rebellions and resistance in the colonial and post-colonial Caribbean, although they have not always been visible in the forefront of those movements.[13]

The point must be made that the overwhelming majority of the 174 admissions to the asylum in 1895–96 were not exhibiting signs of madness, as seen in table 1. The alleged crimes committed by these mainly African Jamaicans had little or nothing to do with mental illnesses. They were predominantly social crimes that they had allegedly committed. Examples of such alleged crimes were arson, murder, praedial larceny, felony, housebreaking, wounding, indecent assault, imbecility and dementia. All these, apart from dementia, have little or nothing to do with weak mental constitution. Dementia and epilepsy are best treated by doctors and do not necessarily involve sending the sufferers to an asylum. Imbecility is clearly not a condition which merits confinement in a mental institution. It seems parochial authorities in the various Jamaican towns dumped their alleged chronic patients in the asylum, as hinted by the chief medical officer of the Jamaica Lunatic Asylum, D.J. Williams.[14] The failure to trap Bedward in 1895 provided the parochial boards of the Jamaican state with an opportunity to get rid of people they considered social outcasts in the various towns under the guise of insanity. This ambiguity shows the fluidity with which the label of insanity could be easily tagged on to African Jamaicans whose behaviour did not fit colonial ideals. No wonder the Bedwardites and the various Revivalists around the country, and later Rastafari members, could be so easily classified as insane. It also explains why in Jamaica the strengthened, revised lunacy law resulted in so many more "sane" people being taken to the asylum.

As an indication of the extent to which the state sought to prosecute African Jamaicans and have them incarcerated for alleged social problems after 1895, table 2 is instructive. It shows a number of African Jamaicans who were eventually acquitted in the courts but were held as criminal lunatics across the gaols in the island to be transferred to Bellevue. Fortunately for them, they were freed in time. Nevertheless, it shows the colonial state's intent.

What table 2 further highlights is the colonial mindset that insanity was the cause of many alleged social crimes. It further highlights the reason the jury of white men could have found Bedward guilty on account of insanity. Unfortunately, there are no surviving written court records explaining the reasons that some of these crimes were attributed to mental problems. It would also be even more enlightening to read the reasons certain illnesses were diagnosed in such a manner. For example, epilepsy accounting for murder, in case number 2,358; "imbecile" leading to murder in case 2,469; and "dementia" leading to murder in case number 1,402. The classification of "imbecile" is particularly interesting. Was this a form of acting to camouflage

Table 2. Persons Deemed as Lunatics across the Island Acquitted up to 1902

Number	Admitted	Age	Crime	Mental State	Court
890	July 1870	69	Arson	Imbecile	Bath Circuit Court
1,402	April 1870	47	Murder	Dementia	Montego Bay Circuit
1,594	January 1872	56	Praedial larceny	Chronic Mania	Falmouth Circuit
2,358	January 1884	40	Murder	Epilepsy	Savanna la Mar Circuit
2,469	August 1885	41	Murder	Imbecile	Kingston Circuit
2,470	August 1885	46	Murder	Chronic Mania	Kingston Circuit
2,730	June 1887	66	Felony	Imbecile	No Information
3,300	August 1891	66	House breaking & larceny	Mania	No Information
3,709	February 1894	73	Wounding	Mania	Santa Cruz Court
3,800	July 1894	30	Murder	Mania	May Pen Circuit
3,803	July 1894	59	Indecent assault	Mania	Mandeville Court
3,569	July 1894	34	Praedial larceny	Epilepsy	Trelawny Court
4,306	January 1897	30	Wounding	Mania	Falmouth Court
4,308	January 1897	49	Assault	Mania	Browns Town
4,396	June 1897	?	Malicious wounding	Mania	St Mary Court
4,913	April 1900	39	Assault	Mania	St Elizabeth Court
5,216	October 1901	19	Arson	Mania	Savanna la Mar Court

the act of murder, as an act of resistance, as it was during the period of slavery? Or was it that the state classified the act as showing the culprit had to be stupid to commit such an act? From whichever perspective it was looked at, the point is that these classifications were rather fluid, and "sane" people could easily be diagnosed as having a mental condition, as was Bedward.

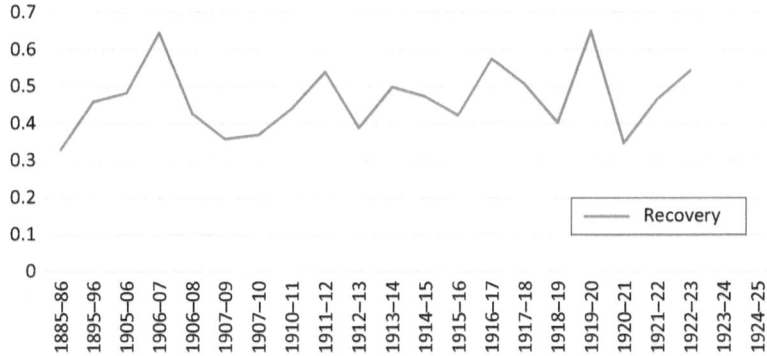

Figure 2. Recovery rate per cent at asylum, 1885/86–1925/26.

This definition of insanity could have been the reason Dr Bronstorph came to the fixed position on Bedward that he was so mentally ill in 1883 that only an asylum could save him. Left to Dr Bronstorph and his medical staff, Bedward would have been put on the streets for the police to detain him and put him in an asylum.[15] It also explains the reason Bedward was so overly critical of European doctors and their diagnoses. Working-class African Jamaicans could be so easily analysed as insane, especially when they endeavoured to reinforce and practise their African culture. Lunacy provided the colonial state with another weapon of control, first, to classify colonial resisters as insane and, secondly, to incarcerate them in an asylum under the pretence of healing. When the data from table 1 is analysed, the average recovery rate of alleged lunatics being cured is 46 per cent, as seen in figure 2.

Although critical factors, such as overcrowding, inadequate resources and inadequate personnel, could affect the asylum's overall recovery rate, one can conclude safely that many people entering Bellevue as mentally ill would never recover. Most criminal lunatics, such as Bedward, once admitted, would never leave the institution and would die there, as Bedward did, having spent nearly nine years there. From the colonial perspective, Bellevue was an ideal place of permanent incarceration for people such as Bedward.

Table 3 contrasts the annual intake of people at the Jamaica Lunatic Asylum and the island's two major prisons at that time, the General Penitentiary and the St Catherine district prison. Of the eight years between 1911 and 1919, six of those years (1911–17) witnessed more people being incarcerated in Bellevue as insane than those incarcerated in the two prisons. Figure 3 speaks for itself, as it is rather strange that more African Jamaicans were declared

Table 3. Contrasting Patients at Bellevue with Prisoners, 1911–19

Years	Bellevue	Prisoners
1911–12	1,439	1,114
1912–13	1,544	1,217
1913–14	1,632	1,440
1914–15	1,670	1,266
1915–16	1,733	1,510
1916–17	1,730	1,575
1917–18	1,637	1,890
1918–19	1,727	2,218

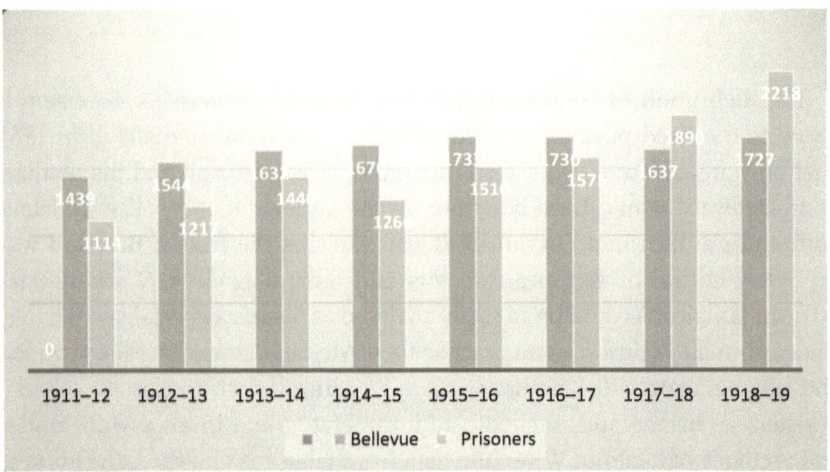

Figure 3. Prisoners versus inmates at Bellevue, 1911–19.

insane and locked away for treatment than those sentenced to prison by the state. The charge of lunacy was so fluid in classifying individuals that it gave the Jamaican state more options to imprison, one way or the other, people who deliberately resisted colonial culture. Colonial thinking about its large African population was that any continued affinity with anything African, when Europeans brought enlightenment, was a viable threat to the health of colonial Jamaica. It was the state's mission to enforce colonial values either by acculturation or by punishment.

Dr Williams, the prominent medical superintendent, in response to the unusually high rate of lunatics in Jamaica, stressed the point continually that the increasing levels of insanity resulted from the Revival meetings indulged in by many African Jamaicans. Williams even argued that this would continue, given the "unstable mental organization" of African Jamaicans.[16] No wonder that in the minds of many Jamaicans who were influenced by the colonial way of life, Bedward's "strange behaviour" was primarily attributed to his Revival tendencies. This colonial view that Revival meetings of Bedwardites and others caused African Jamaicans to become mentally ill was a popular colonial view. However, such a view was not supported by any evidence.

The yearly reports of the lunatic asylum from the 1890s to the 1920s do list "religious excitement" among the African Jamaican class as a factor; however, it was always one of the minor factors in all the yearly reports. The 31 December 1922 report, for example, as seen in figure 4, shows that "religious excitement" was the cause of the detention of only 4 of the 242 persons detained that year.[17] Only 1.7 per cent of those committed to the asylum were recorded as victims of "religious excitement". One also must question what were the criteria used in even determining "religious excitement" as a cause of insanity. But even if it was a legitimate cause, it was always a minuscule factor.

The reports list heredity as the major factor. It would also be interesting to examine their authorities' definition of heredity, as they seemed to be suggesting that African Jamaicans had a natural disposition to insanity, as indicated by Dr Williams. This situation would further suggest the urgency of the European civilizing mission to save African Jamaicans from themselves and their damning African culture. The continued practising of African religion and culture would further push African Jamaicans

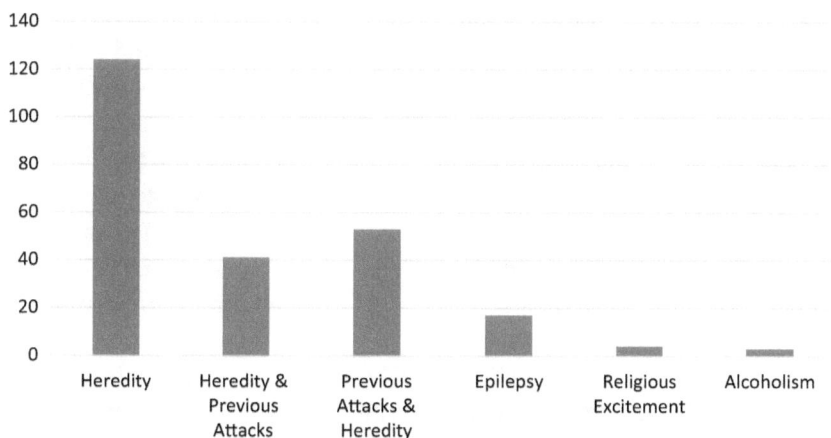

Figure 4. Causes of insanity, 31 December 1922.

into the column of insanity. This position was a view shared by colonial missionaries, such as George Olson, who constantly referred to the natural weaknesses in the black psyche.[18]

Despite the evidence that African Jamaicans and their Revival forms of worship contributed minimally to insanity, the medical authorities at Bellevue continued to denounce the practices of the Bedwardites and the Revivalists in their annual reports. In one such report, they concluded that street preaching, Revival meetings and religious practices in general escalated considerable emotional disturbance in African Jamaicans, primarily among the uneducated class.[19] The 1928 report even adds that "singing in the streets", as practised by Revivalists and Bedwardites, and being "somewhat talkative as these Revivalists are", were also contributing factors leading to detention in the asylum.[20]

No better example of this incorrect assertion can be found than the warning in the 1919 report by Lawson Gifford, the acting superintendent of the asylum. He writes:

> Religious excitement is an undoubted fertile source of insanity in the island. I do not wish to convey that a man's religion is a cause of insanity but persons of unstable organizations who generally revel in revival meetings and nine nights orgies usually terminate their careers within the walls of the lunatic asylum. It may not be amiss to point out that the majority of these cases hail from the backwoods of Manchester, Westmoreland and Hanover. It seems to me that until that apparent impenetrable superstitious darkness is dissipated by the light of compulsory education religious excitement will continue to produce its annual contingent of inmates for the asylum.[21]

It is clear, based on colonial thinking, that Bedwardites and Revivalists and other African Jamaicans who resisted colonial values and lifestyles would easily be diagnosed as crazy. It also means that the classification of insanity was highly subjective and explains the high percentage of African Jamaicans being sent to the asylum. As Margaret Jones opines, confinement in an asylum in a colonial British state like Jamaica in the late nineteenth and early twentieth centuries was more about social control than about the care and treatment of the mentally ill. Thus institutions like the Jamaica Lunatic Asylum, in the colonial context, were an important imposition on the part of the imperial rulers.[22]

Since mental illness was defined legally and not medically in this period in the United Kingdom and her colonies, the criminally insane or potentially violent were housed with the temporarily ill or those infirm through age. The lunatic asylum became massively overcrowded, prompting the

Jamaican governor in the early 1900s to appoint a commission to make a thorough examination of all the asylum's patients. The governor wanted to determine if its inmates were really insane and lawfully detained and whether people could be returned to their families, kindred or their parish almshouses.[23] Not only were older and infirm people sent to the asylum from across the island but also younger people who were committed to African religion and culture. The 1903–04 annual report in table 4 and figure 5 clearly shows the number of people so detained between the ages of twenty and thirty.

Young people aged twenty to thirty continued to be incarcerated in the asylum during the ensuing years of the early twentieth century. While the annual reports from the asylum do not give the specific characteristics of these younger individuals, they were most likely perceived as threats to the

Table 4. Age-Group Profile of Persons Sent to the Asylum, 1903–04

Ages	Males	Females	Total
0–9	0	0	0
10–20	14	14	28
20–30	47	38	85
30–40	21	24	45
40–50	17	14	31
50–60	5	6	11
60–70	1	4	5
70–80	0	1	1

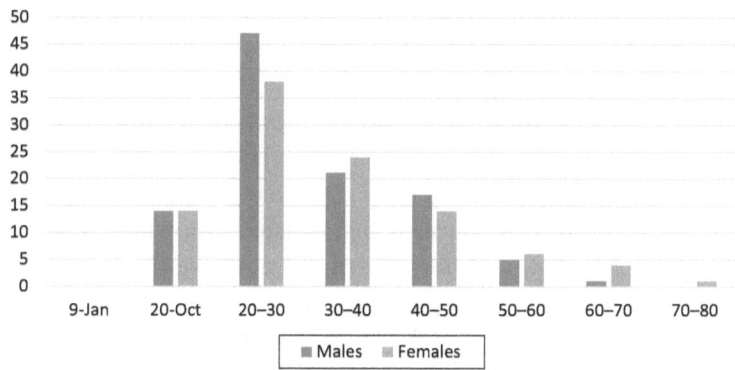

Figure 5. Age-group profile of those sent to the asylum, 1903–04.

colonial religious culture. Leonard Smith thus argues that in the colonial period people admitted to lunatic asylums in Britain and its colonies tended to be those who displayed marked degrees of what was perceived to be dangerous or risky behaviour. Such behaviour manifested itself in violence, threats, self-harm, damage to property or other challenges to social and public order. The legal criteria for admission were laid down separately in each colony, based on earlier English laws subsequently adapted for India and other colonial territories.[24]

In Jamaica, by the late nineteenth to the early twentieth century, the concept of "criminal lunacy" was so fluid that even minor social challenges to the smooth running of the colonial state could result in a verdict of lunacy. In many of the annual reports of the lunatic asylum, the point is constantly made that many more people could have been admitted, swelling the numbers in the asylum in Kingston, had it not been for problems transporting them by public means. One of the reports even proposed building a similar asylum in western Jamaica so that more African Jamaicans could "benefit" from mental care.[25]

Funding the Lunatic Asylum Law Amendment of 1896

While the colonial policymakers in Jamaica all agreed on a strong Lunatic Asylum Law Amendment in 1896 and its importance to the sociopolitical stability of the colonial state, the issue of funding the bill led to bitter controversy and heated exchanges. Central government and local or parochial boards remained deeply divided on the issue. From the very inception of the 1896 bill, when it was being read the second time, one of the big issues for debate in the Legislative Council was the body responsible for funding the cost of supporting criminal lunatics.

The governor insisted that it was the parochial boards; the boards objected vigorously that it ought to be the responsibility of the central government. The parochial boards were of the view that they were already overburdened with the cost of providing material assistance for the poorhouses of the parishes. It was unfair for them also to fund those being sent to the asylum as lunatics. The funding of these criminal lunatics should not come from the parishes' poor people's funds, as they were already inadequate. The governor, through his colonial secretary, insisted that central government would not pay the cost, and the council did not have the legal authority to force central government to pay. The final decision was the governor's, given crown colony government.[26] The bill was passed with a provision for the parochial boards to take on the cost of funding these criminal lunatics in the asylum.

By the following year, 1897, the boards were already finding it difficult to meet the new costs. The outgoing members of the St James parochial board made it clear to the incoming members that it was extremely important for them to use whatever means were necessary to influence the central government to take up the responsibilities of caring for these criminal lunatics. Their records show that over the last two years they had been carrying a greater deficit. They wrote, "At this rate, there will be nothing left to feed the paupers. The very large increase of lunatics, almost 50 per cent since 1896, requires the serious consideration of the government."[27] The central government was even labelled as "extortionists" in using its power to force the parochial boards to pay these additional costs.[28]

In the revision of the 1909 Lunatic Asylum Law, some legislators expressed the concern that central government was still being unfair to parochial boards. It was trying to fast-track the 1909 Lunatic Asylum Law without working on a compromise on costs. These legislators insisted that rounding up criminal lunatics and sending them to the asylum could not be at the expense of the parochial board. The expenses borne by the parishes over the last five years averaged £4,500, in contrast to central government's, which were a mere £1,600.[29]

Despite the strong feeling of the parochial boards that they should not fund the cost of criminal lunatics, they never questioned the relevance of targeting such criminal lunatics. They rhetorically asked, on one occasion, if someone of the stature of an Alexander Bedward were rearrested and sent to the asylum, who would pay his costs.[30] Given Bedward's national prominence, wouldn't the state pay his costs, seeing that Bedwardism was a national problem? Why then were parochial boards being asked to cover the costs of criminal lunatics who threatened the safety and security of the state?

As a compromise to the parochial boards, it was agreed to increase the quarterly refund to each board based on the number of lunatics they sent to the asylum, effective 1 April 1910. The refund would be calculated by the central government at one-half penny per patient per diem. However, the parochial boards would still be responsible for bearing half the costs for all categories of lunatics.[31]

Despite the refunds, the complaints continued. The Kingston and St Andrew parochial board (KSAC) now insisted it should be given far greater concessions. It was the most affected, given the number of impoverished lunatics from all over the country being added to its inmates, resulting in higher operational costs. The Revised Lunatic Law of 1914 sought to address that issue, agreeing with the KSAC. This further enraged the other parochial boards, especially the St Ann board, which stepped up its advocacy on the issue. It complained that for the last twelve years it had not benefited from the refund on duty-free flour to make items such as bread and biscuits.[32]

The St Ann board, joined by other parochial boards, such as Clarendon, continued to argue that despite the importance of the Lunatic Bill for the safety of the island, it was the major financial responsibility of the central government.[33] P. Arscott from the St Ann board, in a circular to all other parochial boards except the KSAC, argued:

> Law 26 of 1914 is unjust and operates unfairly urging a repeal of all parochial boards except for Kingston. Since 1914/15 when the law was passed, without knowing it the burden of Kingston lunatics has been shifted on to the parishes. This undue imposition has been in force now for 11 years. Every parochial board will therefore find it in its interest to have the lunatics removed at the earliest possible date. Based on investigation in 1911, the government besides making large refunds undertook to bear half the cost of the lunatics. For a few years the parochial boards were very greatly relieved. Then came this law of 1914 which gave all the benefit to Kingston. Law 26 of 1914 sought to address a grievance with impoverished people from the parishes drifting into Kingston and becoming a charge on the rates; but the actual number of these would be insignificant as compared with the actual number of lunatics from Kingston. It therefore did not need this drastic measure of the law of 1914.[34]

Although this battle between the parochial boards and the central government persisted beyond 1926, at no time did the parochial boards seek to have the Lunatic Law rescinded. It was clear to the parochial boards, as part of the colonial government, that the Lunatic Bill, as financially unjust as it was to them, was a most important tool in fighting current and future alleged "conspirators" against the state. People such as Alexander Bedward and the Bedwardites and fellow Revivalists had to be contained.

It comes as no surprise that the Lunatic Law was used twice against Alexander Bedward in May 1921, to have him permanently incarcerated in the asylum when he planned his march (manifestation) from August Town to Kingston. His first arrest resulted in the district medical officer utilizing the Lunatic Law to observe him for a week. The medical officer later told the judge that Bedward was of unsound mind and should be detained in the asylum, as he hallucinated that he was the Son of God, that his mother was the Virgin Mary, and his stepfather was Joseph, the carpenter in the Bible. With such a diagnosis, the judge concluded that Bedward was not fit for trial, since he was insane and hence not responsible for his actions. He was freed, to the jubilant cheers of his followers, but was immediately rearrested, as he left the court, by Sergeant Major Williams, on a charge of being a lunatic. He was led back to court and the same district medical officer gave evidence. Bedward was sent to the asylum.[35]

The Obeah and Vagrancy Acts

A Revised Obeah Act of 1898, and a Vagrancy Act, were two other important pieces of legislation produced by the state in tandem with the Lunatic Asylum Law. These bills complemented each other and were used interchangeably by the colonial authorities to attempt to halt the spread of Bedwardism and Revivalism across the island.

Obeah was initially criminalized in Jamaica to discourage enslaved uprisings; the Obeah Act symbolized the colonial government's hostility to African culture and the determination to suppress African Jamaican religion. Obeah was first made illegal in 1760, as part of a sweepingly repressive act passed in the aftermath of Tacky's Rebellion, the largest uprising of enslaved people in the eighteenth-century British Caribbean. The law was a direct response to the fact that the obeahmen advised rebellions' leaders and gave them courage, solidarity and spiritual protection. Along with prohibiting enslaved people from holding weapons and restricting their ability to congregate, the law made obeah a crime punishable by death, if done by any "Negro or other slave".

The law against obeah lapsed with the end of slavery in 1834. The Jamaican government, like other Caribbean governments, acted quickly to ensure that obeah remained a crime. The 1833 Vagrancy Act also prohibited obeah. The first stand-alone Obeah Act was passed in Jamaica in 1854. It made obeah a crime punishable by flogging and imprisonment and equated obeah with "myalism", thus defining obeah not just as acts meant to cause harm but connected more broadly to religions with African origins. Further changes to the Obeah Act took place in 1857, 1892 and 1893, before the Revised Obeah Act of 1898 was introduced.[36]

This latter act (1898) broadened the definition of obeah and introduced a legal category entitled the "Instrument of Obeah".[37] The obeah laws of 1892 and 1893 were indeed weak in contrast to the 1898 obeah law, which gave the state far more power to prosecute. The 1892 law (law 28 of 1892) gave a resident magistrate the authority to impose punishment on individuals who had been found guilty of practising obeah. It also defined the appropriate punishment to be administered. The 1893 act (law 1 of 1893) simply revised the number of lashes to be administered to those found guilty of practising obeah.[38]

The 1898 law, the Obeah Act (law 5 of 1898), still linked obeah to myalism, as in the earlier acts, but in this 1898 act, the assembly defined obeah in its own ethnocentric terms as follows:

> "A person practising Obeah" means any person who, to effect any fraudulent or unlawful purpose, or for gain, or for the purpose of frightening any person, uses or pretends to use any occult means, or pretends to possess any supernatural power or knowledge, and "Instrument of Obeah" means any thing used or intended to be used by a person and pretended by such person to be possessed of any occult or supernatural power.[39]

This revised definition of obeah was extremely broad and obscure. How could the colonial authorities measure precisely one's intention to practise obeah if one was not caught practising it? This was a deliberate attempt by the colonial state to make it easier to charge individuals for practising obeah. If it was proven that they had even attempted to persuade others to practise obeah, they could be charged. If it was proven that they possessed any of the instruments of obeah, even if the instruments were not being used, they would be guilty of practising obeah. Even claiming to have occult or supernatural powers also came under the classification of possessing instruments of obeah.

More important, the burden of proof now fell on those in possession of these "instruments" to prove that they were not practising obeah.[40] Once an individual was charged with obeah, he or she had to prove that there was no such instrument in their possession. People could now be entrapped into committing an offence. Previously the state had to prove the case of obeah, which was difficult. Even if one had in his or her possession the alleged instruments of obeah, the state had to prove they were practising obeah.

This entrapment was clearly noticeable in the discussion surrounding the revisions of the Obeah Act. One of the legislators in 1899 made the point that the Revised Obeah Act of 1898 was indeed helpful in giving the police more powers to make arrests in comparison to previous years. However, the bill was far from perfect and needed to be reread and discussed again to capture more people who were still escaping the dragnet owing to technicalities. "The law should be so framed to catch all the rascals," he concluded, resulting in loud laughter from the other legislators.[41] That is why they also had to address the perceived weakness in legally defining obeah. Its definition must be so comprehensive but specific that the bill targeted all the groups they sought to arrest.

The attorney general, in elaborating on the kinds of people the revised act should target, made it clear that the act would target those street preachers who constantly held meetings in the streets of Kingston. He stressed, "Well, they dance and howl like dervishes and they gave water in little bottles, which was supposed to have magical power, to their disciples (Bedward seems to be the reference); these people ought to be punished for obeah."[42]

Another legislator in agreement argued that while the police could track and catch the regular obeah worker, who was stationary in one space, these other rascals who played on the superstitious minds of others in more subtle ways were the ones whom this law was to catch. Thus, he agreed that the definition of obeah ought to be enlarged.

While some legislators cautioned their colleagues to be careful not to make the bill so large that it became ridiculous and oppressive, one of the other legislators, in supporting the broadness of the definition of the bill, questioned his colleagues, "Whether Bedwardism was not Obeah? Any person who pretended to have supernatural powers, like Bedward, ought to be punished for obeah." He then told the following story of a teacher in one of his schools who brought an "obeahman" into his school at inspection, to ensure that the school got a high rating. This incident occurred because the teacher had become a Bedwardite and was bringing Bedwardism into the school. "He would like the law so framed that every person working on the superstitions of his neighbour could be sent to prison or the Lunatic Asylum."

The very way in which the Obeah Act was framed meant that the police could easily trap suspects with the help of other individuals. As an example of the way Bedwardites were so entrapped, the case of Stewart Carter, a Bedwardite, is instructive. Carter was arrested by a police detective, Wallace, and carried to court. The police relied on one Joseph Barnes, who stated that on 6 October, he, Barnes, went to Carter's house on the Old Church Road, as he had a criminal charge against him for stealing a horse. When he got to Carter's house, he told him that there was a case in court against him and he wanted it dismissed. Carter told Barnes that he could have the case dismissed if Barnes paid him £2. A man who accompanied Barnes, by the name of Learnie, implored Carter to reduce the fee to £1 and Carter agreed. Carter told Barnes to return the following Monday night.

Barnes later testified that on the Monday night, Carter drank rum which he brought with him, then took the rest and sprinkled it on the ground, saying, "Take this and do the work." Carter then took some white powder, mixed it with water in a bottle and gave it to Barnes to sprinkle on the front and back door of the courthouse, as the judge would have to step over it, and the case would have to be dismissed. Carter then asked Barnes to pay the agreed £1, which was given. It was then that Detective Wallace, who was hiding outside, revealed himself and arrested Carter. Several people from the community attempted to rescue Carter from Wallace, testifying that Carter was an "outstanding" member of Bedward's church, had done nothing wrong and must not go to prison. Although Carter made a statement in court challenging the police's narrative, the judge concluded that the charge of obeah was clearly proven.[43] Carter was convicted in the St Andrew parish court in 1899 and sentenced to twelve months at hard labour, with eighteen lashes from the cat-o-nine, which would be administered in prison.[44]

The Revised Obeah Act targeted not only Bedwardites but also balm healers, Revivalists, Garveyites and later Leonard Howell and other members of Rastafari.[45] Diana Paton has shown the high number of people arrested under the Obeah Act, not only in Jamaica but all across the British Caribbean, in the late nineteenth and twentieth centuries.[46] Interestingly, the constitution of the Bedwardites made it clear that they were not Revivalists and should not be confused with them.[47] The colonial authorities, however, made no such distinction and included Bedwardites as people who practised obeah, especially since their leader was known to be selling water in special containers for the purpose of healing.

That is the reason that the 1890s–1930s, the very period of the rise and demise of Bedward, was a time of immense persecution of all African Jamaican religious movements. Diana Paton makes the point that although legislation concerning obeah was present in the early nineteenth century in the Caribbean, the intense period of legislation was from the 1890s to the 1920s. In this period, anti-obeah provisions were adopted or revised by at least Barbados, British Guiana, British Honduras, Grenada, Jamaica, the Leeward Islands, St Lucia, St Vincent and Trinidad.[48]

In attempting to so eliminate African cultural practices by way of the Obeah Act, many innocent Revivalists were included in the police's dragnets and publicly humiliated. Solomon J. Hewitt, affectionately called "Brother Sal", is one such example. Hewitt was dubbed the "Modern Messiah" of Smith's Village (West Kingston) and was considered by many as great as Bedward. He was even categorized in his heyday as one of Jamaica's famous prophets and was the closest to Bedward in terms of influence: more than half of the Revivalists in West Kingston were under his control.[49] Like Bedward, he was accused of having godlike delusions of grandeur and was proclaimed as a "prophet, warner and healer". Hewitt was also known to have the ability to look into the sun without blinking when he was prophesying. As a sign that he was possessed by the Spirit in his preaching, it was said that the spirit made him sound like a cow or a dog.⁵⁰ One journalist commented that Hewitt was the most violent preacher he had ever encountered. Dressed in a white gown, which was his trademark, Hewitt jumped, ran, wheeled and gesticulated while delivering a sermon. "You know that I have caused a commotion in Kingston," he told his followers. "They put me . . . the Lord's anointed . . . in Sutton Street gaol." God surely would bring fire and brimstone to punish those who had tried to stop his work, he promised.⁵¹

Hewitt gained more fame in 1914 by mounting a mock crucifixion, as it was the only way the city of Kingston could be saved from a recurrence of the 1907 earthquake.⁵² On Holy Thursday, his disciples mounted him on a heavy cross, leaving him there until the following afternoon. Then they took him down and wrapped him in a sheet. On Easter Sunday, like the historical Jesus, he "rose from the dead". The police arrested him and charged him with vagrancy.⁵³ In the initial hearing of the case in court, when his case was mentioned and he was not in the courtroom, the judge humorously proclaimed, "Has the Messiah come? Someone shouted out the day was not yet at hand."⁵⁴ The judge (Mr H.C. Robinson) ordered Hewitt to be remanded in custody for medical observation. Despite embarrassing Hewitt, the doctor declared him sane and that he could stand trial. Hewitt was remanded to spend a week in prison under medical observation, as the charge was upgraded to lunacy.⁵⁵

At Hewitt's trial for lunacy, the state's evidence crumbled, as it had no substantial evidence. One Corporal Willacy told how a few weeks earlier he had arrested Hewitt, whom he saw attired in a particular white gown and heard uttering an unknown language. Willacy thought that Hewitt was mad, so he arrested him. Hewitt's lawyer, Mr Lake, after cross-examining Willacy, concluded that Willacy should not have taken exception to the man's dress because he did not like it. They had wrongly targeted him. Furthermore, his client was a Christian, and if he decided to preach, as long as he did not disturb the peace of the community, he had done nothing wrong. The district medical officer's opinion of Hewitt as being of sound mind further led to the case against him being dismissed.⁵⁶

The police were not finished with Hewitt as yet, since they were convinced he possessed instruments of obeah and was an obeah worker. Within a month, he was again arrested and charged with lunacy and the *Daily Gleaner*'s headline again dubbed him the "Self-Proclaimed Messiah again charged with Lunacy". The doctor for the second time declared him sane to stand trial, and again the case against him was dismissed for insufficient evidence. The policemen on this occasion claimed that Hewitt had called down lightning and thunder from heaven to come on them and destroy the station. Two witnesses corroborated Hewitt's story that he had stopped near the station to greet a friend. He was formally dressed to take part in a procession and the policemen detained him, arguing that he had verbally assaulted them. The judge, recognizing that he had no prior convictions and that the police's claims seemed rather spurious, ordered Hewitt to pay £2 or spend thirty days in jail.[57]

Despite other attempts to discredit Hewitt, such as showing how he had female members literally fighting in public, he became a successful minister of religion in Smith's Village, where he founded the Hopewell Baptist Church in 1919 and led the church up to 1928, when it dedicated an organ with much fanfare and publicity. At the organ dedication he was specially congratulated by fellow pastors of traditional churches. One of the pastors was so impressed with Hewitt's leadership and the growth of the congregation that he admitted that Hewitt's church was no longer a Revival church, with jumping up and down and rolling over from fanatical spirits. He was glad to see the orderly manner in which the congregation conducted their worship.[58]

Despite passing stronger laws to defeat "obeahism" in Jamaica, the colonial authorities realized that they were not really winning the battle. Since obeah had to do with healing, the colonial officials even sought to revise the Medical Act so as to convict alleged workers of obeah. The Revised 1908 Medical Law, for example, was used to punish George Forbes and many other individuals. This law was not directly aimed at addressing charges of obeah, or any aspect of religion, but was used when the alleged offence committed did not necessarily fall under the Obeah Act.[59]

The colonial authorities revised the medical laws in 1896, 1905 and 1908.[60] In all three revisions none of the provisions addresses African healers, although mention is made of qualified practitioners of homeopathy. Since the medical laws of Jamaica made no provision to charge Revivalist preachers, why would the colonial authorities use them to convict some Revivalist healers, if it was not for their deep desire to eradicate Africanisms by any means necessary?

The Medical Law was one sure way to charge a Bedwardite or Revivalist for an obeah-related practice, although punishments under this law were significantly less severe than under the Obeah Act. It did not matter, as those convicted could be fined or flogged even if they were not imprisoned. Once an African Jamaican was so fined, even for a lesser offence, it would make a harsher punishment easier the next time they appeared in court.

The story of Mr and Mrs Forbes is a good example, as the wife, affectionately known as "Mama Forbes", was well known nationally as a Revivalist and an excellent African healer.[61] Mr Forbes and his wife

(Rose-Ann) ran a "balming sanatorium" at Blake's Pen, on the border of Manchester and St Elizabeth. The practice, which was started around 1900, became most prominent as Rose-Ann Forbes gradually took the reins of the business. It was believed that people from far and near parishes, suffering from various complaints, travelled by the hundreds to see "Mama" Forbes to ascertain the nature of their disease. A fee was charged, and, on the patient becoming an inmate of the sanatorium, he or she was allegedly washed with the water of various bushes boiled together. Patients paid board and lodging until discharged. Obviously, the police had been watching the establishment for some time.

Rose-Ann Forbes was arrested and prosecuted in 1910 for unlawfully practising medicine. The magistrate, while sentencing her, warned her to "destroy all her implements when she got home, and to dress differently, for if the police found anything, such as bottles and feathers and took them to court, a charge of obeah could be brought against her". She not only was fined two shillings and sixpence but also had to pay much larger costs of £4.17.6.[62]

In their second attempt to entrap Mama Forbes, this time for obeah, the police only succeeded in arresting her husband. The trial took place on 4 April 1917. One Theophilus Doreman, a labourer residing in St Elizabeth, was a witness for the police. He claimed that on 21 February, he went to Blake's Pen with Louisa Granston to the Balm, in the afternoon. A young man came out and asked if he had any case to try. Doreman said, "Yes," and Louisa Granston went behind a screen, where Mr Forbes asked her if she had any money. Two shillings and sixpence was given to him. Mr Forbes had a Bible in his hand which he waved over Louisa Granston's head, while speaking in an unknown tongue. He then dipped his finger in a basin of soapsuds and placed it on her forehead and in the palm of her hand. He spoke again in an unknown tongue and clapped his hands. He gave the woman a tumbler full of whitish stuff and told her to take three sips, which she did, while he said, "Praise Father, praise son, and praise Holy Ghost." No more money was paid. Forbes stated that Louisa Granston's leg was poisoned and would be cured, "and anyone who came to his Balm, no ghost or obeah could trouble them again". Before they left the next day, Forbes gave them two more glasses of bush water to drink.

Mr Forbes's lawyer petitioned the judge to be lenient, since George Forbes was now a poor man and had to depend on his wife for support. Furthermore, his client carried on a meeting house and people with sores came to him for help. The lawyer claimed Forbes had a special gift for helping people of all kinds; some were helped by the bathing and some said they much preferred the herbs to the regular medicine. The judge agreed and charged Mr Forbes under the Medical Law, while the obeah charge was dismissed. The judge then gave a "sound lecturing" to Mr Forbes, then his wife, and advised her to discontinue the practice. If they were ever brought up in court again for a similar charge, they would face a £50 fine and a term of imprisonment.[63]

The colonial authorities even used the Kingston Police Laws of 1881–87, which were amended in 1902 to attempt to curtail the level of Revivalist street preaching in Kingston. Law 12 of 1887, which amended law 36 of 1881, specifically stated that its aim was "to restrict, regulate and control all meetings or gathering of persons in all or any of the streets, lanes, squares, park, roads, thoroughfares or other public places within the city or parish of Kingston, or as to any particular place or places within the said City and Parish, or as to any specified days, times and hours, to prohibit such street meetings or gathering of persons."[64]

These were in turn adopted by the mayor of Kingston and the KSAC. But even in the face of these laws, the Revivalist preachers continued to create what the colonialists dubbed "disturbance" with their preaching and healing, all across the country, especially in Kingston.[65] Despite the state's revisions of the laws from the 1890s to the 1920s to make them adaptable and to increase their efforts to control and eventually destroy both Bedwardism and Revivalism, their attempts failed. The Bedwardites flourished and the Revivalists remained rampant all over the country. Bedward's disciples and admirers were everywhere. Bedward's black wall was encircling the white wall, and it was only a matter of time before he sought finally to crush the white wall.

The Black Wall of Revivalism in Jamaica

One of the major reasons for the colonial administration's targeting of Revivalist leaders, such as Hewitt, was the fear of the growing influence of Revival religion. It was prominent in yards, street corners and lanes all over the island. This situation was particularly troubling as the popularity and presence of Bedwardism strengthened Revival religion. Bedwardism had remained a growing, stable, national movement despite colonial harassment and was a signal of African resistance to colonial culture. The spread of Bedwardism across the island signalled hope for Revivalists, since it showed that blacks could organize themselves and build and sustain a religious movement which was a viable alternative to colonial religion. Bedwardism, its growth and stability had political implications and meant that the myriad of Revivalists and African-Christian religious movements across the island could copy from Bedward's playbook. Historians have commented on the numerous Revivalists scattered across the island building a reputation for themselves as healers. Like Alexander Bedward, they too relied on water rituals for healing. People such as Simon Bygrove of Crofts Hill, Elder Raymond and Alexander Crawford of Bath, St Thomas, were all practising water rituals for healing.[66]

This helps to explain why there was a frantic appeal in the newspapers by Jamaicans committed to British culture who wanted the Obeah Act expanded to catch more Revivalists. A writer, in making his appeal in the *Daily Gleaner*, argued that in the next amendment of the Obeah Act, a stronger provision ought to be implemented to end Revivalism, as this should have been done a long time ago in the previous amendments. The writer stressed:

> During the last session of the Legislative Council we strongly urge our lawmakers to make some steps to put a stop to this thing called Revivalism which flourishes so rampantly in this country and which is one of the most demoralizing influences at work amongst the peasantry. We pointed out that the Obeah law did not touch this evil but did not even mention it, indeed but had curiously confounded myalism with obeah whereas myal and Revival are one and the same thing. You never hear of myalism in Jamaica now simply because it has become Revivalism. Its votaries have changed its name, have appropriated to its own use a word commonly used in Christian phraseology and so are free to indulge in the most degrading practices without the slightest fear of hindrance from the law. Myalism in its essence is what obeah is. Revivalism not only leads to the asylum but is the greatest form of licentiousness. The council is not listening and now the police themselves are loudly crying out against it, and in the last Annual Report of the Inspector General, he states that superstition is still rife amongst some of the people and whether it takes the shape of obeah, belief in bush doctors, medicine, Revivalism etc, the possibilities of serious crimes are always present. While legislation has not yet been made to check Revivalism, this form of religious fanaticism is a blot against civilization and leads its ignorant devotees in many cases to the prisons or the lunatic asylum. Why condemn obeah and allow myalism in disguise as Revivalism to run rampant?[67]

One could understand the writer's fear, as the newspapers, particularly the *Daily Gleaner*, as the largest and most influential, gave numerous examples of the increasing presence of Bedwardism and Revivalism and their sociopolitical impact across the island. It would appear that these notorious Revivalist preachers were either copying Alexander Bedward or being influenced by him in their social critique of the colonial state. These preachers had developed a reputation with their own devoted followers, and like Bedward, the state had already targeted them as insane and kept their activities under a watchful eye. John Higgins is a prime example.

Higgins had developed his reputation as a Revivalist street preacher and had amassed a large following in the city of Kingston. His signature claim was the sword in his hand, which he used to rally God's people. He returned from England to the West Indies with money which the *Daily Gleaner* claimed had been bamboozled from an old lady under the guise of benefiting the "poor heathens" in the West Indies. It is further claimed that he purchased a second-class naval uniform, which he adorned with fresh gold lace. He then obtained an old rusty sword and with this weapon knighted himself "Sir Joshua Higgins". He formed the Royal Millennium Baptist Missionary Society and Associated Millennium Hospital for herbal treatment of illnesses in 1889. He earned the sobriquet "Warrior Higgins" for his fiery denunciations of the mainstream churches and the colonial civil authorities. He even called the Anglican bishop "a damn lazy idle dog", castigated the same bishop and the pope as "damn confounded liars" and called ministers of religion and judges fools, even mocking the king publicly.[68]

He was constantly in trouble with the colonial authorities, and on several occasions he was dragged off to jail. He was charged on two occasions in 1897 for illegally firing a pistol in public, and in 1899 had some of his followers allegedly assault a member of the crowd who jeered Higgins, after threatening the man with his sword.[69]

Higgins worked with Bedward and they conducted mass baptisms together in the Hope River on numerous occasions. However, the rivalry between the two men was often intense, as both had strong personalities, with Higgins attempting to attract Bedwardites to his movement. On one such occasion, he even challenged Bedward's right to call himself a bishop. Higgins also charged that Bedward's chief minister, the Reverend C.C. Carr, was too old and incompetent to perform his duties properly. In reply, it is alleged that Bedward insulted him. But despite their disagreement and temporary stand-off, the two continued to have joint services.[70]

If the *Daily Gleaner*'s account of one such clash is credible, then the encounters between the two men were often heated. The *Daily Gleaner* published on 13 May 1904 the following sensational headline, "Rival Dowies Stirred Jamaica: A New Version of Bedward, Higgins". The story, which was originally printed overseas, highlighted the struggle between the two. While Higgins was preaching at one of his meetings in the Hope River and waving his sword in Bedward's stronghold, he was interrupted by Bedward, proclaiming that he was John the Baptist. "Instantly, there was a free flight as some of the Revivalists stuck to Higgins, but the majority sided with Bedward given his dramatic entrance. This resulted in the two factions quarreling."⁷¹

Higgins tried on several other occasions to challenge Bedward. On one such occasion, he even placed an advertisement in a newspaper for a wife, who had to be brown in complexion like Jamaican mulattoes, or not too black. The strategy, it seemed, was to influence more women to leave Bedward's movement for his. If this story is to be believed, given the penchant of the *Gleaner* journalists to vilify Bedward, the latter responded by making it known that any woman who left to join Higgins would suffer "death in fearful agony". Although Higgins gained a few more female followers elsewhere, all his attempts to weaken Bedward's stronghold were futile.⁷²

After Higgins's death in 1902, Higginism was still a problem for colonial officials. W.F. Dougal took up Higgins's sword and his fierce attack on colonial leaders, to the extent that the Kingston City Council was bombarded by requests from concerned citizens to destroy Higginism once and for all.⁷³

Prince Makaroo, or Uriah Brown, from the parish of St Elizabeth, is another such contemporary of Bedward. While not as flamboyant as Higgins, Makaroo returned from London to Jamaica in 1904 and started preaching, denouncing the government and its unjust laws and calling for his fellow black countrymen to strike and not pay taxes. He pleaded with his followers to end their oppression by the colonialists. He was charged with sedition but luckily received a light sentence of one month's imprisonment with hard labour.⁷⁴

The Consolidation of Bedwardism

Some historians, such as Satchell, opine that the arrest and trial of Bedward in 1895 to some extent stunted the rapid growth of Bedwardism. Such a perspective is plausible if the criterion used is the national paranoia surrounding Bedwardism before and after 1895. The more plausible way to examine the post-1895 period is to view it as a time of institutional consolidation of the movement, as argued by Moore and Johnson. They posit that one major factor accounting for the persistence of Bedwardism was its reorganization post-1895. The decorum of the "dippers" in the Hope River changed, in contrast to previous years. No longer were people "partially nude"; they were now "properly" clothed.⁷⁵ Moore and Johnson seem to be correct, as one of the residents of August Town who knew

Bedward as a child remembers that part of the river was later partitioned by the Bedwardites for dressing, while the other part was for baptisms.[76] It was a clear sign of the movement's attempt at better organization, better structure, polity and doctrines, for greater credibility, especially in the context of immense criticism and harassment by the colonial authorities and their allies.

Even a *Daily Gleaner* reporter who visited Bedward in 1910 spoke glowingly about the impressive chapel, which was almost complete, as were other buildings on the compound. The number of candidates coming forward for baptism was also still very large, and it was clear that Bedwardism was now a "settled" institution in August Town. With stability in the post-1890s period came expansion, as deliberate attempts were made to solidify a national movement with better organized chapters all over the country.

Although national paranoia was not as intense as in the earlier phase of the movement, writers to the *Daily Gleaner* continued to express dismay concerning the stability and growth of the movement after 1895. One writer, for example, in 1907 castigated the Christian churches across the island for their ineffectiveness as one of the main reasons for the increase of Bedwardism. The writer opined that based on Bedwardism's rate of growth, it would shortly become the face of Christianity. Although admitting that "decent people" like himself would not become Bedwardites, he admitted the movement fulfilled a real need in the lives of working-class Jamaicans.[77]

While upper-class Jamaicans were primarily sceptical of Bedwardism, the reporter made it clear that Bedward taught from the Bible and was committed to it for biblical truth, similarly to the Christian church. Bedward's healing in the Hope River was consistent with healing in the Bible; Bedward also believed in the Trinity, as the traditional church did. Furthermore, Bedward also believed in miracles and preached about faith, prayer and baptism by immersion, all of which were taught by the traditional churches. More important, Bedward was diametrically opposed to "obeahism" and witchcraft, as the traditional churches were. The people who flocked to Bedwardism read their Bibles and knew that Bedward was not an obeahman. Thus Bedwardism was bound to grow, as the masses who followed Bedward believed in the Bible, although it was secondary to the leading of the Spirit. The masses looked to Prophet Bedward for biblical interpretation based on their socioeconomic and political conditions. Thus it was quite clear to the Bedwardites that any criticism of Bedward was an attack against them and their Afro-Jamaican culture and hermeneutics.

While the writer views Bedwardism as better and more organized than the old form of myalism, which was too emotional, he cautioned the

Christian churches to take heed quickly so that Bedwardism does not replace them. Bedward deliberately and wisely positioned his movement to reflect traditional Christianity while catering to the needs of ordinary black Jamaicans.

Another writer, in the *Jamaica Times*, reminded his readers in 1905 that Bedwardism was still flourishing, despite the belief that it was weaker than when it began. Pilgrims from all over the country were still finding their way to August Town, their sacred meeting place, to listen to the weekly prophecies and discourses of Bedward. More important, they were still bathing in the healing stream and experiencing its efficacy. To these devotees of Bedward, although they were in thought and rituals miles away and apart from traditional Catholics and Anglicans, it was clear that their movement was authentic, as Bedward also professed great attachment to the major festivals of the church. Special Easter services, such as Good Friday and Easter Sunday, were observed, just as in traditional Christian churches. On those days, hundreds of men, women and children could be observed faithfully and religiously making their way from all the various roads across the corporate area to August Town and going towards their Union Temple.[78]

As an example of their growing influence, he writes:

> I have been around and over this island time and time again and there has never been a spot where I have not found a fervent Bedwardite. And indeed, I have very often met people by the scores, in the most obscure parts of the island, travelling towards the Mona "healing stream" which they look upon with the fervency of the Mohamedan as he turns towards Mecca. These journeys are undertaken in many cases at great personal inconvenience. The attraction of Bedwardism is so strong that it draws its votaries even from the churches; nearly every religious body gives its quota; and even members of the Roman Catholic church I have met who have loudly testified in favour of the virtues of the healing stream.

Given the growth and stability of Bedwardism and the flourishing of Revivalism over the island, the Jamaican authorities combined the use of their laws for more convictions.[79] A charge of lunacy, if it was seen to be too strong, could be changed to vagrancy in the courts, so that if not sent to the asylum, the person could still be punished with a lesser charge. A charge of vagrancy could be upgraded to lunacy, resulting in the individual being sent to the asylum. The decision about which specific charge to bring lay initially with the police and considered the relative seriousness with which the law treated different offences, and the charge that was most likely to result in conviction.[80] However, the final decision resulted in the interaction in the courts, among police, magistrates and prosecution lawyers.[81] Despite the strong arm of the state and the juggling of their laws to crush the black wall, Revival religion was still prominent all over the island. The Bedwardites and the Revivalists remained firm and unshaken. Bedward was about to make his move, however, as the black wall would seek to crush the white wall.

Chapter 5

Judgement Day

Tearing Down the White Wall

French philosopher Michel Foucault argued in his groundbreaking work that the classification of people as "insane" and their separation from the "sane" ones, for hospitalization and treatment, is a product of the European Enlightenment. Before that period, the mentally ill in Europe lived normally in society and were at times admired for their differences. Thus this concept of "madness" is not a natural, unchanging reality but, rather, depends on the society in which one lives.[1] Although some scholars disagree with Foucault's argument, his thesis that culture largely defines insanity within a given society is a critical point. Societies construct the criteria for madness, and hence insanity is a subjective reality.

European colonial societies in Africa, Asia and the Americas constructed such societies, where normality and sanity were tantamount to obedience and conformity to colonial culture. Resistance to European colonialism by exhibiting cultural differences, such as practising one's African culture, resulted in the classification of insanity. It was quite noticeable in the writings of some white Europeans and North Americans living in Jamaica that Africans had a hereditary challenge with "insanity" because they insisted on living their culture. The more Africans practised aspects of their culture, such as Revival religion, the more they were described as insane.

Noted Caribbean psychiatrists Frederick Hickling and Gerard Hutchinson challenge the notion that heredity is a major cause of insanity and argue that it is largely determined by one's environmental circumstances. In their 2011 study of the causes of schizophrenia in African Caribbean males in Europe, they suggested several environmental causes. Their main thesis was that chronic and long-term experience of "social defeat" by African Caribbean males and their subordinate position or their "outsider" status being raised in Europe contributed to their increased risk of schizophrenia. The display of "madness and badness" among African Caribbean youths was in fact an expression of social defiance, which resulted from the five-hundred-year history of European colonialism and oppression of Caribbean culture.[2]

Hickling and Hutchinson presented evidence from contemporary dancehall culture which shows that the artistic expression of these young men was a vehicle of social defiance. These dancehall songs had coded messages legitimizing madness as antidote to the social oppression of urbanization, racism, economic enslavement and marginalization. The message of madness was the symbol of adaptive coping behaviour in contemporary Caribbean societies at home and abroad, reaching deep into the consciousness of Caribbean people living in North America and Europe. In Jamaica, this "mad" message incorporates "violence and abnormal speech and behaviour" as the vehicles of rebellion and is addressed to the youth internationally as a blueprint for liberation. In Trinidad and Tobago, the message of violence is muted, while the message of madness is a perfectly reasonable behavioural response to release the stresses of everyday life. The evidence suggests that "madness", as described by the British colonialists, is an alternative explication of the Caribbean experience and reinforces the philosophy that madness can be accommodated in the community, if it can be positively associated with personal liberation and selfhood.

It is this social defiance or "badness" against the colonized world which Bedward carved out for himself and his followers. This badness or "in-your-face" defiance made his movement attractive, especially to the black working class, nationally and internationally. Bedward portrayed such a sense of badness, barefacedness, audacity in the face of colonial harassment and oppression that he was immortalized in folk culture as someone who should not be interfered with, as he was notoriously bad, thus giving rise to the folk song "Sly Mongoose". The writers of the song and dance correctly historicize the duel between Bedward and the British:

> Sly Mongoose,
> Your name gone abroad.
> Sly Mongoose,
> Your name gone abroad.
>
> Mongoose go inna Bedward's kitchen,
> Tek out one a 'im big fat chicken,
> Put it eena 'im wescut pocket,
> Sly mongoose.
>
> Sly Mongoose,
> Your name gone abroad.
> Sly Mongoose,
> Your name gone abroad.

> Mongoose run inna Bedward's kitchen,
> There go one a 'im big fat chicken,
> Put it eena 'im wescut pocket,
> Sly mongoose.³

Although "Sly Mongoose" is currently a popular folk song across the Caribbean with different variations, the original folk song seemed to have been "Slide, Mongoose, Slide". The latter was a popular song and dance in Jamaica in the early 1900s. In the Jamaican version, the British are identified as the mongoose that interfered with Bedward, by figuratively stealing one of his precious chickens. In so doing, they made a bad error and will have to run, as Bedward will hunt them down and destroy them. The song and dance therefore prophesied the destruction of the British because of Bedward. As performed for local audiences in the 1920s and 1930s, it featured a dance called the "Mongoose Slide", as the mongoose was seen running from Bedward, who was chasing them. This imagery was popular in local dances, as the idea was that mongoose had to run since they troubled Bedward.

"HGD", a journalist from the *Daily Gleaner*, describes the pandemonium of excitement and laughter the song and dance elicited when it was performed in his presence at the Constant Spring Hotel in 1921, as the mongoose was running and sliding and trying not to be caught.

Even in the asylum where Bedward was later housed, Bedward complained to the authorities that he had been teased by fellow inmates ever since a band was invited to play the song and perform the dance at a party.⁴

The song and dance surrounding the "Mongoose Slide" led to the creation of other song-and-dance dramatic pieces, such as "Run Mongoose Run". The latter had become so popular in the island's culture that it was used even at the St Mary's Agricultural Show to promote a membership drive by way of a certificate of membership to attendees. The organizers even brought a live mongoose to parade near the certificates, as a drawing card for membership. The promotion for the certificate drive was carved conspicuously by hand on a wooden frame and read:

> Run Mongoose, Run. If you can't run then slide; if you cant slide then walk and if you cant walk hop, if you cant hop, limp. The Ancient Reckless and the Imprudent Order of the Running Mongoose Certificate of Membership. This is to certify that _____ this day qualified as a member of the above order and is entitled to all the rights and privileges thereof. Given under our hand and seal this day of ___ 19___.
> CMG President
> Secretary.⁵

Some of the British residents of Jamaica were not amused by the folk imagery generally of a running mongoose and the song and dance of the "Mongoose Slide". The folk culture identified them as thieves, and as people who literally harassed and oppressed the black population, just as the mongoose did when initially brought into Jamaica to eat the rats in the cane fields. The mongoose turned on innocent households, eating their chickens and becoming a nuisance across the island. The mongoose multiplied so rapidly and became so devastating to many families, stealing their possessions, destroying the bird population and the natural environment, that the government of Jamaica for years introduced numerous initiatives to rid the island of the horrible mongoose.[6]

But the imagery of the thieving British resonated in African Jamaican culture to the extent that the song and dance were the most popular cultural item performed across the island. Even colonial businesses used sections of the song about the running mongoose in advertisements promoting their products in the *Daily Gleaner*. One such advertisement is as follows:

> Mongoose broke into McKay's drug store
> Stole a bottle of his famous cough cure
> Run Mongoose
> Mongoose from indigestion suffered
> Which prevents him enjoying his supper
> But DIGES-O-VIM cured him
> Slide Mongoose
> Mongoose a corn on his big toe
> Which made him look very sad
> Ideal corn cure made him glad
> Run Mongoose
>
> EGBERT MCKAY, Druggist
> 117 Water Lane, one door east of King Street, Amen Corner[7]

Foreign audiences, such as Canadians, entering the Jamaican space, where Jamaican culture was being paraded, enjoyed the song and dance, although not understanding the language of the song and its implications. It was the African population of the island which owned this interpretation of Bedward and made it one of their favourite folk songs. It was performed even in front of British dignitaries, as noted by the *Daily Gleaner*:

> They came down from the hills and bush bringing with them their handmade drums which were beaten not with sticks but with their fingers and palms in a rhythm that was straight, one felt out of the African bush. They came ready to dance as they danced when the Duke and Duchess of Kent were the guests of

the island; they danced as they danced in the villages on Christmas, when John Canoe galloped through the streets, followed by Horsehead and the Set Girls singing Mango Walk and Slide Mongoose Slide and the other Jamaican tunes that would make Tin Pan Alley marvel and grow jealous.[8]

Hence Bedward's impact was so significant among the African masses that he was immortalized in folk culture as the victim of the British. More important, he was the more powerful of the two cultures and the more dangerous, as the mongoose better run, as Bedward was coming. Alexander Bedward had created an alternative, creolized culture where a semblance of African heritage could be boldly practised without any care for the consequences. To add to Bedward's temerity, he later declared himself "Lord and Master" to inform the colonialists that he, Bedward, and no other oversaw his destiny.

He had the faith to believe that he could cry judgement on his oppressors and to determine when such justice would occur and when his poor victimized black brothers and sisters would be vindicated. He deliberately took on the white colonial establishment indirectly by building his movement, which was both national and international. Directly, he took the fight to the colonial class, as will be discussed shortly, and the only logical conclusion, to a colonial mind, was that he had to be insane to deliberately provoke British colonial power. People who captured his state of being in the court trials of 1895 and 1921 testified to his calm composure. In the preliminary trial of 1895, he held the Bible close to his chest to symbolize his source and hope. In the actual trial of 1895, he left his Bible but remained calm throughout the trial – even when he was pronounced guilty by the jury. He was never rattled, and to the joy of his followers, he was eventually freed.

Bedwardism and the Community of Saints

Towards the end of 1920, the *Daily Gleaner* carried numerous reports highlighting a seismic shift in the status of Alexander Bedward. He was now to be addressed by all as "Lord and Master" and no longer as "Shepherd". More important, he was announcing a day of judgement on British colonialism, as the day of his justice was imminent.[9] The exact time of the change in his title is uncertain, although some Bedwardites believed it was said on a third Sunday at one of his mass baptisms. What seems to have triggered a public discussion surrounding the merit of Bedward's claiming to be "Lord and Master" is a letter from Roman Henry to the Bedwardites. Towards the end of 1920 Henry informed them that Bedward's work was coming to a climax and they should attend a final rally of the movement.

The earthly phase of Bedward's work was closing.[10] The next phase was his return or second advent as the Christ, followed by divine judgement. The *Daily Gleaner* then got wind of the story of Bedward's new title, that of the Christ, and started to sensationalize the story.

This final rally of the Bedwardites seems to have been the main reason for their migration into August Town in droves towards the end of 1920. Of course, the hysteria in the media that Bedward would be flying to heaven made the event more dramatic and exciting, as some of the Bedwardites seemed to have also adopted that view. Bedwardites, such as one Mr Skervin from one of the St Thomas chapters, insist that they were commanded to attend the rally in 1920. The occasion was not an invitation to see Bedward fly to heaven, as the media claimed. They were to close their chapter in St Thomas and gather at their headquarters in Union Temple, August Town, as Bedward's work on earth would be closed shortly. This is why members of his chapter, along with many other Bedwardites, even from overseas, gathered like sand on the ground in 1920, to spend time with their lord and master.[11]

Bedward's declaration of judgement on the colonial order in Jamaica was highly symbolic of his understanding of his messianic status as the "black Christ". He seemed to have been of that view from very early in his prophetic career but claimed that God forbade him to reveal it. Henry acknowledged that Bedward had always had that self-awareness and that his divinity was revealed to Henry in a dream.[12]

Bedward believed that he had to keep it a secret, though in the beginning of his ministry in August Town, he made it known to others, including his mother, that he was the black Christ. He therefore visited the community by going around visiting homes in the mornings and prophesying to people regarding their condition.[13] Bedward was so accurate in his predictions that some people became uncomfortable, and caught him, held him down on the ground and tied him up. He was then flogged mercilessly. People who knew Bedward sent for his mother in Barbican, and when she came and saw him, she cried, "Lord, look me one son Aleck, look what unu do to him." Bedward, lying on the ground, said gently to his mother, "Don't cry over me, I am Jesus." She exclaimed, "Lord, is now I know say you mad." Bedward was disappointed and dejected that his own mother was unable to recognize him. Then God's voice spoke to him: "You see that even your own mother don't know who you are. Stop proclaiming it and do the work that I have called you to do. The work will speak for itself." Bedward therefore stopped proclaiming his divinity and continued his work.[14]

Bedward's understanding of his divinity, which he made public in the latter period of 1920, seems to have been strategic. He got the attention of the entire nation, as he argued that he had fulfilled his mission on earth and that it was now time for his movement to be vindicated. Bedward saw parallels between himself and the historical Jesus, the Christ. Jesus turned water into wine; Bedward turned water into medicine. Jesus spent around thirty-three years on earth ministering; Bedward spent some thirty-two–thirty-three years preaching and teaching as Jesus did. Jesus was crucified by the state and Bedward too was to face his crucifixion. Jesus had built a community of disciples to carry out his work after his death; Bedward had also built a solid community of believers, who were trained to carry on the movement and to remain a model for all to see.

Before 1920, Bedward had built a socioeconomic and independent self-sustaining community of believers. They were a model community of self-discipline, with an excellent work ethic, and were admired and respected by all residents of August Town. Even non-Bedwardites had glowing remarks for the Bedwardites. One such Adventist member in the community testified that when he moved to August Town, long after Bedward's death, he was particularly struck by the Bedwardites' care and concern for each other. He had to admit that the Bedwardites were the first religious movement he had witnessed displaying such a unique model of love and dependence on each other.[15]

Roman Henry, in recalling the nature of their community spirit established by Bedward, made the following remarks.

> It was also patterned on peace and love where all must either not eat but cannot eat at the expense of others. . . . Anything you have is mine and when de work going on we have to bring mat from St Thomas for a ground we sleeping upon. And each parish . . . have a room and of the twenty-five of us in the one room belong to that mission. And all the donkey pad, and everything sister and brother, the whole of we lie down on it. So tight on the mat dat when you get up out a whee you lie down, you cant go deh go lie down pon your back for you pack up so thick you have to go back same way, because you just go in so, sister and brother. And for eight days, you are here. . . . Is what now we're going up into, and Christ government that let you understand that him give eye fe eye, nose fe nose, mouth . . . him give everything that him have fe sinner. So that is. You have to give everything. That's the way Bedward lay de foundation.[16]

They were taught specially by Bedward to work as a team, as unity was most important. If one of the members got a task in the form of a job outside of the community, several Bedwardites would accompany him or her on the job. That was how they survived as a community, as begging was out of the question. They had to be self-reliant. They burnt coal, lime and even made sugar and bammies for sale.[17] One of the elder Bedwardites remarked that Bedward healed not only one's body but also one's mind.[18]

Thus Bedward's headquarters at August Town was a state within a state. Bedward developed social welfare programmes for his followers. Many members of his church, especially those in August Town, lived in a communal camp, and their individual needs were seen as secondary to the community as a whole. Their commune was specially designed in a semicircular shape with the church in the middle, as the latter was the centre of their movement. Various August Town residents estimate that the commune, which seems to have been on two to three acres of land, consisted of fifty to sixty homes. Around two hundred Bedwardites lived in the commune, while others lived outside it, but still in August Town. Across from the commune was the Bedwardite cemetery, which seems to have been on another two to three acres of land. The Bedwardites governed themselves, and their movement could be compared to a fraternal society; outsiders did not know the intricacies of their operations. They had their own shops, their own vegetable gardens, their own farms, their own ironing facilities, their own donkeys and their own washing houses. They washed in their huts on Mondays, and the men carried their own produce to the markets for sale and used the funds to buy groceries their commune needed. Thus all Bedwardites always had enough to eat.[19]

Both men and women who had the strength to work did cooperative farming, especially in a section of August Town known as Tower Hill, where they had various farms, which produced cash crops for sale in the markets. They also burnt wood in the mountains to produce charcoal, which was sold as an affordable alternative for cooking for many working-class Jamaicans.[20]

Together, men and women went to neighbouring communities such as College Common and broke stones, which they would sell to contractors to pave the roads.[21] They would also collect stones from the riverside and from Dawkins Pond near the Mona hotel for sale to others. They would also pick any wild bush they could find which could be used to make tea and offer it for sale in the market in a bundle – popular products, such as cerasee, marigold, vervaine and even ackee, which is now the country's national dish. From the proceeds of the sale of these products they bought meat and fish at the market.[22]

The commune seems to have been designed primarily for Bedwardites who committed themselves to work fully with Bedward. They were provided with a home, as daily prayers started as early as 4.30 a.m. and there were around seventeen different weekly services which required their participation.[23] Secondly, the commune catered for members of the church from other parts of the island who were materially deprived and needed economic assistance. It also catered to members who had returned from overseas and fell on hard times and needed support. Such individuals were given a small plot of land, after which Bedwardite tradesmen helped them to construct a board house. Significantly, the commune seems also to have been an attempt by the movement to create an attractive community of self-reliant believers, who exemplified a visible model of their African tradition and culture.

The fruits grown in the commune were collectively owned, and at crop time they were sold and the proceeds placed in a common fund for welfare purposes. At baptism, the inductees were given a membership card, which attracted an annual fee of one shilling. At Holy Communion services, a further threepence was collected, and periodically other collections were taken to meet specific welfare needs.[24] These monetary contributions went towards providing basic welfare services for the members. For Bedward, "A 'ungry saint makes a wicked sinner."[25]

The Bedwardites also ran a social welfare fund. Whenever a member was in need of anything a leader would be informed, and the goods were purchased from the fund for the individual. A "Burial Scheme" was also established, for which a special fund was collected to meet the funeral expenses of members, especially the most indigent ones. In the absence of government welfare programmes, which were desperately needed at that time, Bedward's Jamaica Native Baptist Free Church provided important services for its members. In fact, no other church or religious movement at that time had a comparable range of social services. This programme was one of the principal foundations of the movement and served to strengthen Bedward's influence over the people.[26]

This programme of the Bedwardites is even more remarkable when one considers that they did not preach a 10 per cent tithing, as practised in many of the Christian churches. The angelic order given to Bedward was that each member was required to pay a penny a month or a shilling for the entire year, which entitled each to a ticket or confirmation of membership. For communion services each member should contribute threepence to assist in buying the wine and bread. An elderly person would bake the unleavened bread for all members and the grape juice would be purchased. All other collections for other projects were not obligatory on the members, as Bedward found the funds to run their commune by raising goats and chickens. He insisted that they had to remain self-reliant and not be governed by the dictates of colonial Jamaica.[27]

Bedward was an effective leader with a vision of where he was going and how to get his members to follow him. As leader, he had to continue to increase his assets, given the growth of his movement. He also knew that he had to maximize the human resources available to him, if he was to remain one step ahead, and if the movement was to remain independent. Overall, it is estimated that Bedward had acquired around four acres of land for himself, which allowed him to build such a self-reliant community.[28] In the early years, he kept buying small pieces of land around him as he saw the movement's expansion.[29] He also received land from his brother-in-law William Burke, who gave him an extra half-acre for the movement and another two acres to remain in the Burke family to be used generationally.[30] It is unclear, however, if Bedward utilized these two additional acres or added it to his acreages.

As the time approached for Bedward's anticipated ascension, August Town was flooded with more believers from all over the island, along with other enquirers and speculators. Numerous misguided Bedwardites were now investing their little earnings with Bedward and literally joining his self-sustaining community because they thought they were witnessing the last days. Day after day, the *Daily Gleaner* carried stories of the working poor and middle-class people selling their possessions and turning over the proceeds to Bedward. Even his critics had to admit that people who chose to give their life earnings to the Bedwardites would be materially taken care of for the rest of their lives.[31] One such critic in the *Daily Gleaner* wrote:

> Make no mistake the Bedwardites will never starve nor will they ever be naked. Bedward has established a huge fund into which all the money of his faithful followers flow . . . of course the expenditure of August Town is no small one. At least six or eight bags of flour have got to be purchased as also saltfish, pickled fish, rice and flour. Fed daily and properly housed, the Bedwardites have no care or responsibility and if their white turbans or costumes get worn they are aided in replacing them. Thus, when you become a Bedwardite and you settle down at August Town you suffer no hardships.[32]

Another critic blamed the government for pussyfooting around the Bedwardites all along, resulting in chaos, as many were now sacrificing their lands, goods and chattels and had nothing left to support themselves. Assuming their self-styled Lord disappeared, these poor unfortunate people would become a charge on the country's revenue. If that should happen, it would lead to a social epidemic and not one more single tourist would come to Jamaica.³³ The Bedwardites were not in the least concerned with the various public commentaries on their material existence, as many of them were convinced that Judgement Day was at hand.

A few people who experienced the socioeconomic impact of Bedward's announcement even sought the assistance of the courts. One Thomas Spencer, for example, a middle-aged black man from St Catherine who was once a Bedwardite but had left the movement, complained to a judge that his wife of thirty-one years had left him and gone to live in August Town with fellow Bedwardites. Worst of all, Bedward was making it clear that all the women in his movement at August Town were his wives. His wife had vowed not to return home. The judge advised him that the state could not get involved in such a personal matter and that he needed the advice of others, such as lawyers, who could better help him.³⁴

Judgement Day

Roman Henry insists that his letter to the Bedwardites was never meant to convey that Bedward would literally fly to heaven, although flying home to his father was not impossible for a person like Bedward. The invitation to the Bedwardites was to be with him as they closed this phase of the work in a great convention. The call was never meant for Bedwardites to believe that they would be shortly taken up to heaven. The call to sell their possessions was grossly misunderstood, Henry argues. The invitation to sell and come to August Town was aimed at members whose possessions prevented them from sharing the occasion with Bedward. They were the ones who should sell their things and bring the money for safekeeping. It was not a general call for Bedwardites to sell their things so casually and come. Those who brought their money for safekeeping would return home with it, where they could repurchase or purchase new commodities. Bedward needed no more money, as he was shortly going home to his heavenly father.³⁵

Henry's explanation contrasts with the *Daily Gleaner*'s account. Based on the latter, Bedward chose Christmas Eve, Friday, 24 December 1920, for his ascension to heaven. He later postponed his flight for a week to Friday, 31 December 1920. The *Daily Gleaner* further reported that after his ascension, he would return three days later to carry his disciples to heaven, rain down judgement on the white race and its collaborators and destroy the city of Kingston.³⁶ With such drama surrounding the end of 1920 and the end of the world, reporters flocked to August Town to interview Bedward. In one such interview on a Monday evening in December 1920, he discussed his manifestation.

The *Daily Gleaner*'s published headline was, "It will be all over by December 31". It stated: "A tired Alexander Bedward pulled himself away from his flock and asked the reporter, 'Now, sir, what do you want to see me about?'"

The reporter replied, "Well, I have come from Kingston . . ."

"Look here," Bedward exclaimed, "I mean to cut white man . . . I mean to wipe all of you out . . . I am going away and I don't care."

Then the reporter broke in, "But Mr Bedward, it is all over Kingston that you are mad, and I have come here to give you an opportunity of contradicting such scurrilous reports."

The reporter surmised that his comment had a somewhat softening effect on Bedward, and his bad language eased for a minute, and Bedward turned his eyes heavenward, paused, stepped down to where the reporter was, placed his hands on his shoulder and said, "You are one of those people from the *Gleaner*, I suppose? Well, you will remember that years ago they wanted to put me in prison?" A brief discussion ensued as the reporter claimed that he was not yet born when that occurred.[37]

Bedward continued, "Yes, sir, you can write it down, I am the Lord of Lords and the King of Kings," while waving his stick.

The reporter continued, "I heard that you have changed your title from Shepherd to that of Lord and Master?"

Bedward replied, "And what of it, am I not entitled to be styled Lord and Master?"

"Certainly," the reporter said, "your following seems large enough and faithful enough to give you any title you deserve."

Bedward was again distracted by his members and used his stick to clear the ground around him, then continued, "Write it, sir, I am going to judgement. This is the last year for you, and the first day of the new year is a Sunday. My work is accomplished, and I am going home."

Then Bedward started a song, some of whose words were, "I have a desire to bring all nations of the earth into one in peace and unity." He then continued speaking: "Oh, I like that hymn, it expresses the thought so well." The singing continued and the reporter was ushered out of Bedward's presence.

Assuming the content of the interview was accurate, the theme of judgement on colonial whites was clear. The date of Bedward's departure and judgement day was not explicitly stated so as to merit the headline. Newspapers like the *Daily Gleaner*, with their sensational headlines, magnified the events surrounding Bedward's closing rally, resulting in further derision and cynicism for Bedward and the Bedwardites. The Bedwardites from all over the country were not deterred, as they were longing for the day of judgement on British colonialism. One reporter overheard a prayer by one of Bedward's leaders fervently asking God clearly to "light dem up the colonial whites with the matches of affliction",[38] as it would soon be time to get away from this oppressive colonial system.

Bedwardites were descending on August Town in droves. Every train brought in many people – men, women and children. They came from Cuba, Colón, Panama, on a steamer travelling across the sea to see their "Lord of August Town" ascend. In King Street, all tram cars travelling to August Town were besieged by people, some with infants in arms, others hardly able to help themselves – but they were all bundling in, with their clothes, baskets and fowls.[39] Downtown Kingston had its fair share of excitement, as two days before Bedward's alleged ascension on 31 December, the *Daily Gleaner* reported that around fifty female Bedwardites were making their way to August Town, bringing their money and all kinds of gifts, such as clothes, drinks, food and even their sewing machines.[40]

But Bedward was still on earth on New Year's Eve. He did not climb any tree attempting to fly to heaven and fall, as was held by many. His manifestation was allegedly postponed from New Year's Eve to an alternative time.[41]

While it is most difficult to confirm what should have occurred at this final convention of the Bedwardites, the concept of flying home to their ancestral land is nothing strange to Africans, in both the Caribbean and the African diaspora. Legends of flying Africans are quite common in African American literature.[42] In 1939–40, for example, the Savannah Unit of the Georgia Writers' Project travelled to towns and villages surrounding Savannah to collect varying versions of the flying-African folktales, as hundreds of such tales originated during slavery in the United States. The project discovered over twenty-five such variations. The strategies recorded which enabled flying included a magic hoe, magic powers from Africa, developing wings, simply rising, magic words or passwords, and spinning. They even noted that flying could occur among some African groups, such as those who have distinguished themselves in contrast to other Africans. Thus it was possible for entire groups to fly and turn into birds.[43]

In Jamaica, such stories of flying home also emerged and were quite popular even beyond slavery, in the indenture period of the 1860s, a few decades before Bedward started his ministry. The common factor which emerged in Jamaica as allowing Africans to fly home was their ability not to contaminate themselves with the various salty proteins given to them to eat by the Europeans. Some of these "uncontaminated Africans" who resisted salt and European culture were believed to have literally flown home. Monica Schuler writes:

> They couldn't go back . . . because they bring down the thing that they call mackerel, herring-a salt – we call mungwa – and after they eat it, they couldn't go back . . . . [But] some fly. They fly a "wing-like a dove and they fly from Jamaica back to Africa . . . . They never eat no salt [in Africa] just in our country . . . ." Schhler highlights two further stories. She writes, "My grandmother had a grand aunt seventeen years old, and one day she in the kitchen, and she blew on her hand – toot, toot – and she disappear. She didn't eat salt and she went back to Africa." George Walker insists that, "Only men fly back to Africa. One flew from Bowden Wharf [at Port Morant] soon after the ship arrive. They never took salt."[44]

The popular belief among the African population in Jamaica about flying home was that any African so committed to his or her homeland by fully resisting European culture had such ability. This belief was the reason African-derived religions, such as Kumina, played a most important role for devout African worshippers in bridging the gap, literally and spiritually, between their ancestral home, on the one hand, and colonial Jamaica, on the other hand. If they were to get across the divide to return home to their ancestral land, they had to be committed to their beloved culture. Since Bedward and the Revivalists were bearers of this African traditional belief, the desire to take the wings of a dove and fly home was a standard belief of their culture. Such an achievement was not impossible for leaders like Bedward, who was at the forefront of an African-inspired movement. Furthermore, since Bedward was convinced he was divine, flying to his father would not have been a difficult feat.

The notion of Bedward's ascension to heaven being so enthusiastically accepted by some Bedwardites shows the popularity of the belief among African Jamaicans, even as late as 1920. The mere fact that some Bedwardites sold their few belongings with the hope of being taken up to heaven by Bedward further cements the point that African Jamaicans were aware that flying "home to glory" was possible. If it were to happen, Lord Bedward was the man best suited to fly and to vindicate his people and to judge colonial Jamaica. Thus Bedward's non-ascension was not an embarrassment to the movement, as his critics like to claim. It was an indictment on colonial Jamaica that so many of its African population were willing to give away their little material comforts and to fly away from this "hellhole" called Jamaica. In their minds, Bedward gave them hope and a chance to say goodbye to their colonial oppression and be received in their ancestral land.

It must also be borne in mind that the rich collection of African religious folk songs in the Americas was fuelled primarily by the Africans' desire to extend their faith to be liberated from their miserable existence in the Americas. Such folk songs as "Fly Away Home", "Crossing River Jordan", "Wade in the Water" and "I Am Going to Lay Down My Burden Down by the Riverside" are not only filled with rich imagery of flying home but are songs of faith in their God to deliver them from their oppressive conditions. For Bedwardites, who were steeped in biblical prophecy, and who believed that Bedward was the black Christ, the possibility of his literally flying was real.

To the disappointment of some of the Bedwardites, it is alleged that Bedward explained that his father was not yet ready to take him, as all such decisions must be approved by his father. It was now his father's will for him to remain a little longer with his believers. His manifestation was still coming, but not yet fulfilled.

That manifestation would occur within a few months, in 1921. Just after the Easter celebrations at the end of March 1921, Bedward claimed that he had been given marching orders by his sovereign master for a public event in the city of Kingston. Having just celebrated Easter, the memory of the historical Jesus's sacrifice on the cross seemed to have inspired Bedward. In making this second momentous announcement, that he and his followers would march into the city of Kingston for a "manifestation", it must have been clear to Bedward that he was provoking the colonial state. He must have known that, like Paul Bogle, who led the Morant Bay War, his march would be similarly interpreted and that he would suffer at the hands of the state.

It seems Bedward knew what danger lay ahead. The most important symbol of the Jamaica Native Baptist Free Church was that of a cross embedded in a crown (figure 6). Bedward knew that without bearing the cross there could not be a crown. He summoned his followers to August Town to prepare for this momentous march. He also sent a messenger to the city to obtain permission from the authorities to use the park for a public meeting. This request was flatly refused. Instead, a senior police officer was sent to August Town to persuade Bedward not to march.[45]

On 27 April 1921, around 5 a.m., Bedward, his elders and over six hundred men, women and children, all dressed in white, gathered at their churchyard and took to the streets of August Town, singing, "Onward, Christian Soldiers". They were making their way to Kingston. One of the Bedwardites who marched with him recounted the ordeal.

Figure 6. Cross and Crown in Rules and Report.

> When we reach Edy Hill in Hermitage, she saw a truckload of police pass and many people as well. When they reach Mona gate, near to the site of the current post office, Bedward said to them, "Children, keep on the left hand." When they reach Mandro gate, the police and soldiers who seemed to have slept all night in the bushes stopped them. Took Bedward away and two ministers in a car.[46]

Another Bedwardite, Mr Skervin, from the St Thomas chapter, who was a young adult at the time, described his experience of the march. He recalled:

> Well . . . and we march out from here, and Bedward lead the bands and him walk from . . . I tell you when I reach to right where the post office dey at Mona there now . . . I remember right there, a van of police come down. Dem send the police say dem must go right back to the back of the congregation that no one turn back. All who march out, everybody must come down. Nobody is to turn back. And when I reach there, when we reach there we were marching four-four in line, four-four, and when we reach there a only see when the police do the van so, and see yu . . . run right into me, me and three more women (I was out and three women to the corner) and it come so, you see . . . bounce me down flat a ground and I drop and him was trying to run the van over me but as I drop I start roll and by the time I ketch to the corner deh one man ketch me hand so wham! And he ketch me right up and raise me up on to the banking. And then pass and go 'way and when I get up, you see, a feel pain all over me body, all over me body. The

men dem say, "Turn back, turn back." I said, "Before I turn back, I die. Before I turn back so help me God, before I turn back I die." And dem say, "Well, go on," and we march on. And when him come out to just above . . . below the reservoir dey, we see police and soldier march out you see, march out . . . And as dem come dem take out Mr Bedward first and fling him in the vehicle and drive away. But there was men who from in the August Town here go out there and point out the parson them, come out and point out the deacons them and so.[47]

Skervin surmises that the state must have had informers in the crowd, as the police knew who the pastors were and took them away after taking Bedward. The plan was to confuse the sheep by taking away their shepherd. When they were being marched to the Half Way Tree courthouse the police were everywhere, in front of them, beside them and behind them.[48]

Governor Sir Leslie Probyn, convinced that the march was dangerous, had convened a meeting with the attorney general and the inspector general of police on the night of 26 April.[49] They agreed that any possible disturbance of the peace should be averted and that no march should take place. However, if Bedward decided to proceed with the march, he should be met with the strongest joint police/military party available and he should be arrested on two trumped-up charges: first, assaulting a constable in the execution of his duties; and second, threatening to commit a breach of the peace in Kingston and inciting others to do so. The first charge was for an alleged offence committed some days before, and the second was anticipatory: the event had not occurred.

Immediately after the meeting, around midnight, Sir Leslie dispatched an urgent telegram to the resident magistrate, Sam Burke, instructing him to go immediately to August Town with the necessary force and firepower to stop the march. He was also instructed to read the Riot Act and fire directly into the crowd if Bedward insisted on proceeding with his march. A serious confrontation was clearly anticipated between Bedward and the police, and the state obviously went on the defensive. These elaborate precautionary measures are indicative of the immense fear and nervous tension Bedward had created among the authorities.[50]

As the Bedwardites marched, Sam Burke, with about sixty well-armed police officers drawn from Sutton Street, Half Way Tree and Matilda's Corner police stations, and a detachment of an equal number of soldiers from two platoons of the Royal Sussex Regiment, waited in ambush at Matilda's Corner, ready to intercept the marchers. The operation was headed by Deputy Inspector General O'Sullivan, "the 'handyman' of the force who is brought forward when the police mean business – when they were up against trouble". On reaching the vicinity of the Mona sugar estate works yard around 6.15 a.m., the marchers were met by Burke with the joint police/military force, who diverted them and escorted them to the Half Way Tree police station.[51]

Trial of the Bedwardites

Nearly seven hundred Bedwardites, in addition to Alexander Bedward, were charged with vagrancy. The burden of proof was on the Bedwardites to show they were not vagrants. Bedward was isolated and carried away separately to the Half Way Tree police station. His leadership team was also isolated from the rest of the membership, as the colonial authorities sought to use this opportunity to destroy the movement. Inside the station yard at Half Way Tree, the rank-and-file Bedwardites were lined up in a rough semicircle made up equally of men and women. For about half an hour, they waited patiently and silently with their wooden crosses, their banners held aloft, with palm leaves in their hands. Around 11.50 a.m., some of the males were organized in fours under heavy police guard. Around two hundred such men were then marched to the court, where they were kept outside. By noon, Bedward was taken into the courtroom from the station to face Judge S.C. Burke, the supernumerary resident magistrate, dressed in his military attire.[52]

"Bring up Mr Alexander Bedward," said Mr Aubrey DeLeon, deputy clerk of the courts. The judge then asked what Bedward was being charged with.

"Assaulting a constable in the execution of his duty," replied the clerk.

"Are you pleading guilty or not guilty?" the judge asked Bedward, but he made no response.

"Under such circumstances, won't your Honour remand him for medical attention?" enquired the clerk.

The judge concluded that he was going to remand Bedward for medical observation for a week. But Bedward made no reply, not even the slightest gesture. His Honour then shouted, "Remand him in custody until next Wednesday." Bedward was thereupon removed from the side bar and escorted back to the lock-up at Half Way Tree.[53]

With Bedward removed for medical observation, some of the males were then pre-selected and organized in groups of nine to ten, as each group was sent to the judge. Around two hundred and twenty of them (appendix 5), except for the leaders of the movement, were quickly convicted and most of them were immediately sentenced to fourteen days with hard labour in the St Catherine district prison. Twenty-five women who were previously separated were also tried as a group, as seen in appendix 6. Twenty-three of them were also quickly convicted and given seven days' hard labour in the St Catherine district prison. The other two women (Cecilia Lewis and Iris Gooden) were warned and released.

Bedward's leadership team (Levi Steele, Benjamin Steele, Isaiah Gooden, Roman Henry, Levi McKenzie, George Burke and Christian Duke) were also tried as a group, and they too were quickly convicted and sentenced. At their trial, the inspector of police, Wright, used his influence to ensure that they were all found guilty. He testified that he had had the Bedwardites under observation for nine months and that these men were the ringleaders. "The court must not be fooled," he argued. "These men are not angels but rogue individuals and are a bunch of good-for-nothing men." Some of them were leaders in the ascension movement and Isaiah Gooden was one of the worst of the lot. Gooden would not listen to reason. Roman Henry was Bedward's second in command and next to Lord Bedward. He was both the secretary and treasurer of the society.

The Jamaican colonial state even provided convenient witnesses to ensure that it had a golden opportunity to secure heavy penalties against Bedward's leadership team. Seeing they were charged under the Vagrancy Law and placed in groups, they did not have the opportunity or privilege to seek legal representation. "Justice" was to be swift, and they were now at the full mercy of the court. One Mr Davis, an overseer at a property in Mona, testified that he knew the members of Bedward's leadership team. They organized gangs to cut the wire fences and stole anything they could find. Even the barbed wire of the fences was not spared from this crime. Their justification was that Bedward, as Lord and Master, was entitled to portions of the commissioner's land. One Corporal Warden of Franklin Town also gave testimony against the men, saying he personally knew Christian Duke, who was a Revivalist. Duke held Revival meetings in his community, and he had to chase him away for the good of the community.

The judge then chimed in.

> So, he came to August Town! I looked upon you fellows in a different light to the others. You are all ring-leaders and if the Inspector chooses he might have charged you with inciting these unfortunate people. You are very leniently dealt with when you are brought up under the Vagrancy Law. You are all idlers and vagabonds and I am going to deal with you differently. I am going to give you the limit. You must be imprisoned and kept at hard labour for two months.

By 5 p.m., another 443 women and children had still not yet seen the judge. His Honour Judge Burke, accompanied by Acting Deputy Inspector General O' Sullivan and Police Inspector Wright, then left the court and went over to the station and addressed the remaining 443 Bedwardites. They were being given a chance to go home without facing the court, but they had to go home quietly, and they had to ensure that they were never caught again, otherwise they would be seriously charged by the court. The authorities emphasized that this act of defiance ought to be a lesson to them to stop the "foolishness" of following a man who had declared himself God.[54]

The comments by his Honour Magistrate Burke were useless, as the Bedwardites claimed that Bedward, who was in the yard briefly with them, stood up and said to them. "Children, oonoo get three months, but it is only three days. In three days' time oonoo coming out back."[55] Those reassuring words were all they needed to hear.

Within a few hours, around 684 Bedwardites had felt the strong arm of the colonial state. Five other Bedwardites – Robert Hinds, Richard Ferguson, Asher Brooks, Ezekiel Martin and Samuel Fisher – however, insisted publicly that Bedward was Jesus Christ, the deliverer. The judge remanded them in custody for medical observation, like Bedward, and their trial date was set for 4 May 1920, for their obstinacy. Veront Satchell, commenting on the swiftness of colonial justice, writes[56]:

> Between 12:30 p.m. and 5:00 p.m., just over four hours . . . persons were tried, convicted and sentenced by one magistrate. Indeed, 30 of those sentenced were able to be transported on the 4:15 p.m. train to Spanish Town to begin serving their sentence. By nightfall nearly 200 were in prison. According to the editor of the *Daily Gleaner*, "Everything went through without a hitch", reflecting the highest credit on the police as well as the court staff.[57]

While some Jamaicans were glad at the punishment of the Bedwardites, others were embarrassed at the jungle justice given to them. A deputation of three prominent men of the city went to the governor and prompted questions in the Legislative Council. The delegation pointed out to the governor that the defendants had not been given a trial in accordance with the strict and true principles of British justice and demanded an enquiry into the matter. In the Legislative Council, the Honourable Reverend George Leslie Young, elected council member for St Catherine's parish, argued: "The exhibition in court did not savour British justice, because the people were given no opportunity to defend themselves. The whole thing looked like a lynch law. All the people were charged under the Vagrancy

Law, yet some were imprisoned while others were freed. Was vagrancy proven among them?"[58]

Young further questioned whether, if one of the established churches had ordered its members to march to Kingston, the authorities would have treated them the same way: "Would they be charged under the Vagrancy Law and imprisoned? It is high time the executive sees that justice is meted out to the masses irrespective of religion." As a result of these protests, the governor pardoned all those convicted.[59]

Bedward's Trial

Resident Magistrate Burke, sitting in the Half Way Tree Petty Sessions Court, took his seat promptly at 10 a.m. on 4 May, the date set for the trial of Bedward and five other Bedwardites. The first case to be called was that involving Bedward for assaulting a policeman in the execution of his duty.[60] Bedward, attired in a white suit, was clearly being set up by the judicial system, to have him finally sent to the lunatic asylum.[61] Dr Charles Edwards, a district medical officer, was first asked to comment on Bedward's mental state, seeing that he had observed him for a week, as provided for by the law. Edwards concluded that Bedward was of unsound mind and should be detained in the asylum, as he had hallucinations. It was clear to him that Bedward really believed he was God.

The judge quickly concluded that since Bedward was insane, he could not stand trial for assault, since a person of unsound mind was not responsible for his actions. He was then freed, much to the jubilant cheers of the Bedwardites. Amid their celebration, they did not realize that freeing Bedward was just the first part of the scheme. While he was proceeding along the main road with his band of happy followers, there was Sergeant Major Williams, who had a warrant for his arrest. This time, he was charged with being a lunatic and immediately led right back to court. Based on the Lunatic Law, once you were seen on the streets "not being productive" in the mind of an officer of the state, you could be arrested on suspicion of lunacy. Bedward had no time even to consider the implications of his initial freedom, as the state's plan was well executed.

In the interim, the judge examined the remaining five Bedwardites, since they too had been remanded in prison for five days to be medically examined. The judge, questioning Dr Edwards, asked, "These people told me that Bedward is Jesus Christ, and for that reason I remanded them. What have you to say about their sanity, doctor?" Dr Edwards responded,

"I have had them under observation and every one of them firmly believes that Bedward is Jesus Christ. In other aspects they are not dangerous."

> His Honour: "But a man who believes that can't possibly be?"
> Dr Edwards: "He is a monomaniac."
> His Honour: "And should he not be locked up?"
> Dr Edwards: "No, except he is dangerous. And as I say, I don't think these defendants are dangerous. Unless they commit in the future some act, I should not be able to testify that they are insane."

His Honour, addressing the defendants, stated:

> The doctor says you are mad on one point and that you believe that Bedward is Jesus Christ. I would advise you to go for a change of air. I believe a little medicine will cure you. I cannot understand how you people can get such extravagant ideas in your head. If you persist in your foolish belief, you are bound to get into trouble. You are certain to commit yourself and you will either be sent to the Penitentiary or the Lunatic Asylum. I may tell you at once that Bedward, your leader, is going to the Asylum, and when that person who you believe is Jesus Christ is locked up in the Asylum, you will realize how foolish is your belief.

The rebellious five, however, continued to be defiant and showed the extent to which they were committed to Bedward and not afraid of the repercussions. Robert Hines, who later became a follower of Rastafari, insisted that he was from Linstead, St Catherine, and should return to his home. Richard Ferguson also insisted that he should return to Lawrence Tavern, from whence he came. Asher Brooks, however, remained devout and stubborn, as seen in the following exchange:

His Honour to Brooks. "Where do you come from, Brooks?"

Brooks, an old man of about seventy years of age, responded, "I was in the Union poorhouse but the Lord Jesus Christ [Bedward] called me to August Town."

Police Inspector Wright then informed the judge that the chairman of the Union Poor House, Mr Myers, was in court, but was undecided if Brooks would return there.

Mr Myers then stated categorically, "No, we don't want him back there."

The judge then continued, "On your own showing, Brooks, you are a vagrant. How do you live?"

> Brooks: "I live in the mercy of our Lord Jesus Christ" – referring to Bedward.
> His Honour: "You are a genuine vagrant and yet you are too old a man for me to deal with."

Brooks: "I want to tell you this, that I feel glad to be able to suffer for our Lord Jesus Christ. The time will come when it will be too late for you all to believe."

His Honour: "Believe what?"

Brooks: "That him whom you now call Bedward is Jesus Christ." (Laughter.)

His Honour: "You silly old man."

One of the five, Ezekiel Martin, informed the court that he came from Richmond, and Spanish Town was the place he would prefer to return. The last of the five, Samuel Fisher, like Brooks, pleaded his case before the judge. "I want to let your Honour know that I am a carpenter and have my own dray and mule. Jail is for a vagrant and the lunatic asylum for people who are not of sober mind. Men who have got their motor cars are allowed to go over any part of the island they desire, and I claim the right to go where I please and will go."

His Honour: "The liberty of the subject must be considered, but I may tell you that none of this nonsense is going to be tolerated. If you persist in your foolish beliefs and ideas, then you will be sent to a place where people who are not of sober minds are detained, the lunatic asylum."

Inspector Wright informed the judge that the other Bedwardites who were grabbed and given a free pardon and released from prison had been told to return to their homes; the judge then discharged them and directed that the police ensure they all returned to their homes.

Bedward was now recalled into court, as his other trial, for lunacy, now commenced. Dr Edwards was again asked to testify. On this occasion, he went into more detail, as he had previously invited the director of Bellevue, Dr Williams, with his considerable experience, to diagnose Bedward. Williams confirmed his opinion that Bedward suffered from hallucination of hearing. Bedward was of the strong belief that God spoke to him and told him what to do. Thus he was extremely dangerous. That is the reason Bedward believed he was the Christ, that his mother was the Virgin Mary and that Joseph the carpenter was his father, as in the scriptures. Bedward also professed to have the power to cure any disease with the water of the Mona River, which he had turned into medicine, and believed those who had used it had been cured of all maladies.[62]

In Defence of Alexander Bedward

The testimony of both Drs Edwards and Williams was not only culturally biased but also intellectually disappointing. Both professional gentlemen were so steeped in British culture that they did not consider the prevailing black theology of the period and realize that Bedward's views were similar to those of fellow black preachers at the time. It was not madness for Bedward to see himself as the black Messiah, especially in the context of an oppressed black community which looked to the Bible for hope and inspiration. By 1920, Marcus Garvey's Universal Negro Improvement Association/African Communities League (UNIA/ACL) and its programmes were prominent all over the world, to the extent that Garvey gathered over three thousand delegates to attend an international convention of Negroes.[63] Importantly, the Anglican clergyman George Alexander McGuire left his Boston pulpit in 1920 to become chaplain general of the UNIA/ACL. McGuire served for many years with the UNIA/ACL and was open to all but under complete black leadership and control. McGuire declared to his followers: "You must forget the white gods. Erase the white gods from your hearts. We must go back to the native church, to our own true God."[64]

Jamaican newspapers and others all over the Caribbean carried these revisionist black concepts promulgated by the UNIA/ACL. More important, its flagship newspaper, the *Negro World*, started publication from 1918 and had a circulation of over two hundred thousand copies. Included in this number were translations into both French and Spanish. Jamaica and the other Caribbean islands were included in its circulation.[65] The content of the *Negro World* was considered revolutionary by many British colonialists, and hence the paper was banned in many places, such as Demerara (British Guiana) and St Vincent in 1919.

Influential people in Jamaica were also writing in the *Daily Gleaner*, advocating a serious examination of these "black" ideas being digested by the Jamaican population. F.M. Kerr-Jarrett, for example, a household name in colonial Jamaica and from a family that is still prominent in independent Jamaica, in 1920 cautioned readers of the *Daily Gleaner* to be critical of the UNIA/ACL. Its ideas, if taken seriously by African Jamaicans, could bring down the colonial government.[66] Obviously, these revolutionary ideas which Kerr-Jarrett mentioned must have been the circulating views of a coming black Messiah and the continued resistance to colonialism. Furthermore, Garvey's call to blacks to awake from their colonial slumber and to take control of their own political, social, economic and religious destiny must have been disconcerting to whites. More significantly, Garvey's views on anthropology and in particular on Christology (Christ) were revolutionary to colonial minds but somewhat similar to those of the Bedwardites.[67]

Garvey believed that Christ was the begotten Son of God, whose special mission was to take the form of man to show man how to rise to the stature of divinity. He also entertained the idea that "Christ" was not a historical person, but a model of faith and love for humans to emulate. Garvey's most significant piece of theology relating to Christ was that he was black. As radical as the idea of a black Christ sounded to colonial minds, this black theological tradition did not begin in the Americas with Bedward or Garvey, but with David Walker, Martin Delany, Alexander Crummell, Bishop Henry McNeal Turner and other liberation theologians. Turner was the first to declare that God is black and indirectly laid the foundation for Bedward and Garvey's thinking of a black Christ.[68]

Furthermore, the African Orthodox Church of which Fr McGuire became bishop was born in 1921, as numerous black clergy, especially in the Episcopalian church, shared McGuire's view that an independent national church for blacks was needed.[69] Such a movement would give black ministers the room to revisit traditional white theology and build a theology for the black church seeking black liberation.

The 1960s Black Power movement further escalated the literature on black theology. These scholars have all credited the pioneering work of Marcus Garvey and his impact on such a theology.[70] Alexander Bedward must be added in tandem with Garvey, as both men had insisted, from the early twentieth century, that the Jesus of the Bible must be understood in one's contemporary sociopolitical and economic context and image. Garvey's and Bedward's views on the relevance of a black theology have borne fruit, as they have become popular among contemporary black theologians who write on the relevance of a "black Christ".

James Cone, for example, one of the prominent black theologians in North America in our contemporary period, writes:

> White conservatives and liberals alike present images of a white Jesus . . . their Jesus is a mild easy-going white American who can afford to mouth the luxuries of love, mercy, longsuffering and other white irrelevances. . . . The black community is an oppressed community primarily because of its blackness, hence the Christological importance of Jesus must be found in his blackness. If he is not black as we are, then the resurrection has little significance for our times. If he cannot be what we are, we cannot be who he is. Our being with him is dependent on his being with us in the oppressed black condition, revealing to us what is necessary for our liberation.[71]

Even before the publication of *Negro World* in 1918, some of the Bedwardites would have been influenced by the work of Jamaican pan-Africanists, such as Theophilus Scholes and Dr Robert Love of the *Jamaican Advocate* newspaper. Some of the Bedwardites were indeed members of local UNIA/ACL branches. Henry acknowledged that he was "Garveyite, Bedwardite, an

African and an Israelite".⁷² Roman Henry and other such conscious blacks were well aware of the literature of Scholes and the perspective that many blacks living in the Americas are genetically connected to Judaism, and more specifically, the lineage of King Solomon and the Queen of Sheba. Veront Satchell endorses this religious position and agrees with the historian Stanley Elkins that Bedwardism was "the nursery of black ideas" which was to develop after World War I, when militant New World Africans in the West Indies began a general struggle for political and social emancipation.⁷³

A.A. Brooks confirms that Bedwardism was the fulfilment of God's prophetic work in both Judaism and Christianity. Judaism has done its part; Christianity has had and is having its triumph: and one of its chief and latest triumphs will be its handing over, from various denominations, creeds and persuasions, the children of God unto Bedwardism. Furthermore, the Bedwardite belief in three heavens was sufficient to include Jewish and Christian believers. The first and second heavens were for those Jewish and Christian believers. The saints of God who died and who had been baptized in obedience to Bedward, whom God had sent, and who had devoted themselves to fasting, would attain the third heaven through obedience.⁷⁴ It was not difficult for devout Bedwardites by 1920 to believe that Alexander Bedward was the black Christ, and God's prophet for this dispensation. They firmly believed that Bedward was sent to deliver the black race from its oppression, given the view that blacks were related to the biblical Hebrews. It was appropriate that Bedward be labelled "Lord", since he was the Christ. His divinity was the reason he could perform so many miracles with the water of the Hope River and why his prophecies were true.

Brooks further claimed that the Bedwardites took the book of Revelation in the Bible seriously, as Bedwardism's existence and distinguishing forms were clearly biblical. The Jesus of the Bible was sent by God; but Bedward was the prophet in whom the light of God's grace would shine in turning men from their iniquity, based on the Bible, as seen in Dan. 10:5 and Rev. 12:1–6.⁷⁵

Roman Henry also confirms that Bedward's divine mission was to free the black man wherever he was being held in bondage. Referring to Gen. 49:10, Henry emphasized that Bedward recovered "the sceptre, the sword, the lion or crown, stolen by the British and kept in England".⁷⁶ These items were returned to Ethiopia, and if Bedward had not come, they would never have been returned. Bedward was therefore the self-appointed political advocate for the black community, and also its voice.

Other scholars who have interviewed Bedwardites concur that Bedward saw himself as the fulfilment of biblical prophecy. Yoshiko Nagashima concludes from her interview with Bedwardites in 1980 that although they were enticed by Bedward's charismatic leadership, his famous healings at the Hope River, his provocative and relevant sermons, what was more crucial was that he was a man full of mysticism and prophecy. Psalm 68:5 was one of Bedward's favourite scripture passages: "Let Ethiopia hasten to stretch out her hands to God." It was also a favourite scripture of the Garveyites, the Rastafari community and black theologians.[77] The Bedwardites saw Bedwardism as the fulfilment of the Psalm 68 passage, as God was building the black wall through Bedward.

The Bedwardites never viewed Bedward as insane. Bedward had revealed to them that he could have been freed from the asylum but knew that he was destined to remain there until the calling would come to him. Though his believers were discouraged by his claim, they were confident in him and faithful to him. Bedward, like the historical "Jesus, the Christ", had to pay the price, since he was fighting the colonial establishment and represented the poor, black working-class community.[78]

The few recorded sermons by Bedward that were based on biblical texts show that he used a hermeneutical principle of a reader-response approach. This approach was common to the black Native Baptist community in Jamaica, and by extension, black religious movements such as Revivalism and Bedwardism. It allowed them to read the Bible through their own experiences of persecution and oppression. This contrasts with the "traditional" methodology of reading the biblical text in its first-century sociohistorical context. In the reader-response approach, there was no historical difference between themselves and the world of the Bible.[79] The black experience was similar to that of the Jews, who were also enslaved and later colonized by various nations for most of their history. The historical Jesus also suffered and was eventually crucified. The biblical stories and prophecies provided for Bedward enough substance with which his audience could easily connect, given their common colonial experiences of oppression.

Biblical passages in Matthew's Gospel and in the book of Revelation were good examples of Bedward's reader-response approach. Matthew 16:1–7 (King James Version) reads:

> The Pharisees also with the Sadducees came, and tempting desired him that he would shew them a sign from heaven. He answered and said unto them, when it is evening, ye say, It will be fair weather: for the sky is red. And in the morning, it will be foul weather to day: for the sky is red and lowering. O ye hypocrites, ye can discern the face of the sky; but can ye not discern the signs of the times? A wicked and adulterous generation seeketh after a sign; and there shall no sign be

given unto it, but the sign of the prophet Jonas. And he left them, and departed. And when his disciples were come to the other side, they had forgotten to take bread. Then Jesus said unto them, Take heed and beware of the leaven of the Pharisees and of the Sadducees. And they reasoned among themselves, saying, it is because we have taken no bread.

Sergeant Nelson testified (chapter 3) that this passage of scripture in Matthew 16 was the source behind Bedward's sermon for which he was charged with sedition. Bedward likened the Pharisees and Sadducees in the passage to white ministers and doctors and labelled them hypocrites, robbers, thieves and liars. The persecuted black community clearly understood and agreed with his analysis, since they too were of that view. Bedward's introduction of the sermon was also a classic form of communication. He stated:

> Brethren, the Bible is difficult to understand. Thanks to Jesus, I am able to understand it. Thanks to Jesus and blessed be his holy name. I can understand it and I, the servant of Jesus will tell you. The Pharisees and Sadducees are the white men. We [the black masses] are the true people. The white men are hypocrites, robbers and thieves. They are all liars. [He then reads Matthew 16:2–3.] "And in the morning, it will be lowering signs of the times." Yes, Brethren, it will be found well. Can we discern the signs of the times? The white men are hypocrites. I can discern the signs of the time. Look over there on the top of the hill, you see white things which you call clouds. I tell you they are not clouds, they are angels and the angels are telling me what I am telling you now. The ministers are thieves and liars and worship the anti-Christ. I am the true servant of the true Christ.[80]

Using another biblical passage, from the book of Revelation, Bedward cited 11:3 (King James Version), which states, "And I will give power unto my two witnesses, and they shall prophesy a thousand two hundred and threescore days, clothed in sackcloth." Bedward linked the two witnesses to himself and Shakespeare, the original founder of the church. He further connected the section of the verse which says, "and they shall prophesy one thousand two hundred and sixty days" to his period of prophecy. By linking the witness to himself, he can bring judgement on his accusers, as the witness is protected by God and vindicated by God. Bedward then can inform his critics that their punishment is ordained by God and that is the reason the black wall will tear down the white wall.

All the colonial officials who interacted with Bedward while he was detained in prison were left with the clear impression that Bedward believed that he was the black Christ. Sergeant Major Williams, a police officer, testified in court that when he first arrested Bedward, he shouted out, "Eli,

Eli," reminiscent of Jesus Christ on the cross. Secondly, since it was part of his duty to visit prisoners in the lock-up daily, he visited Bedward twice daily and conversed with him freely. Bedward kept reiterating that he was the Lord Jesus Christ, that he was the end of the law, and that after that day there would be no more law, and that grace and mercy must reign. More important, Bedward had come as a black man to save his race, he had been going on with his evangelistic work for thirty-three years and five months and the end was now at hand. Today there would be time no more.[81]

Sergeant Williams further testified that on 26 April, the night before Bedward's march, he and Inspector Williams went to Bedward's church to persuade him not to march, as trouble lay before him if he did. A fervent prayer meeting was in session, with an attendance of four to six hundred people. Bedward was insistent that he had to do his father's will and he had to march. Like the historical Jesus in the Garden of Gethsemane, who, when he had become ambivalent about being crucified, and, realizing that it was his father's will, prayed for strength to execute his task, Bedward too had come to a similar conclusion that he had to do his father's will. Bedward stated:

> "I must go. I must obey my father. Do you not know whom I am? I am the Lord Jesus Christ. Must I obey you and disobey the command of my father? The only way I do not take out the children you must cut off my neck or kill me now. It is no good asking me not to go. I must take them out tomorrow. They can shoot me if they like."
>
> After this Bedward's followers broke in with the hymn: "Me no care what Satan da grumble say, we are all going to glory" (laughter) . . . the defendant's followers joined in a tremendous singing, clapped their hands and stamped the floor. The Inspector and him had to leave.[82]

In addition to lunacy, the state also accused Bedward of assaulting two police constables and a census officer. These latter events, which were alleged to have taken place within the two weeks before the march, were added as extra charges, so that if Bedward could not be convicted by way of insanity, there would be other charges to legally trap him and take away his freedom.[83]

Constable Cyril Lionel Cox first testified that on 11 April 1920, he was sent to August Town to make enquiries with reference to three men who were in custody at the Half Way Tree police station, charged with vagrancy. The three men claimed they were on their way to August Town to carry food for their parents, who were in Bedward's camp. Constable Cox was sent to verify their story. He was in uniform at the time and rode his bicycle, and when he got to Bedward's camp, he saw a man at the gate. He asked for the parents of the three men and was initially refused entrance, but was later allowed inside. He stood under an ackee tree in the yard and was approached by Bedward, who drew away the piece of paper in his hand and struck him on the back. Bedward then drew off his cap, crushed it, threw it on the ground and stepped on it. As he attempted to pick it up, Bedward further kicked him. He then took up the cap and hastened away by jumping on his bicycle and riding off quickly.[84]

Secondly, on 16 April 1920 Joseph Paton, a resident of August Town, testified that he was appointed an enumerator under the common law for the district which included August Town. As an agent of the state, he took the census form to Bedward to explain what was required under the Census Law. As he took out the paper to explain, Bedward sharply responded, "Outside with you and your paper." Paton asked him clearly, "Are you driving me out?" and Bedward replied, "Yes, outside." While Paton was making his way outside, Bedward brought out a black stick, ran after him and struck him three blows on his arms. He ran back to his home, but Bedward followed him there and again struck him with the stick. He had to consult a doctor, after which he complained to the police.[85]

Thirdly, District Constable Caleb Campbell also testified that he was stationed at August Town. On the morning of 20 April 1920 he was at work at a tobacco field and was called to arrest a prisoner for praedial larceny. A female prisoner, Jane Thomas, a Bedwardite, was handed over to him for stealing a pumpkin. He arrested her on the charge and was proceeding with her on the parochial road to Half Way Tree. Roman Henry, Bedward's assistant, and several Bedwardites ran after him and impeded his proceeding with the prisoner. Bedward also came on the scene and cursed him, saying, "Look here, boy, you better mind your ——," using some vulgar expressions. Bedward had a black stick, and struck him several times on his arm. Bedward took away the woman he had arrested and said to his followers, "Go on, children." One of his elders also took away the pumpkin.[86]

While the state wanted to get rid of Bedward, it was also clear that Bedward had made up his mind that he no longer cared about the consequences and was deliberately provoking the state. It was a daring confrontation by a "badman", and Bedward was willing to pay the price, since he was ready to die and be united with his father in heaven. Bedward's audacity was also clear to fellow Bedwardites, who nostalgically record the incident with one of the two policemen whom Bedward met. Their version of the story is that when the police came to harass Bedward, he beat them with his stick, took the policeman's hat off his head, and threw it down, stepped on it and asked the policeman, "Who now is your lord and master? Go and tell them that I, your Lord and Master, have done this, and they can do nothing about it."[87]

Bedward played right into the hands of the colonial state. The allegations against him were serious and the state had no concern for natural justice and a fair trial; it wanted swift punishment for Bedward. While some elements of the three testimonies against him seem contrived, the larger point is that Bedward had no constitutional right of self-defence, in contrast to his 1895 trial. A charge of insanity allowed the court full power to decide on his fate, and Bedward was not allowed to defend himself or bring other witnesses for his defence. He found himself in a British kangaroo court, at the full mercy of the judge, who would not allow him even to speak. On one occasion, when Bedward could no longer tolerate the "lies", he blurted out to the inspector, "Please give me fair play, Inspector." As soon as the inspector had finished speaking, the judge instantly declared, "The defendant [Bedward] is committed to the asylum as being a person of unsound mind." Bedward then protested to the judge as he approached him, "Can't I say anything at all?" He displayed reluctance when invited by the policemen to leave the dock, which is in front of the judge. He was then escorted to the police station and then to the asylum.[88]

The injustice done to Bedward in not even allowing him to speak was so noticeable that even the *Daily Gleaner* commented. "An insane person has nothing coherent to say. That was the reason the state made sure that Bedward was declared medically insane, so it could have him trapped."[89] Bedward's capture in the state's dragnet seemed to have resulted from his decision to directly challenge the colonial state. He had consistently taken on the colonial powers and he was quite aware of the consequences. As with Paul Bogle in 1865 and the other African Jamaicans at Morant Bay, Judgement Day had come for Jamaican colonialism, and he was willing to pay the price, as he had become the voice of the black masses.

Sergeant Williams, in his testimony, stated that on the eve of the march, during the attempt to persuade Bedward to postpone his ascension into Kingston, Bedward stated clearly that the time had come. God told him, as his son, to go to Kingston the next day for that purpose. Then Bedward said to his congregants, "Those who were afraid to go could remain behind, and those who were not afraid could follow him. You are prepared to go, Bedward enquired?" and the people replied, "Yes, my lord." Bedward's statement was war on the Jamaican colonial state. Secondly, while he was remanded in prison for the week to undergo medical observation, he prophesied to Sergeant Williams that he was declaring judgement shortly on the colonial state. August Town was the valley of Jehoshophat, and those who wanted to be saved better find themselves there. He also asserted that there would be a tidal wave in Kingston, as the sea would extend as far as the Soldier Camp and as high as the hills of the Long Mountain Road. Only August Town would escape this judgement.[90]

Thirdly, this march into Kingston was clearly a social protest. Like the march of Paul Bogle and the African Jamaicans in 1865 fighting for the rights of blacks to their property. Satchell makes the point that the Commissioner of Lands challenged Bedward's rights to the holdings he had had in August Town for decades. Bedward had to continually defy the government's authority. In an interview he made his position clear: "The police inspector and soldiers with guns and pistols came to my place and told me to get out, but I refuse to do this, because I told them it was my home, where I had lived for thirty-three years."[91]

The symbolism of the over six hundred protesters, singing, "Onward, Christian soldiers! Marching as to war," and carrying palm branches and wooden crosses, is also a clear sign of deliberate social protest. On 25 March 1921, the Bedwardites had celebrated Good Friday, and between Good Friday and 26 April 1921, they had these three major incidents with agents of the state. These clashes must have played an important role in the 27 April march into Kingston, as it was clear to Bedward that this confrontation with the colonial state was inevitable. The Bedwardites were protesting under the banner of the cross and were willing to be crucified like Jesus, the Christ, for standing up for their rights. There could be no crown, no victory, no deliverance from their oppression, if they were not willing to bear the cross.

It was also no secret that Bedward was dissatisfied with the way the colonial state treated him. In his interview with folklorist Martha Beckwith, before his "impending departure" in 1920, she highlighted Bedward's grievances with whites as obvious. Several times he had requested that his own pastors be licensed to perform the marriage ceremony, in order that the fees should come to his own church. This privilege had been denied to him, and he had accordingly decided to bring the world to an end. "I myself am Jesus Christ; I was crucified," he insisted.[92]

Chapter 6

The Impact of Bedwardism

Alexander Bedward's contribution to Jamaica's history as a nationalist and as an anticolonial hero is recognized, although not adequately documented. His contribution to the development of black religion and culture in Jamaica have not been adequately examined in the academic literature, partly because of his death in 1930 and the movement's subsequent decline. The return of Marcus Garvey to Jamaica in 1927 to lead the UNIA/ACL further eclipsed the Bedwardite movement in relation to its national influence. In addition, the birth and growth of Rastafari across the island after 1930 provided another important alternative for black expression and activism. Scholars of both Garvey and Rastafari have made numerous references linking the Bedwardites with the growth of Garveyism in Jamaica and also the development of the early Rastafari movement.[1] Those references, however, are still limited and do not adequately capture the enormous influence of Bedward during the late nineteenth century and the first half of the twentieth. For example, Bedwardism became the face of the Great Revival which swept Jamaica from the 1860s, and which Bedward continued in the early twentieth century. Bedward Jamaicanized European Christianity under a new label (Bedwardism) which further affected the development and spread of an African Jamaican Christianity.

More important, Alexander Bedward, although not formally recognized as a black theologian, must be credited for nurturing and developing a quasi-black theology, which would later be fine-tuned and blossom in the Rastafari movement and other African-centred spirituality.

Alexander Bedward and Black Theology

Scholars who write about or mention Alexander Bedward in their work do not view him as a black theologian or one who engaged in some form of black theology. This omission is primarily due to Bedward's frequent engagement with images and rituals surrounding whiteness as purity. Bedward had developed aspects of a black theology surrounding fundamental doctrines such as Christology (the doctrine of Christ) and, more important, eschatology (the doctrine of the last days). Bedward's concept of the black Christ was far more radical than that of any other "popular and contemporary" native preacher in Jamaica. Bedward's radical affirmation, towards the end of 1920, that he was the "black Christ" and would end the current world order (colonialism) and deliver his black brothers and sisters was based on his concept of eschatology. He was confronting the social injustices of colonialism and providing hope for Africans who felt trapped in the New World and who looked for the demise of the colonial system.

It was clear that Bedward saw his mission in life as fighting white oppression. In his early ministry in 1895, before his arrest for sedition, he made that point clear to a *Daily Gleaner* reporter who interviewed him. The reporter could hardly get to his questions, as Bedward dominated the interview. After getting his Bible and his glasses, for around half an hour, Bedward kept reinforcing the oppression of blacks by whites and showing from the Bible that the whites would soon be judged.

Bedward quoted Matt. 3:3, "For this is he that was spoken by the prophet Esaias saying, 'The voice of one crying in the wilderness, prepare ye the way of the Lord, make his paths straight.'"[2] Bedward emphasized that he was the prophet crying in the wilderness of Jamaica, for the injustice being done to his fellow blacks. Then he told the reporter that he was also Noah. For three years, Noah had preached and not been heard, and when trouble came there was no room for them in the ark. The whites would soon find out that there would be no hiding place for them when judgement came. Bedward then read verse seven of Matthew 23, which highlighted the hypocrisy of the Pharisees and Sadducees. He made it clear to the reporter:

> People of my own colour are not so bad, it is the white and the coloureds. They have tried to kill me but can't do it. I tell you the day of reckoning is coming for them. The people of my own colour are not against me except for my neighbours. Blacks who come from other places believe in me and know that I am a servant of Jesus. The white people are the oppressors. This is a black man's country and black people must rule it.

Turning to Matthew 15, Bedward emphasized that every plant which his heavenly father had not planted would be rooted up. "Yes," he emphasized, "they shall be rooted up, they shall be cleared away, and I tell you that time is coming. You don't know how the black people are treated." Bedward then turned to Matt. 23:4 to reinforce the point of the horrible treatment of his fellow men and women at the hands of whites. He quoted, "'For they bind heavy burdens and grievous to be borne and lay them on men's shoulders, but they themselves will not move them with one of their fingers.' That is what they do the black people but I tell you (reading verse 11), he that is greatest among you shall be their servant (verse 33)." Then, in denouncing the colonial whites and their collaborators, Bedward proclaimed, "Ye serpents, ye generation of vipers, how can ye escape the damnation of hell, judgement is surely coming."

The judgement of the whites which Bedward escalated from towards the end of 1920 to early 1921 is consistent with his black identity as a prophet, a watchman from the 1890s, sent to warn the whites of Jamaica of God's impending judgement on their unjust colonial system. Bedward's form of Revivalism was not just spiritual, but social and political. God had sided with the black race and had seen their oppression, and God would act in bringing healing for the black race and judge the white race. No wonder his believers were convinced of his divinity, as demonstrated in court, with the aged Mr Brooks testifying that he was absolutely sure that Bedward was the "Christ". Even new residents of August Town in the 1950s claimed that the Bedwardites were still convinced Bedward was miraculously sent to them. They had a firm belief in him and believed intensely that their movement was divinely orchestrated by God and that Bedward was the Christ.[3]

August Town, which for many was a sterile and backward little valley, would become the New Jerusalem, a refuge to avoid God's judgement and the spiritual home of the black suffering and oppressed people.[4] This black theology of Bedward's is reminiscent of the liberation theologians of Latin America in the 1960s to the 1970s, who argued on the basis of the suffering of their people that God chose the side of the poor and oppressed and would politically liberate them, as God had exercised a preferential option for the poor of Latin America.[5]

Bedward's black theology must not be compared with the black theology of Rastafari. Rastafari scholars like Chevannes argue that Bedwardism propagated Eurocentric ideas, given the discussion between Bedward and Beckwith.[6] Although Rastafari members can boast that they built an indigenous black theology with their own vocabulary, culture and with the appropriate symbols, Rastafari is multifaceted and is still evolving. Rastafari theology has so developed over time, from its earliest doctrines in the 1930s, that in the twenty-first century it has become far more palatable to some Europeanized Jamaicans than in the early twentieth century. Bedwardism under Bedward became the vanguard of resistance to colonialism and had not had that chance to evolve.

The Great Revival from which Bedwardism sprang had numerous fundamental ideas, such as the importance of healing, either by myal medicine or through the instrument of the leader or shepherd; the rereading and the reinterpreting of the Bible from their African Jamaican context of race; the fight for social justice for the black oppressed community against an unjust colonial order; and the assurance of their return to Africa, since their entrapment in the New World was harsh and oppressive.[7]

Bedwardism must be credited for carrying the torch of Ethiopianism into early twentieth-century Jamaica. Bedward was the most popular head of a black religious organization and was the most successful black religious leader fighting British colonialism. Bedwardism nurtured the seeds of millenarism, with the hope of a black Christ and a God who witnessed the affliction of blacks and was committed to changing it. Thus, after Bedward's death in 1930, of the thousands of Bedwardites across Jamaica, those who left the Bedwardite movement could easily identify with other African-derived movements, such as the various streams of Rastafari, Garveyism and other Ethiopian-led churches.

Bedward's contribution to the cause of Ethiopianism in Jamaica is even more profound when you examine the traditional religious landscape of the 1890s–1920s. Among the native churches, the Native Baptists represented the largest black indigenous movement in the island, with a membership of over eight thousand by 1839.[8] These churches were founded by the exploits of North American freed slaves George Leile and Moses Baker and included Paul Bogle and George William Gordon by 1865. The Native Baptists, as a black independent church, carried the seeds of Ethiopianism in Jamaica in the late eighteenth century and were initially dubbed the Ethiopian or Black Baptists.[9]

By the early twentieth century, however, their numbers had declined, and they had become generally theologically moderate, although they still carried the torch of Ethiopianism, organizationally and liturgically. Their decision to invite the English Baptists (European missionaries) to assist them in Jamaica in 1814 resulted in a continuous struggle to assert their independence in managing their own affairs and the right to be in charge of their own property. They fought to preserve their own form of worship, to control their own funds and to implement their own rules of governance. They were well organized, but by relating with the English Baptists, they had become more orthodox in their theology.[10] The Great Revival pillars of social protest and social justice were still core pillars of the Native Baptists, but unlike Bedwardites, the Native Baptists generally had no preferential option for a distinct black theology; no reference to a black Christ; and no specific judgement on whites and colonialism.

This absence is not to suggest that the Native Baptists, who were predominantly from the lower class and theologically untrained, did not develop their own interpretation of the Bible, and their own understanding of God; they were highly critical of the European interpretation of the Bible. They remained African-conscious by insisting on the use of their native language in their liturgy and by practising their form of management. They did not display marked African beliefs, like myalists and other African-led religions in Jamaica.[11] The other native black-led churches, such as the Methodists, were never as large and influential as the Native Baptists, and hence did not have the sociopolitical sting that the Bedwardites had.

Obviously, there were other individual preachers who were highly African-centred in their theology and in their rituals. Such individuals never developed a strong and sustaining political force like Bedwardism. This distinction is the reason Bedwardism, with its seventy-three stations across the island and with its charismatic and daring leader in Alexander Bedward, became the genuine hope of oppressed Africans in Jamaica.

Alexander Bedward and the Garvey Movement

Given the black consciousness promoted by Bedward, many of his disciples found affinity with the teachings and programmes of the UNIA/ACL, while others became and remain members of the movement after Bedward's death. The inner leadership core of the Bedwardites viewed Marcus Garvey and Bedward as prophets working together and reinforcing each other. As one Bedwardite proclaimed, "Garvey is lawman and Bedward is graceman, Garvey is water and Bedward is gas. Is two, but Garvey is man call and Bedward is God call . . . Garvey is on the temporal side while Bedward is on the spiritual side."[12]

Roman Henry argues that God commanded Bedward, who was then in the lunatic asylum, to guard Garvey spiritually when he returned to Jamaica in 1927. The Bedwardites argue that Garvey's assault on the colonial system was so intense that the Jamaican colonialists would have killed him, if he were not spiritually protected. So two of the leading Bedwardites spiritually guarded and protected Garvey by way of prayer.[13] It is highly possible that Henry and the Bedwardites were indeed instructed by Bedward to pray for the protection of Garvey. While Bedward was in Bellevue from 1921 until his death in November 1930, he was allowed to meet with his core leadership of ten to twenty people every Monday for half an hour, when they received instructions from him.[14] On Henry's last such visit, Bedward asked him to stay alone with him and was allowed to spend two and a half hours with him. In that session, Bedward poured his heart out to Henry and gave him final instructions.[15] One of those instructions could have been praying for Garvey, since their missions coincided.

At the height of Garvey's work in Jamaica from 1927 to 1930, Bedward was still incarcerated in Bellevue and must have heard of Garvey's continuing influence among the black masses and the attempts of the colonial class to silence him. Garvey's People's Political Party was successful in winning a seat in the KSAC in October 1929, and he was immediately charged with seditious libel. Bedward died in November 1930 and thus was most likely aware of Garvey's legal troubles.

It is possible that the Bedwardites saw the Garvey movement as a continuation of their work and thus Garvey had to be supported. As the Jamaican colonial class had criticized Bedward, so too they criticized Garvey. Missionary George Olson, for example, remarked that the whole of Jamaica was now caught up with Marcus Garvey and his movement, and he could not understand how Garvey was so influential among the masses.[16] Therefore Henry's claim is possible, especially in the context that he and other Bedwardites were also Garveyites and attended his meetings. Furthermore, it was in the Bedwardites' interest to support the Garveyites. The long and arduous work done by Bedward in watering and nurturing the seeds of Ethiopianism and the redemption of the black race could finally be a reality under Garvey.

Given the paucity of archived data on the full membership lists of both the Bedwardites and the UNIA/ACL chapters across Jamaica, it is difficult to identify the number of Bedwardites who formally joined the UNIA/ACL. But if the comments by Roman Henry are to be used as a marker, the Bedwardites saw Garvey as Bedward's successor. Henry offered glowing praise of the achievements of Garvey in promoting the black race, and the interpretive lens he used to analyse public events was largely because of Bedward's constant teaching. His Bedwardite training in the importance of seeing things from the black man's perspective was clear.

In commenting on the rise of the charismatic leader Michael Manley and his brand of democratic socialism in the 1970s, Henry makes the observation that Manley's agenda was averse to Bedward and Garvey's black nationalism. Manley, Henry argues, is a mere creole nationalist. Henry opines:

> Michael is not an African nor an Englishman. Is mother is English and him daddy black so he is a come-between. Him can't point we to Africa for him don't come from there and him can't point we to England for him is not a European.

Right now him and our own brethren now is selling us back to Cuba. Cuba a no African; Cuba a no Russian. Michael no have it. Garvey and Bedward stand up for the black man. That's the black man age. That is the first word that God tell Bedward. The black wall shall crush the white wall.[17]

Henry further argues that the excellent work done by both Bedward and Garvey in crushing the white wall and in empowering the black man was hijacked by the largely creole nationalist agenda of the Jamaican politicians. They were the ones who betrayed Marcus Garvey, as they planted all kinds of obstacles in his way. Garvey in 1928 made the case for the importance of the black race historically at the renowned Royal Albert Hall in London before English dignitaries. While Garvey was described as the greatest black man they ever met, Jamaica discards its prophets: first Bedward and now Garvey.[18]

Alexander Bedward and Rastafari

Scholars who write on Rastafari generally agree that Bedwardism and Revivalism were among the many streams shaping the early development of Rastafari. The Revival influence as described by Chevannes, for example, was both direct and indirect. Directly, Revivalism influenced Rastafari by its ritual structure: its meetings; its instruments, such as drumming, singing, Bible reading and preaching; divination (the power of the Bible to expose evil); and the power ascribed to herbs for healing and visions, which are usually rich with symbolic meaning. Indirectly, Revival influenced Rastafari in the power of the spoken word; the designation of women as a source of evil; and the belief in the divinity of man.[19] While other scholars have identified other influences of Revivalism, such as Kumina and Burru music, on Rastafari, the specific impact of Bedwardism on Rastafari has not been adequately highlighted, except for the contribution of Robert Hinds.[20] While it is still difficult to precisely highlight Bedward's influence on Rastafari, enough secondary evidence is available for more recognition to be given.

The first influence is that several key Bedwardites became members of Rastafari in its early years. Since Bedwardism had developed strong millenarian views on the coming of a black Christ, and the nearness of his coming to judge the world, it was easy for Bedwardites to be open to the teachings of Rastafari, especially after Bedward's death in 1930. It is not coincidental that with the coronation of Haile Selassie as emperor of Ethiopia on 2 November 1930 and the death of Bedward six days later,

Howell found fertile ground among Bedwardites, who were some of his earlier converts. The Bedwardites were just replacing one Christ (Bedward) with the other (Selassie).

The renowned historian of Garvey Robert Hill argues that one of his key sources claims that when he first attended an open-air meeting to hear Leonard P. Howell speak at Redemption Ground in Kingston, many of the old-time Bedwardites were with Howell on his platform that evening. Furthermore, those who accepted Howell's teaching of Rastafari as Jesus Christ included both old and new Bedwardites.[21] Hutton and Murrell, in acknowledging the contribution of Bedward's Revivalist stream to early Rastafari, highlight that several Bedwardites, including Robert Hinds, who marched in social protest with Bedward in 1921, became significant members of the Rastafari movement.[22]

I am of the view that Robert Hinds was not just an assistant to Howell in preaching Rastafari but was critical in introducing former Bedwardites and fellow Revivalists to Howell. Although Hinds was not listed as one of the assistant leaders to Bedward, he distinguished himself in the group of five who stubbornly refused to deny Bedward as the Christ at Bedward's second trial in 1921. The judge was so outraged with the defiant five that they were remanded in prison for a week, to be medically examined and to reappear before him. All five were locked up with Bedward in the same prison at Half Way Tree and reappeared before the same judge on the same day. The day they sent Bedward to the asylum was the day Hinds was sent to Linstead, where he was born and raised. It is alleged he told the judge in Half Way Tree that if he were sent home that evening he would be back in Kingston the following day.[23] Hinds's reputation, then, as a sincere and committed Bedwardite would have been so elevated that he would have an easier time contacting former Bedwardites and Revivalists across Jamaica and introducing them to Howell.

In St Thomas in the 1930s, for example, Hinds would probably have been in contact with many of those leaders, given his Bedwardite network and its proximity to Kingston. Howell, on the other hand, had just returned to Jamaica in 1932 and would not have had that extensive network of Bedwardites with strong millenarian views within a year, when he started preaching in 1933. Hinds must have been one of Howell's main contacts in finding audiences of Bedwardites, Revivalists and Garveyites for Howell. It is also not coincidental that at the meeting in Trinityville, St Thomas, where Hinds, Howell and others were all charged with sedition, Howell was invited specifically to preach. That meeting was described in the *Daily Gleaner* as a Revival meeting at Maud

Wray's house. It is not clear, however, if Maud Wray was a Bedwardite, a Revivalist or a Garveyite.

What must also be noted is that in the 1920s, Bedward had nine strong chapters in areas of St Thomas: Bethsaida, Union Hill, Hephzibah, Mount Happy View, Unity, Mount Humble, Bethany, Beulah and Mount Prospect. By 1934 it is not clear if these chapters still existed, and if they did, how strong they were, and whether Hinds was able to convince some of these former Bedwardites to listen for themselves to the good news of the black Christ. As was stated by one of the witnesses at the trial in St Thomas, they thought that Howell was a Christian minister, as he was specially invited to speak. Although the *Daily Gleaner* did not state specifically who invited Howell to that meeting, the assumption must be made that it was most likely Robert Hinds. It is not surprising then, that, given Hinds's extensive Bedwardite and Revivalist network, Chevannes highlights Hinds as the most successful Rastafari preacher in the early years, with over eight hundred solid believers.[24] If the mantra is true among the Bedwardites that Bedward preached that Garvey and himself were reincarnations of Moses and Aaron respectively, the one lawgiver, the other high priest, and that in the hands of both was the destiny of Israel, the African race, then it is not difficult to imagine that Hinds was instrumental in bringing Bedwardites to Rastafari.[25]

Secondly, the Bedwardite emphasis on millenarism and Ethiopianism must also have influenced early Rastafari teaching. Since Bedward was viewed as the Messiah by Bedwardites, as evidenced by 1920, and Bedwardism was destined to replace Christianity, it is not coincidental that with the death of Bedward, Rastafari in the 1930s embodied a similar belief in the coming redemption of the black race by Haile Selassie. Howell, in his early years of preaching of Rastafari, spoke much on prophecy and the imminent return of the black Christ, as the Bedwardites previously did. Howell even gave a date, 1 August 1934, when believers of Rastafari would be repatriated to Africa.[26] Howell would later modify some of his prophetic views and avoided giving precise timelines for the coming of the Christ.

What was even more remarkable in Howell's response in court for sedition after the Seaforth meeting was the way he quoted extensively from both the Old and New Testaments. On each occasion he showed how the myriad of biblical texts were linked to historical events culminating in the coronation of Ras Tafari. Hence Howell's case before his initial audience in Seaforth would be most convincing for Bedwardites, Revivalists and other Ethiopianists.[27] Furthermore, as a mark of confidence in his millenarian position, Howell informed the court that even if it condemned him, he would be shortly vindicated when the final judgement came. Ethiopia would rule the world and he would be one of its judges, as his saviour would have delivered him.[28] At this early stage in Howell's preaching, his millennial doctrines from the Bible cast him in the same mould as Alexander Bedward. It must be more than a coincidence that Howell and Bedward were using the same playbook and adopted the black Revivalist tradition of prophetic protest against the colonial state.

It is not surprising that some Rastafari scholars see a clear similarity between the ministries of Alexander Bedward and Leonard Howell. Hélène Lee makes the point that the sermons of both had the same tone of arrogance, as a form of resistance against colonial culture.[29] Both were severely criticized and persecuted by the various arms of the state, arrested and jailed and sent to the lunatic asylum. Their similarity transcends their defiant sermons and persecution, however, as they created authentic communities of believers, which consisted primarily of the working poor and the black downtrodden in Jamaican society. It can even be argued that Bedward's successful model of a self-reliant community of believers in August Town also had an impact on Howell. Some Bedwardites in August Town claim that Bedward's community served as a model for Rastafari communes.[30]

Given the Bedwardite influence on Howell and the dire material needs of the working poor whom Howell met, it must have been clear that he too had to build a community of believers who lived, worked, supported each other and worshipped together. Even the harshest critics of Bedward admired the peaceful and hard-working Bedwardite community. They were described as model citizens of August Town, could be relied on for their industry and work ethic, and troubled no one.[31] Such a community, of believers who pooled their resources and practised self-reliance as a model to the outside community, must have been in Howell's mind.

Chevannes argues that from the earliest years, it was Howell's intention to establish such a community. This is the reason he moved to St Thomas in 1933, a parish with a proud history of anticolonial resistance. This was also his reason for later buying and settling on Pinnacle Estate in St Catherine in 1940. Between living in these parishes, he lived with a small community in Kingston, which earned its living by running a bakery. When a poor man went and purchased a piece of bread he got a little free sugar and a little parcel of cornmeal.[32] Howell seems to have been replicating Bedward's successful model in St Thomas, which seems to have further infuriated some of the leading citizens of the parish, thereby leading to the 1937 riot.

On the night of Saturday, 9 January 1937, a crowd of angry residents of Harbour Head, Port Morant, raided and destroyed Howell's premises and mercilessly whipped numerous Rastafari brethren, and the police later escorted Howell and a few others out of the parish for their own protection. Around five hundred Rastafari brethren had already gathered to celebrate the Ethiopian Christmas on Thursday, 7 January. The Rastafari members were celebrating for four days, from that day to Sunday, 10 January, which would climax with the wearing of their uniforms and a love feast. All Rastafari members were to be adequately clothed and fed as they worshipped together. This was a sign of a self-reliant community in the making, as members came as far away as the parish of Clarendon and brought with them their food to be shared. One Rastafari brother reluctantly informed the angry mob that he had brought a fowl (chicken) as his gift to add to the pool. In advance, the Rastafari brethren had already stored food for the love feast. Howell complained that among the food looted by the mob was over 15 chickens, 200 pounds of rice, 48 quarts of coconut oil and over 450 enamel plates for the love feast.[33]

On the Sunday evening, when Howell was finally rescued by the police, news had also spread that two additional truckloads of Rastafari brethren had arrived at Leith Hill, a district about two miles from Port Morant. On hearing this, the mob came together in bands and invaded Leith Hill. Police had to rush to the scene to save those Rastafari members too.[34] The *Daily Gleaner* reported that the wanton destruction of Howell's property and the beating of Rastafari members could only be compared to what occurred in 1865 in the Morant Bay Rebellion, as some members of the Port Morant community, aided by the police, it seems, decided that Howell's community of Rastas was becoming too prominent and the movement had to be crushed immediately, before it was too late.[35] Most likely, the disappointment of Port Morant must have been a deciding factor for Howell to set up his community of believers in Pinnacle, St Catherine, rather than in St Thomas.

Robert Hinds's conversion to Rastafari and his success as one of the religion's earlier leaders is a good example of the ease with which Bedwardites became followers of Rastafari. The precise time Hinds became convinced that Ras Tafari was Jesus Christ is unclear. What is known is that he was converted by Howell and became one of Howell's early and most important lieutenants in spreading the news of Ras Tafari. Hinds, at one of his trials in a St Thomas Court in 1934, made the point that his biblical training (obviously in Bedwardism) and millenarian views before meeting Howell prepared him easily to accept Ras Tafari as the black Messiah.

In the early part of the trial in St Thomas, Hinds spoke strongly of his belief in angels, although he was now a believer in Ras Tafari. He warned the court that his angels protected him and would vindicate him. Hinds adopted Bedward's and Howell's daring and courage at the trial by warning his accusers that his God had the last word, and he could call on him to vindicate him. Hinds stated, "Anyway I go with my angels, flood come. I went to Kingston, flood come, and I went to St Elizabeth, [flood come] and now St Thomas. You better mind I don't call down my angels and let flood come!"[36]

Hinds repeatedly made the point in court that many of his current beliefs about a "black Christ" were formed long before Howell's influence. The court disagreed and blamed Howell for his enormous influence on Hinds, resulting in Hinds's foolish views and arguments. Hinds argued strongly that the historical Jesus was a black man like himself. So too were all Israelites in the Bible, and by extension, they were all Ethiopians. In making his point that Jesus was black, Hinds recited from memory Jeremiah 8:20–22. In response to an observation in court that Christ would come in the spirit, Hinds reiterated that Jesus would come in the flesh and quoted John 4 from memory to make his point. Hinds concluded that the historical Jesus had to have a son when he came to earth again to reign. If he came in the spirit, he would not have a son. If he came in the spirit, he would not wear a crown. That was the reason Ras Tafari came in the flesh and was inaugurated with his crown.

Hinds then held up a picture of Ras Tafari and showed the court the crown of gold on the head of the king. He quoted Revelation 12 to show that the crown had to contain twelve stars and showed them the twelve stars on the king's crown in the picture. Then he urged all members of the court to repent, pray, fast and not to blaspheme. In response to Howell's continuing influence on him, Hinds further revealed that he read of the King of Kings in the Bible, and then was shown a picture of the crowned king by a man from Cuba, followed by a magazine with pictures. It was later that he saw Howell's picture and was convinced that Ras Tafari was the black Jesus he had been looking for all along.

Hinds then traced his knowledge of the black Christ to his Bedwardite days, in response to the suggestion that it was Howell who told Hinds that he was a Jew. Hinds asserted that he found that evidence in the Bible long before meeting Howell. Seeing that he could not read, those who were literate in the religious community of which he was a part searched the Bible, used a dictionary, and all concluded that black people were Ethiopians. This community of which Hinds spoke who searched the scriptures had to be the Bedwardite community. Hinds further asserted that he was preaching long before he met Howell.

The court then asked him, "You didn't preach about Rastafari before?"

Hinds responded, "No, sir, but I found out that afterwards that Ras Tafari was the Christ."

Hinds's preaching before his preaching of Ras Tafari was when he was a Bedwardite. Hinds then reminded the court that he was one of the Bedwardites who marched in Bedward's final public demonstration in April 1921.[37] Thus his understanding of a black Christ predates Howell's preaching.

Hinds's assertion is correct. Although Alexander Bedward generally withheld the claim that he was the black Christ until 1920, the Bedwardites were aware of such a coming black Christ. That is the reason prominent Rastafari activists, such as Bongo Jerry, argue that, based on their oral history, Bedward was known to have preached of a coming black Christ as early as the 1890s.[38] The concept of a black Christ to Bedwardites such as Hinds would be most familiar. With the death of Bedward and the coronation of Haile Selassie, with his international prominence, it was easy for Bedwardites to become believers of Rastafari.

Rastafari doctrine, culture and rituals have evolved since the 1930s and continue to evolve, as argued by Michael Barnett, to the point where it has become very distinguishable from Bedwardism and Revivalism.[39] Nevertheless, the Bedwardite impact on Rastafari is still long-lasting. Hinds's death on 12 May 1950 did not halt his King of Kings Missions. Although the latter had disintegrated even before Hinds's death, his message and his Revivalist practice of Rastafari have been partly copied by some of Hinds's own lieutenants, each setting up his own group.[40] Thus Hinds's Bedwardite practices, such as quarterly baptisms for new initiates of Rastafari, still occur, given Rastafari's decentralized structure. As a matter of fact, there are still Rastafari believers whose doctrines and theology are like those of Hinds and its early leaders.[41] The latest is the School of Vision, founded in 1997 by Dermot Fagan. His followers have set up camp in the Blue Mountains overlooking Kingston, awaiting the return of the King of Kings to repatriate them in spacecraft, thus signalling the end of the world.[42] In this tendency towards decentralized engagement with the society, the Rastafari movement very closely resembles the movement from which it could be said to have emerged, Revivalism.

Bedwardism and Revival Religions

Scholars who write on Revivalism have identified the similarities and dissimilarities between two of the well-known Revivalist streams, Revival Zion Sixty and Revival Zion Sixty-One. What has not been identified, however, is the influence of the Bedwardite stream of Revival on the other forms of Revivalism and in particular Zion Sixty, which is operated similarly to a Christian church.[43] Since both Revival Sixty and Sixty-One have largely decentralized organizational structures, the possibility exists that Revival bands, although having much of their rituals, tables and iconographic elements in common, also have unique characteristics, given their geographical and ecological contexts. This makes the impact of Bedwardism on Revivalism even harder to trace.

One Bedwardite ritual, however, which seemed to have influenced some of the bands of Revival Sixty is the Vow Ceremony, which was held before baptism. This Vow Ceremony was the first step for initiates to be formally recognized as members of the Revivalist Sixty bands. Simpson describes this particular Revivalist Sixty meeting in West Kingston in the church sanctuary, in which the members used the Bedwardite Vow Ceremony, which he personally witnessed. The ceremony started with the deacon or one of the leaders handing each candidate a white candle, and the new members kneeling, while a song from the Sankey hymnal, number 123, was sung, and the candles were lit. Interestingly, one of the two opening songs mentioned by Brooks in the Bedwardite Vow Ceremony was sung in the Revivalist Sixty ceremony Simpson witnessed. It reads:

> Behold the wretch whose lust and wine
> Had wasted his estate
> He begs a share among the swine
> To taste the husks they eat!
> "I die with hunger here," he cries,
> "I starve in foreign lands;
> "My father's house has large supplies
> "And bounteous are his hands."[44]

The same Bedwardite ritual which Brooks described was said afterwards by the shepherd as the candidates knelt and repeated after the minister the short prayer:

> Lord take me down to hell
> Show me my sins and my condemnation
> Help me to abstain from them
> And do them no more
> Witness me men and angels,
> Before the Lord I kneel
> To thee I make a solemn vow
> A vow I dare not break.[45]

The Hope River where Bedward performed his baptisms became the popular baptism spot for many Revival Sixty bands and other Revivalist groups. Even Christian churches used Bedward's sacred space for baptisms. Interestingly, the Roman Catholic Church in August Town also performs adult baptisms for requested members of the congregation.[46] It is common knowledge that the Roman Catholic Church in general does not practise adult baptism by immersion. Bedward's impact on adult baptism by immersion had become so embedded as a cultural practice that it has even transcended traditional ecclesiastical norms.

The Bedwardites were known to march in processions before the break of dawn to the Hope River for their baptisms. Simpson further describes some West Kingston Revivalists in the 1950s making the seven–ten-mile procession to the Hope River after the Vow Ceremony. They started out after midnight to have early-morning baptismal services. The Hope River became the Revivalist popular spot for such baptisms, to the extent that a man-made dam was created in 1953 for that purpose.[47]

Rituals were not the only impact of Bedwardism on the Revival movement. Chevannes argues that Bedwardism was the poster child for the Revivalist movement, given its popularity, numerical strength and, most important, national and international appeal. Bedward's success in building a stable and viable movement must have had a positive impact on the Revivalist movement generally. Fellow Revivalists understood that their religion was viewed negatively by colonial adherents and seen as a scourge on the society and a serious hindrance to the moral and social development of Jamaica. Thus all Revivalists shared a common identity as outcasts. Bedward's success in the face of harsh persecution meant that they too could succeed, as Bedward and his movement remained a model of resistance.

Not only was Bedwardism a poster child, but it was also an aspirant to the Revival movement, as argued by anthropologist George Eaton Simpson. The fluidity of the Revival movement in Jamaica, where bands were primarily autonomous and decentralized, meant that groups which were struggling to remain independent had the option to look to larger Revival groups for support, stimulation and even models. Smaller groups could even merge with larger, more successful groups for their own survival, seeing that most groups had similar rituals and litanies. This is attested to in the Bedwardites' 1920 annual report, where the point is made that numerous splinter Revivalist groups have separated themselves from them and were now on their own. Despite Bedwardism having a strong centre and a hierarchy, its decentralized structure aided autonomous Revivalist groups. Such groups could freely associate with the Bedwardites and receive support. Later, the same groups could disassociate themselves if it was in their best interest or face disassociation by the Bedwardites for not following their doctrines.

Chevannes, commenting on the fluidity of Bedward's polity, notes:

> The Bedward movement comprised a network of loosely attached Revival groups, besides having a church organized around Bedward himself. Mother Burke, Dixon's aunt and foster parent, was herself the leader of one of those groups. The groups functioned autonomously of their centre of gravity but paid recognition and allegiance by visits to August Town for baptism and other rituals. That was why, no doubt, Minister Dawson was among those deputized by the prophet Bedward to baptize.[48]

It is important to note that the Revivalist groups which became disassociated from the Bedwardite movement were still influenced by its theology, organizational practices and litanies, such as baptism, fasting and the important role of healing, as the latter was what made Bedward famous. Although these disassociated bands would be adapting and recreating themselves, as argued by Chevannes and Besson, to remain relevant in their environment, their association with the Bedwardites left lasting legacies.

Bedwardism also had an impact on the Revival movement by providing a blueprint of what a successful indigenous Jamaican religion ought to resemble. The Bedwardites' retention of some of the core doctrines of the post-1865 Great Revival was indeed one of the secrets behind their success.

Another fundamental doctrine the Bedwardites imparted in their Jamaican version of Christianity was the important role of healing, either by myal medicine or through the instrument of the leader or shepherd. So was the rereading and reinterpreting of the Bible in their African Jamaican context and not from the perspective of the privileged European missionaries. This reinterpretation allowed the African Jamaican community to make visions and dreams a doctrinal priority in their lives, rather than the hermeneutical interpretation of the white missionaries, who studied the Bible as literature, while not allowing the spirit of the Bible to reveal itself.[49] Robert Stewart took the following observation from one such Revival leader, Pennock:

> He told me that if he laid down to sleep, and put the prayerbook or Bible on his breast, the spirit would not speak to him, but if these were not there, he would have dreams, visions, voices etc., and that when he had the spirit, if he opened either of the above books, the paper would appear perfectly white and clean – no

print could be seen. Pennock acknowledged that the bible would teach him many good things, but he was firm in his doctrine, that God by his spirit taught him many things which could not be found in the bible.[50]

Thirdly, the African Jamaican community viewed the fight for social justice for the black oppressed community against an unjust colonial order as another important tenet of the Great Revival. These native churches led by their own leaders spoke on their behalf and even planned social programmes, initiating their own courts and alleviating their own socioeconomic problems. Fourthly, they were sure of their return to their home in Africa, since their entrapment in a New World was harsh and oppressive. They wanted to be assured that their sins were washed away by their baptism, and they were saved and healed, and most important, at death, they would return to their motherland.[51] Bedwardism seemed to have captured these four core elements of the Great Revival, and this recognition seemed to have accounted for its attraction for the working-class black community.

The Jamaica Native Baptist Free Church, from its birth with Shakespeare as head, had its own organizational structure of twenty-four elders. Alexander Bedward further complemented it with seventy-four. Bedward, as hierarchical leader, had full control of the movement and played a similar role to an African religious leader, since he was prophet, healer and advocate of his people. With Bedward providing water from the Hope River as holy medicine, his healing ministry authenticated him as an outstanding shepherd who genuinely had the gift of prophecy and healing.

Bedward also skilfully articulated the role of the Bible. He did not downplay its relevance, as some other Revivalists did, but used it as an important source of prophecy, as the Bible authenticated Bedwardism. Bedward taught that both Judaism and Christianity were his forerunners, and hence the Bible, especially the sections on prophecies, was most important. Despite highlighting the Bible's relevance, Bedward made the caveat that his visions and dreams by way of revelation were what really mattered as inspiration and guided his decision-making. Thus, on the one hand, he could not be legitimately described as being against the Bible, since his sermons and prophecies were all biblically based. On the other hand, he was able to maintain his Revivalist tradition by giving divine revelation priority over the written scriptures. Bedward's sermons, which were based on the Bible, were highly contextualized to address societal injustices done to blacks, and as a sign of social protest, which was a tradition of the Revival movement. This biblical mandate distinguished Bedward and made his movement attractive to the persecuted black community, who knew they had a leader who would die for them and was their watchman. The millenarian role which Africa played was central to Bedwardism and found resonance with the African population. Bedwardism was also a space where Ethiopianism was central, where black people were related to the ancient Hebrews and where its leader was later to be seen as the black Christ. Bedwardism was the full package of a contextual black Jamaican religion, with a black Christ and a hope that the black man would find his final resting place in Africa.

Bedwardism embodied a genuine Jamaican black religion and was a stimulant for the other Revivalist movements. This made the Revival movement most difficult to distinguish in the population, despite the myriad attempts by the colonial government to do so. Bedward's bold resistance to the colonial authorities must have also emboldened fellow Revivalist leaders, such as Higgins and others, who were very harsh in their rhetoric against the colonial order. Revivalist leader Dr David Bell is a classic example:

> Marching to the tune of Onward Christian Soldiers, a column of people carrying Christian flags entered May Pen . . . they were joined by several hundred persons . . . the leader of the group Doctor David Bell, a preacher and healer, prophesied the impending doom of the town by flames. Raising up their hands the entire crowd yelled, "Fire! Fire! Fire!". From a collection of onlookers nearby the Reverend W.B. Esson, a Congregational minister, came forward and spoke to Bell, "Who are you that I should hear you?" Bell asked. "I am a representative of the King, a member of the Legislative Council and a Justice of the Peace." "I don't care who you are," Bell shouted, "you are nothing but a little white boy . . . you hypocrite, you liar, everybody preach Christ, but it is different to do the work of Christ . . ." Bell then picked up some trash and said, "I don't count the man as I count this trash."[52]

The Pentecostal Impact

Diane Austin-Broos argues that Revivalism had a direct influence on Pentecostalism in Jamaica. I would further argue that Pentecostalism in Jamaica also benefited from the Revival paradigm which the Bedwardites made popular. Pentecostalism is acknowledged by scholars as the fastest-growing version of Christianity in the Americas and in Africa. The birth of the Pentecostal movement in Jamaica is dated around the early 1920s, a period when Bedwardism was still at its height as a popular national religious movement islandwide. Although Bedward was sent to the asylum in 1921, the Bedwardite movement was still relatively strong. It was the death of Bedward in 1930 which would have had a major impact and led to the decline of the movement. A number of those Bedwardite members would have found refuge in the growing Pentecostal movement, which has healing practices similar to the Revivalist movements.

Bedwardism affected the Pentecostal movement in two ways. First, Pentecostalism continued the Bedwardite orientation towards one Spirit, the Holy Spirit, the third person in the Christian Trinity, rather than accommodating heavenly and earthly spirits as some Revivalist groups do. Bedwardism had already distanced itself from such Revivalists in not entertaining such spirits. Despite Bedward's attempt at locating Bedwardism as a "normal religious movement" which believed in the Trinity, and not entertaining the various African spirits, the movement was still viewed negatively by many who were influenced by colonial values.

The Pentecostal emphasis on God as the Holy Spirit, and allowing the Holy Spirit alone to manifest itself, outside of other spirits, was its way of gaining legitimacy as a genuine Christian movement. Thus the Pentecostal movement never had the stigma of practitioners of obeah, as the Bedwardites and other Revivalists were tagged. Secondly, however, the Pentecostals continued the important Revivalist and Bedwardite tradition of holistic healing in their litanies. The socioeconomic and political plight of the black working poor made the process of healing a priority in Pentecostal services over the ethical appeal for right living. This feature of the Pentecostal church was not that dissimilar to Bedwardism. Bedward's ability to heal all kinds of diseases was a major contributory factor to its growth and spread. Divine healing became labelled the most important aspect of Pentecostal worship. An elderly Pentecostal in northern Clarendon made this critical point, given the movement's expansion in the 1920s:

> Why the people flowing to the New Testament Church of God the more, it was divine healing. Anywhere we went and preached, that brought people that were sick, and we prayed for them, and they got healing, you see. Then the people them believe the church for the healing more, even more than the preacher. That goes a lot for the physical, you know, because many of the people them want that power. Yes, man, when the spirit preaches you feel it all over your body. The body feels good. I mean, if you go in the church and the spirit of God is not in the church, you can't operate. You just sit down listening, but when the Spirit of God come in, you can turn the body in the Spirit.[53]

Austin-Broos argues that the impact of Bedwardism and other, smaller, less recognized African religious movements in emphasizing the work of the Holy Spirit provided the blueprint for the Pentecostal movement. Secondly, the Pentecostal movement was further authenticated by its North American linkages, as the Jamaican colonial class generally tolerated it as a "legitimate church". This legitimacy given to the Pentecostal church is not to suggest that the colonial elites would become members, as it was clear that the Pentecostal movement comprised largely the poorest people in society. Like Bedwardism, Pentecostal Christianity became attractive to the Jamaican poor over traditional Christianity, as it engendered a more intimate connection with their own creole traditions. One Pentecostal elder observed:

> The Pentecostal churches gave more freedom to the individual to be identified in worship, while [in] the other, what we say "established churches," it was just a pastor, the pastor, the preacher that did the preaching. The Baptist churches had a certain amount of life in it, in their songs, and some of them would even offer a little shout – an "amen" or a "hallelujah" in their service, but normally the churches were sort of straight, you know, just regimented. No way in the Pentecostal. It was all expression. Maybe too, with our African background and our emotional response, we would have more tendency to go towards the Spirit, to receive the Holy Spirit.[54]

The Pentecostal movement and other charismatic movements have also engaged in prophesy. Given its North American theological influence, its prophecies are usually conservative, and like many other traditional Christian movements, it has stayed away from race-based critique and analysis, in contrast to the prophecies of Alexander Bedward.[55] Generally, the Pentecostals give support and privilege to the status quo, that is, the prevailing sociopolitical system. They engage in a withdrawal from society as they prepare their members for life in the next world.[56]

Impact on August Town

Alexander Bedward also had a significant impact on the social development of the August Town community. August Town seems to have been first settled by runaway enslaved Africans who occupied an area known today as Bottom River, lower (August Town). Local historians argue that Bottom River was a wasteland which was used as a burial ground for enslaved Africans.[57] Given the topography of much of the August Town lands – sloping, with intermittent streams and rock – it was not suited for sugar cane cultivation but had numerous cattle estates, such as Hermitage Pen and Latimers Pen. These estates were smaller in size, with fewer enslaved Africans, in comparison with the neighbouring plantations of Mona and Papine. In 1831, for example, the Hermitage Pen had an enslaved population of only seventy enslaved Africans in contrast to 177 at Mona with its stock of seventy-seven. The Papine Estate, on the other hand, had an enslaved population of 144 enslaved Africans with a stock of 146.[58]

By the middle of the nineteenth century, the cattle estates in August Town seemed to have folded, as many Jamaican plantations did, given the 1846 Sugar Duties Act. Hermitage Pen and Latimers Pen were purchased when Lewis Verley bought the Mona Estate in 1860.[59] Verley also purchased the Papine Estate to enlarge his acreage at Mona. The Mona Estate became the main economic hub in this section of the Liguanea Plains. This economic opportunity explains the reason labourers like Alexander Bedward and others living in the environs of Mona found work on the estate. It also explains how Shakespeare was able to purchase a lot of land in August Town for the Jamaica Native Baptist Free Church, since August Town had ample marginal land for sale, given the abandoned estates in the community.

One Englishman, William Platt, was the person Bedward bought pieces of land from on different occasions. Platt divided his land in August Town into small pieces for sale. He sold hillside land with flat land to ensure that his land could be sold.[60] By the late nineteenth century the inhabitants of August Town were Bedwardites, descendants of runaway Africans and freed enslaved Africans, along with Indian immigrants who had served their indentureship. Generally, the residents of August Town were poor, and the community was considered an inhospitable place to live.

The main road was lined with bush and dildo macka trees to the extent that you often had to walk with a machete to cut them down, as they were over one's head. The community also had plenty of wild hogs, cows and goats, decrepit creatures with swollen feet, caused primarily by chiggers.[61] The community never had any good roads for vehicular traffic, as donkeys or bicycles were the common means of transport other than walking.[62] Bedward, who lived in Barbican before August Town, opened the community to others, since many people were attracted by his popularity and wanted to become members of his church.

Bedward made it clear, however, that anyone who wanted to live in August Town and be provided with a home had to be called specifically for that task, and he had to be so convinced. One Manchester woman, for example, claimed that God called her specifically to leave her husband and work with

Bedward and to live in August Town. Bedward accepted her and she became the church's caretaker. The arrangement was that the woman would devote herself to the movement's fasting and prayer on Mondays, Wednesdays and Fridays. The other days of the week she was free, apart from the early-morning call for all Bedwardites to pray.[63]

Other Bedwardites, especially from the parishes of Portland and St Thomas, also came to live in August Town as full-time workers. They too claimed a call to the movement to support Bedward at Union Temple, their headquarters. The parishes of Portland and St Thomas had thriving Bedwardite chapters, as some of them came through Newcastle into August Town.[64] The influx of Bedwardites living in August Town to support Bedward was the primary reason the Bedwardites built their communes adjacent to Union Temple.

Other Bedwardites who were serious about their faith but were not categorized as full-time workers also moved to August Town. They did not live in its commune but bought land to build their homes, and they too received assistance from fellow Bedwardites in building them. The many disappointed Bedwardites who sold their possessions to depart with Bedward in 1920 and were embarrassed to return home were also accommodated in the commune, along with others who could return home, but chose to remain in August Town and live with their fellow Bedwardites. One Bedwardite estimates that by 1921 around a thousand Bedwardites lived in the commune and its environs.[65] This led to August Town becoming more of a religious town, with the temple in the centre, and homes on one side.

As the community grew, so did the homes that were built and refurbished. Before Bedward's grass house was rebuilt in stone, the houses were primarily grass with a little wattle and daub, and grass-thatched roofs. Only two buildings in the community, it is believed, had shingle roofs, one being the St Cyprian Anglican Church, a well-built stone structure.[66] The grass houses were so flimsy that one Bedwardite said you could actually push your hand in and pull people out of their homes. The Bedwardites later transformed many of them into board structures, with appropriate roads and other necessary infrastructure.

After the Bedwardites built their religious town, non-Bedwardites flowed in, as the community had become a decent place to live. Chinese businessmen also came to ply their trade and live there. The Indian community had become so large numerically that they planned Hosay celebrations on what is today Manley Avenue.[67]

The 1951 Hurricane Charlie, which devastated Jamaica's south coast, left around nine thousand people homeless, including many citizens of August Town. The Jamaica Labour Party took the initiative in organizing a hurricane-rehabilitation housing scheme for these residents, who were given tents to live in temporarily. The scheme improved the quality of houses in August Town, as it benefited low- and medium-income residents.[68] The quality of homes and an increasing housing stock was further enhanced by the People's National Party government of 1955–62, especially as August Town was in the constituency of Chief Minister Norman Manley. He completed the last batches of the Jamaica Labour Party's hurricane-rehabilitation homes on Bedward Crescent in 1957 and initiated a new housing scheme in Hermitage, half a mile away.[69]

The Hermitage homes were in such heavy demand, not only by residents of August Town but from people within the KSAC region, that in 1959 the *Daily Gleaner* described chaos at the housing office in Kingston over a fight to get them. Thousands of people appeared at the office to apply for and pay down on one of the precious houses, only to discover that the advertisement in the paper was for those who had previously applied and had been chosen for the sixty houses built that year. These new enquirers were informed that the waiting list already had around seven hundred names on it.[70]

It was evident by the 1950s that August Town was being transformed into a comfortable place to live and do business, especially for low- and middle-income earners. The Kingston metropolitan bus service (JOS) added August Town to its route and a North American shoe company, Wellco, built its factory on eight acres of land between the junction of the Hope River and the August Town gully.[71] In 1959, Wellco shipped 5,000 pairs of shoes to the United States.[72]

August Town had come of age and Alexander Bedward was its conceptualizer. It was he who first brought a level of organization to the community, with his church at the centre, its low-income houses spread in a semi-circular pattern, spaces for farming, its cemetery and its various shops, all on his estimated four acres of land.[73] Bedward motivated the Bedwardites and with their spirit of self-reliance and cooperation opened the door to the further development of a larger town. The Bedwardites opened it up as a viable community to live and work, and both the Jamaica Labour Party and the People's National Party governments added to and improved the community's housing stock and infrastructure.

But August Town, which was Jamaica's religious mecca for over thirty years because of Alexander Bedward, would face dark and difficult days by the end of the twentieth century. The country's two major political parties had built their enclaves in different sections of August Town and now competed for votes and for political power. The gun replaced the Bible and the gunmen had replaced the peaceful Bedwardites.

Appendix 1
Berry, the Independent Stream Flowing from a Huge Rock

Appendix 2
The Rock from which Bedward Preached Many of His Sermons

Appendix 3
Remnants of Union Temple, Shown from Three Angles

Appendix 4
The Churches of the Jamaica Native Baptist Free Church, 1920

Churches & Parishes	Managers	Members
St Andrew		
1. Union Camp	Rev. A. Bedward	405
2. Batheran	Mr D.E. Walker	261
3. Little Zion	" Percival Carnegie	101
4. Union Hill	" Simon Edwards	29
5. Mt Parau	" Alexander Stewart	37
6. Mt Luz	" Alexander Nelson	40
7. New Refuge	" Oscar Oddiman	30
8. New Beulah	" Enos Moore	36
9. Mt Haloth	" Alfred Hamilton	14
Portland		
10. Bethalla	" Josiah Summers	56
11. Trinity Vale	" Zechaia West	83
12. Church Hill	" Richard Anderson	38
13. Zion	" Alexander Smith	14
14. Mt Gracious	" Amos Edwards	19
15. New Hall	" Chas Smith	36
16. Mt Olives	" Daniel Brown	24
17. Mt Dasah	" Bartholomew Simpson	27
18. Bethsaida	" Timothy James	10
St Mary		
19. Beulah	" F.A. Smith	115
20. Mt Pleasant	" Josiah Mitchell	25
21. Mt Moriah	" John Wade	25
22. Mt Havilah	" Zachariah Mendes	
23. Pleasant Vale	" A.A. McLennon	15
24. Mt Ephraim	Mrs Isabella Barrett	27

Churches & Parishes	Managers	Members
25. Mt Hermon	Mr Henry Brown	8
26. No name	Mr David Lewis	15
27. No name	No name	
St Catherine		
28. Lighbourne	" Samuel Fisher	40
29. Bethbeva	" Joseph Shaw	20
30. Refuge	" Francis Burrell	59
31. Faith View	" Joseph Bell	40
32. Watch Tower	" Constantine Bell	16
33. Ebenezer	" Thomas Stanley	42
34. Mt Hollack	" Arthur Moore	47
35. Mt Nebo	" Richard Walker	90
36.	" James Grant	43
37. Mt Jerusalem	" Thomas Brown	36
38. Jordan Vale	" Edward Hamilton	15
39. Homestead	" John Hayles	7
40. Mt Hablon	" William Anderson	14
41. Salem	Mrs Ann Halstead	48
42. Mt Privilege	Mrs Lucian Paige	0
43. Tranquility	Mrs Zipporah Smellie	0
44. Bethany	Ms Niami Dixon	14
St Thomas		
45. Bethadia	Mr Samuel Skervin	59
46. Union Hill	" Charles Fraser	59
47. Hephezebah	" Irving Roberts	13
48. Mt Happy View	" George Edmonston	20
49. Unity	" Elisha Smith	9
50. Mt Humble	" Edward Bailey	23
51. Bethany	" James Allen	44
52. Beaulah	" Edwards Payton	7
53. Mt Prospect	Mrs Melvina Hensley	18
Clarendon		
54. Bethlehem	Mrs Mary McLean	25

Churches & Parishes	Managers	Members
St Ann		
55. Ebenezer	Mr Isaac Scott	27
Kingston		
56. Union Band	Mr I. Gordon	9
57. Little Samaria	Mrs C. Ellis	10
58. Hope Hill	Mr Joseph Stewart	15
59. Bethrome	Mr James Bogle	11
60. Mt Zion	Mr George Ellis	15
61. New Carmel	Mr James Bogle	14
62. No name	Mr Charles Bennett	9
63. Refuge	Mr Solomon Graham	13
64. No name	Zachaeus Dawkins	8
65. Mt Airy	Mr Charles Dacres	0
66. Moore Park	Mr Charles Davis	0
67. Hyltonside	Mrs Catherine Ivy	11
68. Water Lane	Mrs Ann Bennett	26
69. Mt Olive	Mrs Dorothy Keith	11
70. No name	Mrs Victoria Roye	12
71. Mt Grace	Mrs Alice Hyde	5
72. Hope Road	Mrs Rebeca Carter	0
73. Fortune Corner	Emily McLean	26
74. New Monkland	Mr David Ford	0

Appendix 5
List of Males Who Marched with Bedward and Were Imprisoned

Leaders
Levi Steele
Benjamin Steele
Isaiah Gooden
Roman Henry
Levi McKenzie
George Burke
Christian Duke

Batch One	Francis Burrell, Jas French, David Lewis, Francis Rutherford, Charles Bell, Caleb DaCosta, Rainford Allman, Alfred Dennis, Naboth Stewart
Batch Two	George Ballentine, James Myers, Charles Hyatt, Adolphus Ranger, Samuel Henry, George Jones, Edward Edmonson, Thomas Britton, Naaman Dennis
Batch Three	John Mowatt, Obadiah Bryan, Isaac Scott, Joseph Broadbelt, Samuel Malabre, Emanuel Reuben, James Harris, Joseph Dennis, Josiah Jackson
Batch Four	Daniel Ricketts, Nathan Williams, Ezekiel McLean, Simeon Thompson, John Henry, Ernest DuCas--, Beniah Taylor, Samuel Hause, Robert Fyffe
Batch Five	Charles Nelson, Emanuel Gibson, Richard Foster, Joseph Foster, Arthur Grant, David ———, Albert Thompson, William Johnson, George Martin
Batch Six	Nathaniel Brown, George Sherrington, Charles Williams, Joseph Dixon, Eustace Edwards, William Burke, Ivanhoe Burke, Frederick Donaldson

1. Ivanhoe McCarthy
2. Samuel Male
3. Simeon Bicknell
4. Robert Hinds
5. David Johnson
6. Joseph Gibson
7. Irving Nathaniel Roberts
8. Edward Hamilton
9. Theophilus Gooden
10. Hubert Wynter
11. George Williams
12. Richard Henry
13. Charles Smith
14. Samuel Smith

15.	Charles Watson	52.	Theophilus Stewart
16.	Geo Clark	53.	Richard Burrell
17.	Chas Moore	54.	James Shore
18.	Constantine Broadbelt	55.	Wm Bethune
19.	Levi Thompson	56.	Jonathan David Steele
20.	Benjamin Haughton	57.	William Cole
21.	Marcus Coleman	58.	Claud Shand
22.	William Harvey	59.	Ezekiah Martin
23.	Theophilus Skirven	60.	Christie Skirven
24.	Nathan Osbourne	61.	Sam Chambers
25.	Nathaniel Briggs	62.	Lyons
26.	John Graham	63.	Bell
27.	Daniel Malabre	64.	Gowdie
28.	Michael Harriman	65.	Watson
29.	James Henry	66.	Alfred Mais
30.	George Roberts	67.	Levy
31.	Augustus Donald	68.	Brown
32.	Donald Rainford	69.	Cephas Nethersole
33.	Samuel McIntosh	70.	David Walsh
34.	Chas Harding	71.	David Brown
35.	James Coward	72.	Zachariah West
36.	Daniel Hinds	73.	William Cole
37.	Henry Thomas	74.	Asher Brooks
38.	Henry Richards	75.	The old man
39.	George Fraser	76.	Lewis Foster
40.	Stephen Bryan	77.	Jacob Calvin
41.	Zachariah Drummond	78.	Elisha Drummond
42.	Joseph Reynolds	79.	Reuben Blackwood
43.	James Shepherd	80.	Edward Hibbert
44.	Joseph Francis	81.	James Bodie
45.	Samuel Hamilton	82.	Robert Ivey
46.	James Johnson	83.	Colin Maloney
47.	Uriah Jones	84.	Richard Addison
48.	Richard Brown	85.	John Chamberlain
49.	Charles Easy	86.	Uriah Deannie
50.	Richard Ferguson	87.	Alexander Nelson
51.	John Lewis	88.	Lionel Dixon

89. Stedman Lawrence
90. Alexander Rule
91. William Lewis
92. Dexter Walker
93. Isaac Cruickshank
94. Robert Wilson
95. Michael Campbell
96. Azariah Maloney
97. Percival Robinson
98. Methuselah Baugh
99. Isaac Brown
100. Percival Carnegie
101. Henry Thompson
101. Richard Walker
102. John Squire
103. John Edwards
104. Emanuel Dickens
105. Luther Mendes
106. Eustace Brown
107. Samuel Johnson
108. Richard Henry
109. Charles McCatty
110. George Malcolm
111. Zachariah Mendes
112. Alfred Hamilton
113. Nimrod Bryan
114. Jonathan Roberts
115. Wilmot Foster
116. Daniel Henry
117. Ephraim Wright
118. Alexander Smith
119. William Harris

Appendix 6

List of Twenty-five Females Who Marched with Bedward and Were Imprisoned

1. ——— Beckford
2. Roslyn Taylor
3. N. Wilson
4. Adina Salmon
5. Catherine Hill
6. Elizabeth Foster
7. Jane Johnson
8. Hernice Clayton
9. Henrietta Dixon
10. Margaret Dunn
11. Helen Campbell
12. Iris Gooden
13. Agnes Boyd
14. Elizabeth Small
15. Sarah Thomas
16. Mabel Sinclair
17. Eliza Enie
18. Cecilia Lewis
19. Clarice Grant
20. Helen Melvin
21. Ann McKenzie
22. Mariah Goldson
23. Jemina Patterson
24. Charlotte French
25. Annie Scott

(Gooden and Lewis were discharged with a warning but the others were given seven days' hard labour.)

Appendix 7
Rules and Report of the 1920 Convention

RULES
—AND—
REPORT
—FOR THE—
Jamaica Native Baptist Free Church
SOCIETY

—AND FOR—
The Churches that are connected therewith
FOR THE YEAR 1920.

JAMAICA:
Printed at Gray's Book Room,
98 Oxford St., Kingston,—970

1. That the name of this Union shall be called The Jamaica Native Baptist Free Church Society.
2. Its Object shall be to promote unity in whatever may best serve the cause of Christ in general, and the interest of this Baptist Denomination in particular.
3. The Society shall be managed by the President, Ministers, Secretary and Elders.
4. It is also understood that every separate Chapel has within its power and authority to exercise all evangelical discipline, rules and government, and to put in execution all the laws of Christ necessary for edification, and to carry out the rules given from the mother Church, in setting apart three days in the week for spiritual worship in fasting and prayer for one or two hours in each day.
5. It is requested that each Church send in their reports to the Secretary three days before the time of the Annual meeting.
6. It must be understood that the meeting of this Society shall be held annually between the first and Second week in June, at the mother Church, Union Camp, August Town, St Andrew. Any Evangelist or Elder who fails to send in their report or neglect in attending the meeting for two years, shall be considered as having withdrawn from the Society.
7. It is requested that each Chapel is to make a subscription or the provision of the Evangelist and Elders during that time of the meeting.
8. No member is excluded from the Lord's supper because they hadn't the 3d to pay immediately. They are permitted to take the Supper and another time pay for it, when they get same.
9. It is also requested that on the first Monday of each month that all Stations in Kingston and lower St Andrew be closed, and leaders and people meet at the mother Church to celebrate the Memorial Day of the Shepherd.
10. It is requested that on the second Sunday of each month in all the Churches in the Country that a special fast Table be spread immediately after Divine Service, and all members meet around the board at the time of the celebration of the Lord's Supper at the mother Church when there is no appointment for a Minister to visit in such month.
11. No member is exempted from their monthly duties, save those that are afflicted, or in any extreme poverty or children under age that cannot help themselves.

12. No Harvest Festival meetings, Flower Services or any other meeting to raise money or the help of building Chapels will be accepted in this Society. All money must be by Freewill offerings to the Lord. "For the building of the Lord's House, let the people of God build their Master's House. As God hath prospered them, let them give every man as he purposeth in his heart let him give" 2 Cor. 9:7.
13. The Society strictly prohibits what is commonly called revival of shaking the head and tramping the ground and wallowing on the earth and saying: "It is the Spirit." Such are not Spirit that the Lord teach us to pray for those are the Spirit that works in the children of disobedience. God want is the revival of the heart, a revival from sin to grace, and a surrendering of the heart to God, that the Spirit of truth and grace may reign therein.
14. Special attention is called to all Leaders and Leadresses to beware of the many so-called Bedwardites, who are going about as deceivers, saying that they are preachers sent from August Town, and are performing works contrary to the rules of the Society. By their fruits you must know them, and go not with them nor alter them. Unless any one can show a certificate as a recognized Evangelist from the Church, don't receive him. For many are gone from us and has become enemies to the cause by evil works.
15. Any Leader or Evangelist receiving land for the erection of any Mission in connection with this Society, must first see that the land from which they receive such piece, be a well settled property, and that a deed of gift be given with proper stamp from the giver and signed by all who may be heirs of the said property.
16. ORDER OF FASTING: - Mondays, Wednesdays and Fridays, Table spread at 11 o'clock, service begins at 12 o'clock, a hymn sung, reading of the Holy Scriptures, exhortation, hymn and prayer, the cups turn and the food bless and break, a hymn sung, prayer and dismissal.
17. Candle march, balm yards and the spreading of the so-called mourning tables are strictly prohibited. Candles are only to be used for vowing or any other special matter approved by the Society.
18. ORDER OF DIVINE SERVICE: -Service begins at 11 a m., Hymn, Prayer, Hymn, Psalm, response Chant, reading from Old Testament, Chant, reading from New Testament, Chant, Prayer, Hymn, exhortation, Hymn, Prayer, Closing.
19. Prayer meetings begin at 7 p.m., and closes at 9 o'clock.
20. No station should be erected in any parish or district where there is less than seven to twelve members living near to carry on the work.

21. Any member who backslides or fall away from grace whether by actual or practical sin, and is returning back to the Church, the Leaders must see that such a member attend Prayer meetings and fast table for three months as a penitent before they are allowed to fellowship again as a full member of the Society.
22. It is requested that all members in connection with this Society take notice that no money is changed in the Church.
23. It is also requested that all Leaders and Leadresses who may desire to erect new buildings are to send their money to the Shepherd and that the Ministers may approve first the situation of the spot and the rest of the proposed.
24. Please to take notice that any Mission that was already built, or will . . ., and no Minister who is connected to the Society has approved of the works that are being carried on, such Station will not be reported as recognized.
25. Please take notice that all small Stations that are two to three miles off, is to attend the larger one for Divine Service on first Mondays until they are strong enough to stand their own foundation.

NOTICE

All workers of this Society will observe that there is in our report this year an additional column of small stations to be improved.

Appendix 8
Bedward's Manifestation into Kingston in 1921

Notes

Introduction: Lies, Distortion and Colonial Memory

1 Chris Barker, *Cultural Studies: Theory and Practice*, 4th ed. (London: Sage, 2012), 91.
2 George Olson to Secretary Phelps of the Missionary Board, February 1921, MS, 1835, no. 1.
3 Ibid.
4 Ibid.
5 Ibid.
6 Ibid.
7 Ibid.
8 Brian L. Moore and Michelle A. Johnson, *Neither Led nor Driven: Contesting British Cultural Imperialism in Jamaica, 1865–1921* (Kingston: University of the West Indies Press, 2004), 81.
9 Louis Marriott, "Dip them, Bedward, Dip them . . .," *Gleaner*, 22 February 2003, 1.
10 Henry Beauclerk, *Jamaica's Negro Prophet*, Woodstock letters, Maryland, Institute of Jamaica, vol. 23, 1894, 354–55.
11 Patrick Bryan, *The Jamaican People 1880–1902: Race, Class and Social Control* (1991; reprint, Kingston: University of the West Indies Press, 2000).
12 Colin A. Palmer, *Freedom's Children: The 1938 Labor Rebellion and the Birth of Modern Jamaica* (Chapel Hill: University of North Carolina Press, 2014), Kindle.
13 Edward White, "Rise Up: Alexander Bedward's Mystical Powers of Flight", *Paris Review*, 5 October 2016, https://www.theparisreview.org/blog/2016/10/05/rise-up/.
14 Moore and Johnson, *Neither Led nor Driven*, 80.
15 Bryan, *Jamaican People*, 41.
16 Moore and Johnson, *Neither Led nor Driven*, 80.
17 Ibid., 81.
18 Roman Henry interviewed by Ena Campbell, The Bedwardite Papers, African Caribbean Institute of Jamaica, 1980, T 251, 6; Veront Satchell, "Early Stirrings of Black Nationalism in Colonial Jamaica: Alexander Bedward of the Jamaica Native Baptist Free Church 1889–1921", *Journal of Caribbean History* 38, no. 1 (2004): 83. Satchell gives a membership of over seven thousand Bedwardites in its heyday.

19 A.A. Brooks, *The History of Bedwardism* (Kingston: Gleaner Company, 1917).
20 Randolph Williams, B/N, Institute of Jamaica, 1.
21 Ibid., 2.
22 Leroy Thompson, *Star*, 23 October 1972, 1. The *Star* is the Gleaner Company's evening tabloid.
23 Ibid., 2.
24 Ibid., 3.
25 Martha W. Beckwith, *Black Roadways: A Study of Jamaican Folk Life* (New York: Negro Universities Press, 1929), 169.
26 May Gordon, "Little Lives: The Beggar", *West Indian Review* (1950): 29.
27 Satchell, "Early Stirrings", 77.
28 He was arrested in 1895 and twice in 1921. At the second trial in 1921 he was freed by the court but rearrested within minutes for another trial to face the same judge who had released him.
29 Barry Chevannes, *Rastafari: Roots and Ideology* (New York: Syracuse University Press, 1994), 39, Kindle.
30 See D.A. Dunkley, "The Suppression of Leonard Howell in Late Colonial Jamaica", *New West Indian Guide* 87 (2013): 62–93; Clinton Hutton, Michael Barnett, D.A. Dunkley and Jahlani Niaah, eds., *Leonard Percival Howell and the Genesis of Rastafari* (Kingston: University of the West Indies Press, 2015); Michael Barnett, ed., *Rastafari in the New Millennium: A Rastafari Reader* (New York: Syracuse University Press, 2012).
31 Rupert Lewis, "Garvey's Forerunners: Love and Bedward", *Race and Class* 28, no. 3 (January 1987): 29–40.
32 Yoshiko S. Nagashima, "Rastafarian Music in Contemporary Jamaica: A Study of Socio-religious Music of the Rastafarian Movement in Jamaica", in *Contemporary Jamaica: A Study of Socio-religious Music of the Rastafarian Movement in Jamaica*, ed. Yoshiko S. Nagashima (Tokyo, Japan: Institute for the Study of Languages and Cultures of Asia and Africa, 1984), 27.
33 Roxanne Watson, "The Native Baptist Church's Political Role in Jamaica: Alexander Bedward's Trial for Sedition", *Journal of Caribbean History* 42, no. 2 (2008): 231.
34 Bryan, *Jamaican People*, 42.
35 Louis Marriott, *Bedward: A Play in Two Acts* (Kingston: Institute of Jamaica, 1960).
36 Kei Miller, "That Story Keeps on Repeating Itself", interview by Erin MacLeod, *Hazlitt*, 4 October 2017, https://hazlitt.net/feature/story-keeps-repeating-itself-interview-kei-miller.
37 Palmer, *Freedom's Children*; Ken Post, *Arise Ye Starvelings: The Jamaican Labour Rebellion of 1938 and its Aftermath* (The Hague: Martinus Nijhoff, 1978).
38 Moore and Johnson, *Neither Led nor Driven*.
39 Philip M. Sherlock, *Norman Manley* (London: Macmillan, 1980), 35.

40 Jürgen Osterhammel, *Colonialism: A Theoretical Overview* (Princeton: Markus Wiener, 1997), 4.
41 Frantz Fanon, *The Wretched of the Earth* (New York: Grove Press, 2004), 2; Kofi Barima, "Obeah to Rastafari: Jamaica as a Colony of Ridicule, Oppression and Violence, 1865–1939", *Africology: Journal of Pan African Studies* 10, no. 1 (March 2017): 163–86.
42 Rosco M. Pierson, "Alexander Bedward and the Jamaica Native Baptist Free Church", *Lexington Theological Quarterly Journal* 4 (July 1969): 65.

Chapter 1. Revivalism and the Birth of Bedwardism, 1860s–90s

1 Beautiful Feet, https://romans1015.com/jamaican-Revival/ (accessed 09 March 2021).
2 Ibid.
3 Ibid.
4 Ibid.
5 Ibid.
6 Monica Schuler, *"Alas, Alas, Kongo": A Social History of Indentured African Immigration into Jamaica, 1841–1865* (Baltimore: Johns Hopkins University Press, 1981), 87.
7 Edward Bean Underhill, *The Life of James Mursell Phillippo, Missionary in Jamaica* (London: Yates and Alexander, 1881), 314.
8 Shirley Gordon, *Our Cause for His Glory: Christianisation and Emancipation in Jamaica* (Kingston: University of the West Indies Press, 1998); Robert Stewart, *Religion and Society in Post-Emancipation Jamaica* (Knoxville: University of Tennessee Press, 1992); Philip Curtin, *Two Jamaicas: The Role of Ideas in a Tropical Colony, 1830–1865* (Cambridge, MA: Harvard University Press, 1955).
9 Curtin, *Two Jamaicas*, 162.
10 William Gardner, *The History of Jamaica: From Its Discovery by Christopher Columbus to the Year 1872* (London: Routledge, 1971), 456.
11 Curtin, *Two Jamaicas*, 164–65.
12 Ibid., 91.
13 Gardner, *History*, 460.
14 Ibid., 454–55.
15 Ibid.
16 Mary Turner, *Slaves and Missionaries: The Disintegration of Jamaican Slave Society, 1787–1834* (Kingston: University of the West Indies Press, 1998).
17 K. Asare Opoku, "Religion in Africa during the Colonial Period", in A. Adu Boahen (ed.), *The UNESCO General History of Africa; Africa under Colonial Domination 1880–1935*, vol. 7 (London: James Currey, 1990), 218.
18 John S. Mbiti, *African Religions and Philosophy*, 2nd ed. (London: Heinemann, 1980).

19 Maria Robinson-Smith, *Revivalism: Representing an Afro-Jamaican Identity* (Kingston: University of the West Indies Press, 2018), 44, Kindle.
20 Asare Opoku. "Religion in Africa during the Colonial Period", 225.
21 Clinton Hutton, *Colour for Colour, Skin for Skin: Marching with the Ancestral Spirits into War Oh at Morant Bay* (Kingston: Ian Randle, 2015), 97, Kindle.
22 See Martha Beckwith, "Some Religious Cults in Jamaica", *American Journal of Psychology* 34, no. 1 (January 1923): 39–40, in her discussion on the Isaiahs; Dianne M. Stewart, *Three Eyes for the Journey: African Dimensions of the Jamaican Religious Experience* (Oxford, New York: Oxford University Press, 2005); Nathaniel Samuel Murrell, "Myal and Kumina in Jamaica Past", in *African Caribbean Religions: An Introduction to their Historical, Cultural and Sacred Traditions* (Philadelphia: Temple University Press, 2010). Murrell refutes Leonard Barrett's claim that Kumina is a product of the 1860s.
23 Schuler, "*Alas, Alas, Kongo*", 86.
24 John Francis Danbe, "The Jamaican Rebellion of 1865: Its Causes, Course and Consequences" (MA thesis, University of Southern California, 1950), 35.
25 Thomas C. Holt, *The Problem of Freedom: Race, Labor, and Politics in Jamaica and Britain, 1832–1938* (Baltimore: Johns Hopkins University Press, 1992).
26 Ibid., 274.
27 Ibid., 275.
28 Ibid., 276.
29 Hutton, *Colour*, 52.
30 Ibid.
31 Holt, *Problem*, 277.
32 Curtin, *Two Jamaicas*, 170.
33 Barima, "Obeah", 8; Hutton, *Colour*, 180.
34 Bryan, *Jamaican People*, 166.
35 Ibid., 192.
36 Ibid., 167.
37 *Daily Gleaner*, 14 October 1901, 7.
38 Bryan, *Jamaican People*, 168–69.
39 Ibid.
40 *Daily Gleaner*, 29 March 1905, 10.
41 Ibid.
42 Bryan, *Jamaican People*, 167.
43 David Picking and Ina Vandebroek, "Traditional and Local Knowledge Systems in the Caribbean: Jamaica as a Case Study", https://www.researchgate.net/publication/335731386 (accessed February 2020).
44 Ibid.; see also Arvilla Payne-Jackson and Mervyn Alleyne, *Jamaican Folk Medicine* (Kingston: University of the West Indies Press, 2004).
45 Payne-Jackson and Alleyne, *Jamaican Folk Medicine*.
46 Ibid.

47 W.F. Elkins, *Street Preachers, Faith Healers, and Herb Doctors in Jamaica, 1890–1925* (New York: Revisionist Press, 1977), 3–4.
48 Ibid., 92.
49 Diana Paton, *The Cultural Politics of Obeah: Religion, Colonialism and Modernity in the Caribbean World* (Cambridge: Cambridge University Press, 2015), 229, Kindle.
50 "Convince" is a religious expression of the enslaved Africans of Jamaica. It is believed to have Central African origins in its beliefs and practices. It comes from Christian teaching about "conviction", and the term "convince" was used for myal possession.
51 Elkins, *Street Preachers*, 4.
52 Ibid., 5.
53 Ibid., 6.
54 Ibid., 8.
55 George Eaton Simpson, "Jamaican Revivalist Cults", *Social and Economic Studies* 5, no. 4 (1956): 321–442.
56 Beckwith, *Black Roadways*, 167.
57 Watson, "Native Baptist", 232.
58 Brooks, *History*, 3.
59 Ibid.
60 Ibid., 3–4.
61 Ibid.
62 Ibid., 5.
63 Ibid., 10.
64 Louis Marriott dates his birth to 1840–46 (*Daily Gleaner*, 21 November 2014) while others date his birth to 1848–50.
65 Ibid.
66 Ibid.
67 George Eaton Simpson, "Jamaican Revivalist Cults", *Social and Economic Studies*, 5, no. 4, *Jamaican Revivalist Cults* (December 1956): 337.
68 Elkins, *Street Preachers*, 10.
69 Kei Miller, *Augustown* (New York: Vintage Books, 2016), 112.
70 Ibid.
71 White, "Rise Up".
72 Diane Austin-Broos, *Jamaica Genesis: Religion and the Politics of Moral Orders* (Chicago: University of Chicago Press, 1997), 25–26.
73 Brooks, *History*.
74 Miller, *Augustown*, 112–13. This humorous account is most likely historically incorrect, as Miller's account is fictional.
75 Brooks, *History*, 7.
76 Ibid.
77 Ibid.
78 Ibid.
79 Ibid.
80 Ibid.

81 Ibid.
82 Ibid.
83 Ibid.
84 Ibid.
85 Ibid.
86 Ibid.
87 Ibid.
88 Elkins, *Street Preachers*, 10.
89 Ibid., 11.
90 Ibid., 6–8.
91 Ibid.
92 Roman Henry interviewed by Ena Campbell, 19 September 1980, T 246, 22.
93 Adina Donalds interviewed by Ena Campbell, 23 September 1980, T 247, 1–2.
94 Elkins, *Street Preachers*, 11.
95 Roman Henry interviewed by Ena Campbell, 14 October 1980, African Caribbean Institute of Jamaica, T 250, 2.
96 Theodore Skervin interviewed by Ena Campbell, 23 September 1980, T 247, 7–8.
97 Beckwith, *Black Roadways*, 44.
98 Personal interview with Duane Daley, 18 January 2020.
99 Mrs Peyton interviewed by Ena Campbell, 1980, T 263.
100 Esta Perkins interviewed by Ena Campbell, 18 May 1980, T 2074, 1981.
101 See Moore and Johnson, *Neither Led nor Driven*, for a further discussion highlighting the importance of river maids as a source of healing for Africans.
102 Chevannes, *Rastafari*, 79.
103 Brooks, *History*, 28.
104 George Olson, "Bedward: A False Prophet", *Gospel Trumpet*, February 1921, 16.
105 Chevannes, *Rastafari*, 83.
106 Wikipedia, wikipedia.org/wiki/1907_Kingston_earthquake (accessed 22 October 2019).
107 George Olson to Secretary Phelps of the Missionary Board; *Chanting Down Babylon: The Rastafari Reader* (Philadelphia: Temple University Press, 1998), ed. Nathaniel Samuel Murrell et al. Rowan Williams interviewed by Ena Campbell, 14 October 1980, T 249, 1. Fourteen hundred people are listed as being baptized after the earthquake.
108 Roman Henry interviewed by Ena Campbell, 14 October 1980, T 249, 1; Theodore Skervin interviewed by Ena Campbell, 23–24 September 1980, T 247, 17.
109 Chevannes, *Rastafari*, 80.
110 Brooks, *History*, 8–9.
111 Ibid., 15.

112 Roman Henry interviewed by Ena Campbell, 12 October 1980, T 248, 36–40.
113 Ibid., T 244, 19–20.
114 Mrs Peyton interviewed by Ena Campbell, 1980, T 263.
115 Ibid.; White, "Rise Up".
116 Moore and Johnson, *Neither Led nor Driven*, 82.
117 CO/137/566, 291. Dr Cargill's evidence was on page 291 in the original document and he is in the text as Jasper Cargill.
118 Randolph Williams, "The Prophet of August Town, Bedward – Reformer and Blasphemer".

Chapter 2. The Fundamental Pillars of the Jamaica Native Baptist Free Church

1 Roman Henry interviewed by Ena Campbell, 19 August 1980, T 244, 12–13.
2 Ibid., T 251, 14.
3 Ibid.
4 Ibid., 12–13.
5 Mrs Peyton interviewed by Ena Campbell, 23 November 1980, T 263.
6 Veront Satchell, "Religion and Protest in Jamaica: Alexander Bedward and the Jamaican Native Baptist Free Church in August Town, Jamaica, 1889–1921". Paper presented at the Second Conference on Caribbean Culture in Honour of Kamau Braithwaite (University of the West Indies, Kingston, Jamaica, 8–12 January 2002), 15.
7 Beckwith, "Some Religious Cults", 42.
8 Roman Henry interviewed by Ena Campbell, T, 244, August 19, 1980, 10.
9 Ibid., T 248, 17.
10 Chevannes, *Rastafari*, 80.
11 Ibid., 82.
12 Brooks, *History*.
13 Ibid.
14 Roman Henry interviewed by Ena Campbell, 19 September 1980, T 246, 22.
15 Brooks, *History*, 21–22.
16 Chevannes, *Rastafari*, 79.
17 Roman Henry interviewed by Ena Campbell, 1 September 1980, T 245, 11.
18 Ibid., 22 November 1980, T 251, 9.
19 Ibid., 19 August 1980, T 244, 18.
20 Governor Henry Blake to the Colonial Office, 28 May 1895, CO/137/566.
21 White, "Rise Up".
22 Post, *Arise*, 8.
23 Ibid., 7.
24 Satchell, "Early Stirrings", 86.

25 George Eaton Simpson, *Jamaican Cult Music* (Washington, DC: Smithsonian Institution, 1954), 3.
26 Joseph G. Moore, "Acculturation in Morant Bay and West Kingston", in *Religious Cults of the Caribbean: Trinidad, Jamaica and Haiti*, ed. George Eaton Simpson (Rio Piedras, Puerto Rico: Institute of Caribbean Studies, 1980), 183.
27 Ibid.
28 Olive Lewin and Kenneth Bilby, "Kumina", in *Encyclopedia of Caribbean Religions* (Champaign: University of Illinois Press, 2013), 487–91.
29 Appendix 7, Rules and Report of the 1920 Convention.
30 Ibid.
31 Governor Probyn to the Colonial Office, 27 September 1921, CO/137/750, 224.
32 Chevannes, *Rastafari*, 28.
33 Theo Sundermeier, *The Individual and Community in African Traditional Religions* (Piscataway: Transaction, 1998), 45–46.
34 Mbiti, *African Religions*, 56.
35 Steeve O. Buckridge, *The Language of Dress: Resistance and Accommodation in Jamaica, 1760–1890* (Kingston: University of the West Indies Press, 2004), 160.
36 Interview with Fanny Knight or Mother Knight, local leader of the August Town Church of Christ. Personal interview with Fanny Knight or Mother, local leader of the August Town Church of Christ, April 2020.
37 Roman Henry interviewed by Ena Campbell, 14 October 1980, T 250, 6 and 12.
38 Satchell, "Religion and Protest", 12.
39 Ibid., 13.
40 Olson, "Bedward"; Beckwith, *Black Roadways*; Olive Senior, *Dying to Better Themselves: West Indians and the Building of the Panama Canal* (Kingston: University of the West Indies Press, 2014).
41 Pierson, "Alexander Bedward and the Jamaica Native Baptist Free Church", 65.
42 Satchell, "Religion and Protest", 13.
43 Roman Henry interviewed by Ena Campbell, 14 October 1980, T 250, 12–13.
44 Beckwith, "Some Religious Cults", 41.

Chapter 3. The Arrest and Trial of Alexander Bedward

1 Governor Henry Blake to the Colonial Office, 28 May 1895, CO/137/566, 278–80.
2 Brooks, *History*, 10.
3 *Daily Gleaner*, 23 January 1895, 7.
4 Brooks, *History*, 10.
5 Ibid. Bedward's reasons are unclear for first denying Stern's invitation and later changing his mind and accepting him as his lawyer. The most

plausible reason is that the Lord revealed to Bedward that he should do so. Bedward usually relied on divine revelation in making major decisions.
6 Ibid.
7 Satchell, "Early Stirrings", 88.
8 Governor Henry Blake to the Colonial Office, 28 May 1895, CO/137/566, 286.
9 Governor Henry Blake to the Colonial Office, 28 May 1895, CO/137/566, 281–85.
10 Ibid.
11 Ibid., 287.
12 Ibid., 288.
13 Ibid.
14 Ibid.
15 Ibid.
16 Ibid., 290.
17 Ibid.
18 Ibid.
19 Ibid.
20 Ibid., 292.
21 Ibid.
22 Ibid., 286. (The jury consisted of Messrs Archibald Munro, foreman; Frederick C. Henriques; C.N. Cobbold; John W. Middleton; C.H. Lewis; J.J.G. Lewis and Jacob DePass.)
23 Ibid.
24 Ibid.
25 Ibid., 293.
26 Ibid.
27 Watson, "Native Baptist", 242.
28 Governor Henry Blake to the Colonial Office, 28 May 1895, CO/137/566, 297.
29 Ibid.
30 Ibid.
31 Ibid.
32 Ibid.
33 Ibid., 293.
34 Ibid., 290.
35 Watson, "Native Baptist", 240.
36 Governor Henry Blake to the Colonial Office, 28 May 1895, CO/137/566, 293.
37 Ibid., 294.
38 Ibid.
39 Ibid.
40 Ibid.
41 Ibid.
42 Ibid., 292.

43 Ibid.
44 Ibid.
45 Ibid., 294.
46 Ibid. His disappointment in their testimonies must be the reason they were not called to the preliminary hearing and were transferred. Nelson was the best witness, as he had been following Bedward for three years.
47 Ibid., 295.
48 Ibid.
49 Ibid., 296.
50 Ibid.
51 Ibid.
52 Ibid., 296. The judge, who is the chief justice, is prejudicing the case with his own opinions and hence casting doubts on Stern's arguments, such as the strange collusion between Inspector Calder and Mr Lanigan, and concluding there was no ulterior motive in their meeting. Secondly, how could Mr Lanigan's notes be verbatim when he could not understand some of the unique expressions of the Jamaican language? Why not allow the jury to decide for themselves on these important issues of interpretation?
53 Ibid., 297.
54 Ibid.
55 Ibid.
56 Ibid., 296.
57 Ibid.
58 *Daily Gleaner*, 6 October 1938, 12.
59 Ibid.
60 Ibid.
61 Brooks, *History*, 11.

Chapter 4. Bedwardism, Revivalism and the Jamaican State

1 Governor Blake to the Colonial Office, 28 May 1895, CO/137/566, 278–80.
2 Ibid.
3 Jamaica, "The Laws of Jamaica", 1896, 26, https://ecollections.law.fiu.edu/jamaica/59.
4 Jamaica, "The Laws of Jamaica", 1890, 24, https://ecollections.law.fiu.edu/jamaica/59.
5 Ibid., 1896, 95.
6 Acting Attorney General T. Bancroft Oughton to the Colonial Office, 8 April 1896, CO/137/573, 155.
7 Ibid., 328–29.
8 Leonard Smith, "Caribbean Bedlam: The Development of the Lunatic Asylum System in Britain's West Indian Colonies, 1838–1914", *Journal of Caribbean History* 44, no. 1 (2010): 5.

9   Jamaica Annual Report with Departmental Reports, 1895–96, 148. The designation of "brown" implies people who are described as mulattoes in the Jamaican context. Such brown individuals are legally categorized as blacks.
10 Ibid., 100.
11 Ibid., 173.
12 Unnamed female of August Town interviewed by Ena Campbell, 1982, T 261.
13 See Verene Shepherd, ed., *Women in Caribbean History* (Kingston: Ian Randle, 2012); Rhoda Reddock, *Women, Labour and Politics in Trinidad and Tobago: A History* (London: Zed Books, 1994).
14 Ibid., 121.
15 Brian L. Moore and Johnson, *Neither Led nor Driven, Contesting British Cultural Imperialism in Jamaica*, 1865–1921, (Kingston: UWI Press, 2004), 82.
16 Jamaica Annual Report with Departmental Reports, 1906, 106.
17 Jamaica Annual Report with Departmental Reports, 1922, 586.
18 Missionary Stiemla to Secretary Phelps, 28 November 1924, 4/28/11.
19 Jamaica Annual Report with Departmental Reports, 1928, 266.
20 Ibid., 245.
21 Ibid., 274.
22 Margaret Jones, "The Most Cruel and Revolting Crimes: The Treatment of the Mentally Ill in Nineteenth-Century Jamaica", *Journal of Caribbean History* 42, no. 2 (2008): 290–309.
23 Jamaica Annual Report with Departmental Reports, 1906, 106.
24 Smith, "Caribbean Bedlam", 9.
25 Jamaica Annual Report with Departmental Reports, 1885–1926.
26 *Daily Gleaner*, 7 March 1896, 7. Crown colony government was introduced in Jamaica and several other British Caribbean islands after the Morant Bay War of 1865. The British government, through its governors in each of the islands, ruled the colonies directly, as all the houses of assembly in the respective colonies surrendered all their rights and privileges in making their own decisions, a right they had enjoyed for over two hundred years.
27 *Daily Gleaner*, 7 September 1897, 7.
28 *Daily Gleaner*, 2 April 1909, 13.
29 Ibid.
30 *Daily Gleaner*, 30 July 1910, 1.
31 *Daily Gleaner*, 26 July 1910, 3.
32 *Daily Gleaner*, 24 November 1913, 3.
33 *Daily Gleaner*, 24 June 1926, 13 and 14 July 1926, 13.
34 *Daily Gleaner*, 24 June 1926, 13.
35 *Daily Gleaner*, 5 May 1921, 6.
36 Diana Paton, "The Racist History of Jamaica's Obeah Act", *Daily Gleaner*, 16 June 2019, D 10 or 49.

37 Jamaica, "The Laws of Jamaica", 1892, 108, https://ecollections.law.fiu.edu/jamaica/59.
38 Ibid., 1893, 14.
39 Ibid., 1898, 24.
40 Paton, "Racist History".
41 *Daily Gleaner*, 12 May 1899, 6.
42 *Daily Gleaner*, 12 May 1899, 6.
43 "Cases Brought before the County Courts", *Daily Gleaner*, 30 June 1916, via Caribbean Religious Trials, https://www.caribbeanreligioustrials.org/CaseSource/Details/1056.
44 *Daily Gleaner*, 17 October 1899, 6.
45 "Cases Brought before the County Courts", *Daily Gleaner*, 30 June 1916, via Caribbean Religious Trials, https://www.caribbeanreligioustrials.org/CaseSource/Details/1056.
46 Paton, *Cultural Politics*.
47 See the Rules and Report of the 1920 Convention, appendix 7.
48 Diana Paton, "Obeah Acts: Producing and Policing the Boundaries of Religion in the Caribbean", *Small Axe* 13, no. 1 (March 2009): 5.
49 *Daily Gleaner*, 20 June 1954, 8.
50 Elkins, *Street Preachers*, 47.
51 Ibid.
52 *Daily Gleaner*, 29 June 1935, 25.
53 Elkins, *Street Preachers*, 46.
54 *Daily Gleaner*, 2 June 1914, 13.
55 *Daily Gleaner*, 24 April 1914, 3.
56 *Daily Gleaner*, 2 June 1914, 13.
57 *Daily Gleaner*, 24 July 1914, 6.
58 *Daily Gleaner*, 31 January 1928, 16. It is not clear if Hewitt's Hopewell Baptist had become an independent Baptist church or was linked to the Jamaica Baptist Union. Inez Sibley's book *The Baptists of Jamaica 1793-1965* (Kingston, Jamaica: Jamaica Baptist Union, 1965) lists a Hopewell Baptist church as part of a circuit of churches with Hanover Street and Denham Town. The Jamaica Baptist Union no longer has a Hopewell Baptist church in West Kingston, but in the parish of Hanover. It can be concluded that if Sibley's mention of a Hopewell Baptist was indeed Hewitt's church, then it seemed to have discontinued its association with the Jamaica Baptist Union.
59 Paton, *Cultural Politics*, 230.
60 Jamaica, "The Laws of Jamaica", 1896, 1905, 1908, https://ecollections.law.fiu.edu/jamaica/59.
61 See Beckwith, *Black Roadways*; Paton, *Cultural Politics*; Simpson, "Jamaican Revivalist Cults".
62 Caribbean Religious Trials, https://www.caribbeanreligioustrials.org/CaseSource/Details/1056, 13–14, 1916.
63 Ibid., 1917.

64 Jamaica, "The Laws of Jamaica", 1902, 114, https://ecollections.law.fiu.edu/jamaica/59.
65 Moore and Johnson, *Neither Led nor Driven*, 76.
66 Ibid., 70; Elkins, *Street Preachers*, also has a list of known Revivalists.
67 *Daily Gleaner*, 2 October 1905, 12.
68 Moore and Johnson, *Neither Led nor Driven*, 76–77.
69 Elkins, *Street Preachers*, 20.
70 Ibid., 22.
71 *Daily Gleaner*, 13 May 1904, 6.
72 Ibid.
73 Moore and Johnson, *Neither Led nor Driven*, 77.
74 Frank Jan Van Dijk, *Jahmaica: Rastafari and Jamaican Society, 1930–1990* (Utrecht: Isor, 1993), 70.
75 Ibid., 83.
76 Mrs Peyton interviewed by Ena Campbell, 1980, T 263.
77 *Daily Gleaner*, 10 August 1907, 6.
78 *Jamaica Times*, 26 April 1902, 5.
79 Paton, *Cultural Politics*, 151. Paton highlights the numerous cases of Revivalists and others convicted under the Obeah Acts and other legislation.
80 Ibid., 192.
81 Ibid., 194.

Chapter 5. Judgement Day: Tearing Down the White Wall

1 See Michel Foucault, *Madness and Civilization: A History of Insanity in the Age of Reason* (New York: Vintage, 1988).
2 Frederick W. Hickling and Gerard Hutchinson, "Madness as Social Defiance in African Caribbean Youths: Evidence from the Dancehall", *Wadabagei: A Journal of the Caribbean and Its Diaspora* 13, no. 3 (Fall 2011): 3–25.
3 https://www.mamalisa.com/?t=es&p=4089, accessed 1 November 2019.
4 *Daily Gleaner*, 19 July 1921, 6. The initials HGD most likely stand for Herbert George de Lisser.
5 *Daily Gleaner*, 18 August 1921, 3.
6 *Daily Gleaner*, 16 July 1906, 10.
7 *Daily Gleaner*, 27 August 1921, 13.
8 *Daily Gleaner*, 25 February 1937, 9.
9 *Daily Gleaner*, 15 December 1921, 1; 17 December 1921, 10.
10 Roman Henry interviewed by Ena Campbell, 22 November 1980, T 251, 22.
11 Theodore Skervin interviewed by Ena Campbell, 23–24 September 1980, T 247, 3.

12 Roman Henry interviewed by Ena Campbell, 9 August 1980, T 244, 9–10.
13 Ibid., 9.
14 Ibid., 9–10.
15 Ibid., 35.
16 Roman Henry interviewed by Ena Campbell, 14 October 1980, T 249, 37–38.
17 Theodore Skervin interviewed by Ena Campbell, 23–24 September 1980, T 247, 33–34.
18 Ibid., 34.
19 Interview with an unnamed male Bedwardite, 29 October 1981, T 262.
20 A community member of August Town, interviewed by Ena Campbell, 1982, T 261, and an unnamed female Bedwardite, T 264.
21 Theodore Skervin interviewed by Ena Campbell, 23–24 September 1980, T 247, 30–31.
22 Ibid., 31.
23 Roman Henry interviewed by Ena Campbell, 12 October 1980, T 248, 17.
24 Satchell, "Religion and Protest", 15.
25 Ibid., 16.
26 Ibid.
27 Roman Henry interviewed by Ena Campbell, 19 August 19, 1980, T 249, 2.
28 Ibid., T 244, 15.
29 Theodore Skervin interviewed by Ena Campbell, 23–24 September 1980, T 247, 10.
30 Ibid., 41–42.
31 *Daily Gleaner*, 3 May 1921, 1.
32 Ibid.
33 *Daily Gleaner*, 30 December 1920, 4.
34 *Daily Gleaner*, 6 April 1921, 6.
35 Roman Henry interviewed by Ena Campbell, 22 November 1980, T 251, 20–22.
36 *Daily Gleaner*, 17 December 1920, 10.
37 *Daily Gleaner*, 15 December 1920, 1.
38 *Daily Gleaner*, 20 December 1921, 1.
39 Beckwith, *Black Roadways*, 169.
40 *Daily Gleaner*, 29 December 1920, 8.
41 Marriott, *Bedward*.
42 See Wendy W. Walters, "'One of Dese Mornings, Bright and Fair,/Take My Wings and Cleave De Air': The Legend of the Flying Africans and Diasporic Consciousness", *Melus* 22, no. 3 (Fall 1977): 3–29; "Drums and Shadows: Survival Studies among the Georgia Coastal Negroes." *Savannah Unit Georgia Writers' Project*, Works Progress Administration. Foreword by Guy B. Johnson. Photographs by Muriel and Malcolm Bell, Jr. (Athens:

University of Georgia Press, 1940) is by far the greatest collection of flying African tales ever published.
43 Samantha Hunsicker, "Fly Away Home: Tracing the Flying African Folktale, from Oral Literature to Verse and Prose" (Honours thesis, Ball State University, 2000), 14.
44 Schuler, *"Alas, Alas, Kongo"*, 93.
45 Satchell, "Early Stirrings", 91.
46 Unnamed female Bedwardite interviewed by Ena Campbell, 1980, T 264.
47 Theodore Skervin interviewed by Ena Campbell, 23 September 1980, T 247, p. 4.
48 Ibid., 5.
49 Satchell, "Religion and Protest", 24.
50 Ibid.
51 Satchell, "Early Stirrings", 92.
52 Ibid.
53 *Daily Gleaner*, 28 April 1921, 1.
54 Ibid.
55 Theodore Skervin interviewed by Ena Campbell, 23–24 September 1980, T 247, 6.
56 An error seems to have been made in the original reporting as in this case Ezekiel is used and in the appendix Ezekiah is used.
57 Satchell, "Early Stirrings", 93.
58 Ibid.
59 Ibid.
60 Ibid.
61 *Daily Gleaner*, 3 May 1921, 1.
62 *Daily Gleaner*, 5 May 1921, 6.
63 *Daily Gleaner*, 16 August 1920, 7.
64 Rachel Gallaher, George Alexander McGuire 1886-1934, https://www.blackpast.org/african-american-history/mcguire-george-alexander-1866-1934/.
65 *Daily Gleaner*, 5 July 1919, 6 and 9 September 1920, 4; Van Dijk, *Jahmaica*, 72.
66 *Daily Gleaner*, 4 September 1920, 12 and 9 September 1920, 4.
67 See Dave Gosse, "Garvey's Black Theology and Its Impact on the UNIA/ACL", *Caribbean Quarterly* 62, no. 2 (2016): 178–92.
68 Nathaniel Samuel Murrel and Lewin Williams, "The Black Biblical Hermeneutics of Rastafari", in *Chanting Down Babylon*, 330.
69 Byron Rushing, "A Note on the Origin of the African Orthodox Church", *Journal of Negro History* 57, no. 1 (January 1972): 37–39.
70 See Rupert Lewis and Patrick Bryan, *Garvey, His Work and Impact* (Trenton: Africa World Press, 1991).
71 James H. Cone, *A Black Theology of Liberation*, Twentieth Century Edition (Maryknoll: Orbis Books, 1997), 111, 120.
72 Satchell, "Religion and Protest", 22.
73 Satchell, "Early Stirrings", 84.
74 Brooks, *History*, 17.

75 Ibid., 27.
76 Satchell, "Early Stirrings", 85.
77 Nagashima, "Rastafarian Music", 15.
78 Ibid.
79 Devon Dick, *The Cross and the Machete: Native Baptists of Jamaica – Identity, Ministry and Legacy* (Kingston: Ian Randle, 2009), 163.
80 Satchell, "Early Stirrings", 85.
81 *Daily Gleaner*, 5 May 1921, 6.
82 Ibid.
83 *Daily Gleaner*, 3 May 1921, 1.
84 *Daily Gleaner*, 5 May 1921, 6.
85 Ibid.
86 Ibid.
87 Theodore Skervin interviewed by Ena Campbell, 23–24 September 1980, T 247, 30.
88 Ibid.
89 Ibid., 1.
90 Ibid., 6.
91 Satchell, "Religion and Protest", 23.
92 Beckwith, *Black Roadways*, 169–70.

Chapter 6. The Impact of Bedwardism

1 See Rupert Lewis, "Marcus Garvey and the Early Rastafarians: Continuity and Discontinuity", in *Chanting Down Babylon*, 145–58; Chevannes, *Rastafari*; Noel Leo Erskine, *From Garvey to Marley: Rastafari Theology* (Gainesville: University Press of Florida, 2005); Robert Hill, "Dread History: Leonard P. Howell and Millenarial Visions in Early Rastafari", *Epoche* 9 (1981): 30–71; Van Dijk, *Jahmaica*.
2 *Daily Gleaner*, 22 January 1895, 6.
3 Personal interview with Mrs Francis and Mrs Walker, 1980, T 263.
4 Brooks, *History*, 13.
5 See the work of the following priests: Gustavo Gutiérrez, *A Theology of Liberation: History, Politics, and Salvation* (New York: Orbis Books, 1973); Leonardo Boff, *Jesus Christ Liberator: A Critical Christology of Our Time* (New York: Orbis Books, 1978); Juan Luis Segundo, *The Liberation of Theology* (New York: Orbis Books, 1976); Jon Sobrino, *Jesus the Liberator* (Maryknoll: Orbis Books, 1993). They popularized the phrase "Preferential option for the poor".
6 Barry Chevannes, "Rastafari and the Exorcism of the Ideology of Racism and Classism", in *Chanting Down Babylon*, 57.
7 Shirley Gordon, *Our Cause for his Glory*, 74.
8 Ibid., 52.
9 Van Dijk, *Jahmaica*, 66.

10 Dick, *Cross*, 90–91.
11 Ibid., 126.
12 Roman Henry interviewed by Ena Campbell, 19 August 1980, T 244, 11.
13 Ibid., September 1980, T 245, 13.
14 Ibid., 14 October 1980, T 249, 12.
15 Ibid., 14.
16 George Olson to Secretary of the Missionary Board, 4/28/11, 19 October 1929, 2.
17 Roman Henry interviewed by Ena Campbell, 19 September 1980, T 246, 18–19.
18 Ibid., 12.
19 Barry Chevannes, *Rastafari and Other African-Caribbean Worldviews* (The Hague: Institute of Social Studies, 1995), 33–37.
20 Neil J. Savishinsky, "African Dimensions of the Jamaican Rastafarian Movement", in *Chanting Down Babylon*, 127; Verona Reckord, "From Burru Drums to Reggae Ridims", in *Chanting Down Babylon*, ed. Nathaniel Murrell et al., 238.
21 Hill, "Leonard P. Howell", 38.
22 Clinton Hutton and Nathaniel Samuel Murrell, "Rastas' Psychology of Blackness, Resistance, and Somebodiness", in *Chanting Down Babylon*, 45.
23 Chevannes, *Rastafari*, 127.
24 Ibid., 127.
25 Ibid., 126.
26 Ibid., 150.
27 *Daily Gleaner*, 15 March 1934, 20.
28 *Daily Gleaner*, 16 March 1934, 16.
29 Hélène Lee, *The First Rasta: Leonard Howell and the Rise of Rastafarianism* (Lawrence Hill Books, 2003), 51.
30 Albert Bailey interviewed by Ena Campbell, 23 October 1980, 28.
31 Mrs Peyton interviewed by Ena Campbell, 1980, T 263.
32 Chevannes, *Rastafari*, 121–22.
33 *Daily Gleaner*, 18 January 1937, 28.
34 *Daily Gleaner*, 14 January 1937, 12.
35 *Daily Gleaner*, 18 January 1937, 28.
36 *Daily Gleaner*, 17 March 1934, 6.
37 Ibid.
38 Hutton and Murrell, "Rastas'", 45.
39 Barnett, *Rastafari*.
40 Barry Chevannes, "Rastafari and the Coming of Age: The Routinization of the Rastafari Movement in Jamaica", in *Rastafari in the New Millennium*, edited by Michael Barnett (Syracuse: Syracuse University Press, 2012), 16.
41 See Chevannes, *Rastafari*. Hinds had baptisms twice a year in the Ferry River on two important liturgical feasts, 1 April, the beginning of the Ethiopian year, and 1 August, Freedom or Emancipation Day.

42 Chevannes, "Rastafari and the Coming of Age", 27.
43 See Stewart, *Three Eyes*. She argues that Kumina and Revival Zion have far more in common and meet more frequently for services than the general literature says; Colinnet Wiltshire-Brown, "God Is Best Understood through the Familiar: An Exploration of Revivalism in Light of Exodus 32:1–6", MA Thesis, Caribbean Graduate School of Theology, 2019. She shows that Kumina rituals are most evident in Zion worship.
44 George Eaton Simpson, "Religious Cults in Jamaica", *Social and Economic Studies* 5, no. 4 (December 1956): 369.
45 Ibid., 370.
46 Personal interview with Duane Harris of August Town, 25 March 2020.
47 Simpson, "Jamaican Revivalist Cults", 370–71.
48 Chevannes, *Rastafari*, 80.
49 Gordon, *Our Cause*, 74; Stewart, *Religion*, 143.
50 Stewart, *Religion*, 143.
51 Ibid.; Gordon, *Our Cause*, 74.
52 Elkins, *Street Preachers*, 42.
53 Austin-Broos, *Jamaica Genesis*, 79.
54 Ibid., 80.
55 See Garnet Roper, "The Impact of Evangelical and Pentecostal Religion", *Caribbean Quarterly* 37, no. 1 (March 1991); Ashley Smith, "Pentecostalism in Jamaica", *Jamaica Journal*, no. 42 (1978): 2–13. Thompson highlights other positives and also negatives of Pentecostal Christianity in Jamaica.
56 Robert Stewart, "Religion, Myths and Beliefs: Their Socio-Political Roles", in *General History of the Caribbean*, ed. Bridget Brereton, Teresita Martínez-Vergne, René A. Römer, Blanca G. Silvestrini, vol. 5 (New York: Palgrave Macmillan, 2003), 590.
57 The History of August Town (Hill an Gully Ride 1994), https://www.youtube.com/watch?v=8wLqr4yvSz0, accessed 12 July 12, 2020.
58 *The Jamaica Almanack of 1833*, Kingston, Printed by W. Cathcart [etc.] [n.d.].
59 Suzanne Francis-Brown, *Mona Past and Present: The History and Heritage of the Mona Campus, University of the West Indies* (Kingston: University of the West Indies Press, 2004), 9.
60 Roman Henry interviewed by Ena Campbell, 19 September 1980, T 246, 21.
61 Ibid., T 247, 44–45.
62 Personal interview with Fanny Knight, Mother Russell, January 2020.
63 Roman Henry interviewed by Ena Campbell, 12 October 1980, T 248, 33–35.
64 Ibid., 14 October 1980, T 250, 28–29.
65 Ibid., T 248, 46.
66 Ibid., 40.
67 Ibid., 53.

68 Ibid., 55; *Daily Gleaner*, 13 November 1957, 8.
69 *Daily Gleaner*, 12 October 1956, 12.
70 *Daily Gleaner*, 10 December 1959, 12.
71 *Daily Gleaner*, 11 January 1958.
72 *Daily Gleaner*, 16 June 1959, 1.
73 Roman Henry interviewed by Ena Campbell, 19 August 1980, T 244, 15.

Bibliography

Primary Sources

Daily Gleaner, 1895–1930.
The Laws of Jamaica, 1861, 1873, 1885, 1890, 1892, 1893, 1896, 1898 and 1902.
Jamaica Times, 1902.
The Star.
Institute of Jamaica.
West Indian Review, 1950.
The Bedwardite Collection, African Caribbean Institute of Jamaica.
Church of God in Jamaica Missionary Papers.
Colonial Office Papers CO/137/566, CO/10331, CO/137/573.
The Handbook of Jamaica.
Jamaican Censuses.
Jamaica Annual Report with Departmental Reports, 1890s-1920s.
Caribbean Religious Trials Database. https://www.caribbeanreligioustrials.org/.

Secondary Sources

Austin-Broos, Diane J. *Jamaica Genesis: Religion and the Politics of Moral Orders.* Chicago, IL: University of Chicago Press, 1997.
Barima, Kofi. "Obeah to Rastafari: Jamaica as a Colony of Ridicule, Oppression and Violence, 1965–1939". *Africology: The Journal of Pan-African Studies* 10, no. 1 (March 2017): 163–87.
Barnett, Michael. "Differences and Similarities between the Rastafari Movement and the Nation of Islam". *Journal of Black Studies* 36, no. 6 (July 2006): 873–93.
———, ed. *Rastafari in the New Millennium: A Rastafari Reader.* New York: Syracuse University Press, 2012.
Barrett, Leonard E. *The Rastafarians: A Study in Messianic Cultism in Jamaica.* Rio Piedras: Institute of Caribbean Studies, University of Puerto Rico, 1968.
Beckles, Hilary. *Natural Rebels: A Social History of Enslaved Women in Barbados.* New Brunswick, NJ: Rutgers University Press, 1989.
Beckwith, Martha W. *Black Roadways: A Study of Jamaican Folk Life.* 1929. Reprint, New York: Negro Universities Press, 1969.
———. "Some Religious Cults in Jamaica". *American Journal of Psychology* 34, no. 1 (January 1923): 32–45.
Boahen, A. Adu, ed. *The UNESCO General History of Africa: Africa under Colonial Domination 1880–1935.* London: James Currey, 1990.

Boff, Leonardo. *Jesus Christ Liberator: A Critical Christology of Our Time*. New York: Orbis Books, 1978.
Bogues, Anthony. *Black Heretics, Black Prophets: Radical Political Intellectuals*. New York: Routledge, 2003.
Brooks, A.A. *The History of Bedwardism*. Kingston: Gleaner Company, 1917.
Bryan, Patrick. *Jamaican People 1880–1902: Race, Class and Social Control*. 1991. Reprint, Kingston: University of the West Indies Press, 2000.
Campbell, Horace. *Rasta and Resistance: From Marcus Garvey to Walter Rodney*. Trenton, NJ: Africa World Press, 1985.
Chevannes, Barry. *Rastafari: Roots and Ideology*. Syracuse, NY: Syracuse University Press, 1994. Kindle.
———. *Rastafari and Other African-Caribbean Worldviews*. The Hague: Institute of Social Studies, 1989.
Chevannes, Barry, and Jean Besson. "The Continuity-Creativity Debate: The Case of Revival". *New West Indian Guide* 70, nos. 3–4 (January 1996): 209–28.
Curtin, Philip. *Two Jamaicas: The Role of Ideas in a Tropical Colony, 1830–1865*. Cambridge, MA: Harvard University Press, 1955.
Danbe, John Francis. "The Jamaican Rebellion of 1865: Its Causes, Course and Consequences". MA thesis, University of Southern California, 1950.
Dick, Devon. *The Cross and the Machete: Native Baptists of Jamaica – Identity, Ministry and Legacy*. Kingston: Ian Randle, 2009.
Dijk, Frank Jan Van. *Jahmaica: Rastafari and Jamaican Society, 1930–1990*. Utrecht: Isor, 1993.
Dunkley, D.A. "The Suppression of Leonard Howell in Late Colonial Jamaica". *New West Indian Guide* 87 (2013): 62–93.
Edmonds, Ennis B. *Rastafari: From Outcasts to Culture Bearers*. Oxford: Oxford University Press, 2003.
Elkins, W.F. *Street Preachers, Faith Healers, and Herb Doctors in Jamaica, 1890–1925*. New York: Revisionist Press, 1977.
Erskine, Noel Leo. *From Garvey to Marley: Rastafari Theology*. Gainesville: University Press of Florida, 2005.
Fanon, Frantz. *The Wretched of the Earth*. New York: Grove Press, 1963.
Foucault, Michel. *Madness and Civilization: A History of Insanity in the Age of Reason*. New York: Vintage, 1965.
Gardner, William. *The History of Jamaica: From Its Discovery by Christopher Columbus to the Year 1872*. London: Routledge, 1971.
Gordon, Shirley. *Our Cause for His Glory: Christianisation and Emancipation in Jamaica*. Kingston: University of the West Indies Press, 1998.
Gosse, Dave. "Garvey's Black Theology and Its Impact on the UNIA/ACL". *Caribbean Quarterly* 62, no. 2 (2016): 178–92.
Gutiérrez, Gustavo. *A Theology of Liberation: History, Politics, and Salvation*. New York: Orbis Books, 1973.
Hickling, Frederick W., and Gerard Hutchinson. "Madness as Social Defiance in African Caribbean Youths: Evidence from the Dancehall". *Wadabagei: A Journal of the Caribbean and Its Diaspora* 13, no. 3 (Fall 2011): 3–25.

Hill, Robert. "Leonard P. Howell and Millenarian Visions in Early Rastafari". *Jamaica Journal* 16, no. 1 (1981): 24–39.
Holt, Thomas C. *The Problem of Freedom: Race, Labor, and Politics in Jamaica and Britain, 1832–1938*. Baltimore, MD: Johns Hopkins University Press, 1992.
Hunsicker, Samantha. "Fly Away Home: Tracing the Flying African Folktale from Oral Literature to Verse and Prose". Honours thesis, Ball State University, 2000.
Hutton, Clinton. *Colour for Colour, Skin for Skin: Marching with the Ancestral Spirits into War Oh at Morant Bay*. Kingston: Ian Randle, 2015. Kindle.
Hutton, Clinton, Michael Barnett, D.A. Dunkley, and Jahlani Niaah, eds. *Leonard Percival Howell and the Genesis of Rastafari*. Kingston: University of the West Indies Press, 2015.
Jones, Margaret. "The Most Cruel and Revolting Crime: The Treatment of the Mentally Ill in Mid Nineteenth-Century Jamaica". *Journal of Caribbean History* 42, no. 2 (2008): 290–309.
Lee, Hélène. *The First Rasta: Leonard Howell and the Rise of Rastafarianism*. Translated by Lily Davis. Chicago, IL: Lawrence Hill Books, 2003.
Lewis, Rupert. "Garvey's Forerunners: Love and Bedward". *Race and Class* 28, no. 3 (January 1987): 29–40.
———. "Marcus Garvey and the Early Rastafarians: Continuity and Discontinuity". In *Chanting Down Babylon: The Rastafari Reader*, edited by Nathaniel Samuel Murrell, William David Spencer and Adrian Anthony McFarlane, 145–58. Philadelphia, PA: Temple University Press, 1998.
Lewis, Rupert, and Patrick Bryan. *Garvey: His Work and Impact*. Trenton, NJ: Africa World Press, 1991.
Marriott, Louis. *Bedward: A Play in Two Acts*. Kingston: Institute of Jamaica, 1960.
Mbiti, John S. *African Religions and Philosophy*. 2nd ed. London: Heinemann, 1980.
Miller, Kei. *Augustown*. New York: Vintage Books, 2018.
———. "That Story Keeps on Repeating Itself". Interview with Erin MacLeod. *Hazlitt*, 4 October 2017. https://hazlitt.net/feature/story-keeps-repeating-itself-interview-kei-miller.
Moore, Brian L., and Michelle A. Johnson. *Neither Led nor Driven: Contesting British Cultural Imperialism in Jamaica, 1865–1920*. Kingston: University of the West Indies Press, 2004.
Moore, Joseph G. "A Comparative Study of Acculturation in Morant Bay and West Kingston, Jamaica". In *Religious Cults of the Caribbean: Trinidad, Jamaica and Haiti*, edited by George Eaton Simpson, 157–200. Rio Piedras, Puerto Rico: Institute of Caribbean Studies, 1980.
——— "Religions of Jamaican Negroes: A Study of Afro-Jamaican Acculturation". PhD Dissertation, Northwestern University, 1953.
Morris, Brian. *Religion and Anthropology: A Critical Introduction*. Cambridge: Cambridge University Press, 2006.
Morrison, Toni. *Song of Solomon*. New York: Knopf, 1977.
Murphy, Joseph. *Working the Spirits: Ceremonies of the African Diaspora*. Boston, MA: Beacon Press, 1994.

Murrell, Nathaniel Samuel, William David Spencer, Adrian Anthony McFarlane, and Clinton Chisholm, eds. *Afro-Caribbean Religions: An Introduction to Their Historical, Cultural, and Sacred Traditions*. Philadelphia, PA: Temple University Press, 2010.

———, eds. *Chanting Down Babylon: The Rastafari Reader*. Philadelphia, PA: Temple University Press, 1998.

Nagashima, Yoshiko S. "Rastafarian Music in Contemporary Jamaica: A Study of Socio-religious Music of the Rastafarian Movement in Jamaica". In *Contemporary Jamaica: A Study of Socioreligious Music of the Rastafarian Movement in Jamaica*, edited by Yoshiko S. Nagashima, 1–227. Tokyo: Institute for the Study of Languages and Cultures of Asia and Africa, 1984.

Niaah, Jahlani, and Erin MacLeod, eds. "Negotiating the African Presence: Rastafari Livity and Scholarship", *Caribbean Quarterly* 59, no. 2 (June 2013): 1–9.

Osterhammel, Jürgen. *Colonialism: A Theoretical Overview*. Princeton, NJ: Markus Wiener, 1997.

Owens, Joseph. *Dread: The Rastafarians of Jamaica*. Kingston: Sangster's, 1976.

Palmer, Colin A. *Freedom's Children: The 1938 Labor Rebellion and the Birth of Modern Jamaica*. Chapel Hill, NC: University of North Carolina Press, 2014.

Paton, Diana. *The Cultural Politics of Obeah: Religion, Colonialism and Modernity in the Caribbean World*. Cambridge: Cambridge University Press, 2015.

———. "Obeah Acts: Producing and Policing the Boundaries of Religion in the Caribbean". *Small Axe* 13, no. 1 (March 2009): 1–18.

Pierson, Rosco M. "Alexander Bedward and the Jamaica Native Baptist Free Church". *Lexington Theological Quarterly* 4 (July 1969): 65–76.

Post, Ken. *Arise Ye Starvelings: The Jamaican Labour Rebellion of 1938 and Its Aftermath*. The Hague: Martinus Nijhoff, 1978.

Price, Charles. *Becoming Rasta: Origins of Rastafari Identity in Jamaica*. New York: New York University Press, 2009.

Robinson-Smith, Maria. *Revivalism: Representing an Afro-Jamaican Identity*. Kingston: University of the West Indies Press, 2018. Kindle.

Roper, Garnet. "The Impact of Evangelical and Pentecostal Religion". *Caribbean Quarterly* 37, no. 1 (March 1991): 35–44.

Satchell, Veront. "Early Stirrings of Black Nationalism in Colonial Jamaica: Alexander Bedward of the Jamaica Native Baptist Free Church 1889–1921". *Journal of Caribbean History* 38, no. 1 (2004): 75–105.

———. "Religion and Protest in Jamaica: Alexander Bedward and the Jamaican Native Baptist Free Church in August Town, Jamaica 1889–1921". Paper presented at the Second Conference on Caribbean Culture, University of the West Indies, Kingston, Jamaica, 8–12 January 2002.

Schuler, Monica. *"Alas, Alas, Kongo": A Social History of Indentured African Immigration in Jamaica, 1841–65*. Baltimore: Johns Hopkins University Press, 1980.

Segundo, Juan Luis. *The Liberation of Theology*. New York: Orbis Books, 1976.

Senior, Olive. *Dying to Better Themselves: West Indians and the Building of the Panama Canal*. Kingston: University of the West Indies Press, 2014.

Shepherd, Verene, ed. *Women in Caribbean History*. Kingston: Ian Randle, 2012.

Sherlock, Philip M. *Norman Manley*. London: Macmillan, 1980.

Simpson, George Eaton. "Jamaican Revivalist Cults". *Social and Economic Studies* 5, no. 4 (December, 1956): 321–442.

———, ed. *Religious Cults of the Caribbean: Trinidad, Jamaica, and Haiti*. Rio Piedras: Institute of Caribbean Studies, University of Puerto Rico, 1980.

Smith, Ashley. *Pentecostalism in Jamaica: A Challenge to the Established Churches and Society*. Mandeville, Jamaica: Eureka Press, 1993.

Smith, Leonard. "Caribbean Bedlam: The Development of the Lunatic Asylum in Britain's West Indian Colonies, 1838–1914". *Journal of Caribbean History* 44, no. 1 (2010): 1–47.

Stewart, Dianne. M. *Three Eyes for the Journey: African Dimensions of the Jamaican Religious Experience*. Oxford: Oxford University Press, 2005.

Stewart, Robert. *The Bible as Ideology: Ethiopianism in Jamaica, 1930–38*. African Perspectives. Cambridge: Cambridge University Press, 1970.

———. *Religion and Society in Post-Emancipation Jamaica*. Knoxville, TN: University of Tennessee Press, 1992.

Underhill, Edward. *The Life of James Mursell Phillippo, Missionary in Jamaica*. London: Yates and Alexander, 1881.

Walters, Wendy W. "'One of Dese Mornings, Bright and Fair,/Take My Wings and Cleave de Air': The Legend of the Flying Africans and Diasporic Consciousness". *MELUS* 22, no. 3 (Fall 1997): 3–29.

Watson, Roxanne. "The Native Baptist Church's Political Role in Jamaica: Alexander Bedward's Trial for Sedition". *Journal of Caribbean History* 42, no. 2 (2008): 231–254.

Wiltshire-Brown, Colinnet. "God Is Best Understood through the Familiar: An Exploration of Revivalism in Light of Exodus 32:1–6". MA thesis, Caribbean Graduate School of Theology, 2019.

Index

Page numbers followed with "n" refer to endnotes.

African: enslavement, 17, 19–20, 97, 162, 163; healing, 27–28; religion, 20–21
African Jamaicans, 17–19, 22–23; acquittal of criminal lunatics, 87–88; alleged crimes, 87; colonial thinking, 90, 92; natural weaknesses to insanity, 91–92; religion and culture practice, 91–92; Revivalist religion, 21; Revival meetings, 89–90, 92; social justice for, 159; sociopolitical maturity, 24
Afro-Christian religion, 20
Allen, Deacon, 44
American Missionary Society, 15
Arscott, P., 96
August Town, 2, 31–32, 142, 145; Bedward's impact on, 162–166; cattle estates, 163; community's housing, 165; Hurricane Charlie of 1951 and rehabilitation, 165; as religious town, 164
Austin-Broos, Diane, 160, 162

badness, 111, 112
baptism, 2, 18, 36, 38, 41, 45–46, 48, 54–55, 108, 157–159
Baptist church, 17–18
Barbados, lunatic asylum, 84
Barima, Kofi, 23
Barnes, Joseph, 99
Barnett, Michael, 155
Beckwith, Martha, 8, 46, 53, 54, 56, 142, 145
Bedward, Alexander, 1, 22, 23, 30–32, 44–46, 49, 50, 82, 95, 96, 100, 105, 108, 109, 112, 113, 115, 116; after death of, 117, 146, 147, 149; among the poor black masses, 4–5; ascension, 2–3; audacity, 140–141; authenticity, 40; baptism, 36, 38, 41, 48, 54–55, 157; belief (of flying home, 121, 124, 125; as Jesus/black Christ, 8, 12, 116, 125, 130–133, 135, 136, 138, 139, 144, 145, 155); biblical prophecy, 136–137; black nationalism, 51; black theology, 135, 143–147; black wall destroying the white wall, 50–51, 61–63, 69, 72, 75, 79, 139, 149; charged with vagrancy, 128; as charismatic leadership, 137; colonial resistance, 160; colour white identity and, 53–54; community spirit of believers, 117; comparison with Jesus, 117; *Daily Gleaner's* interview with, 121–122, 144; death of, 151, 155, 161; in defence of, 133–142; divinity, 116–117, 136, 159; earthquake of 14 January 1907, prediction of, 40–41; as an effective leader, 120; Ethiopianism and, 146; evidence/testimony (Campbell, Caleb, 140; Cox, Cyril Lionel, 139; Edwards, Charles, 131–133; Paton, Joseph, 140; Williams, Major, 97, 131, 138–139, 141–142); experience of racial discrimination, 33; fighting white oppression, 144; followers, 2; fund/earnings of Bedwardites given to, 120; and the Garvey Movement, 147–149; healing services, 5–6, 108, 159, 161; healing stream, 36–39, 42–43, 50; health complications, 33–34; hermeneutical principle

of a reader-response approach, 137; Higgins, John and, 106–107; hospitalization and, 42; and Howell, Leonard, 152; impact on August Town community, 162–166; incarceration in asylum, 89, 96–97; insanity, 6–10, 12–14, 42, 81, 87, 89, 141; interpreting the Bedwardism and, 6–14; as "King of Kings", 2, 122; as leader of a colonial resistance movement, 12–14; leadership team under Vagrancy Law, 129; as "Lord and Master", 115; as "Lord of Lords", 2, 122; marching orders of Bedwardites, 125–128; as the Messiah by Bedwardites, 151; mind healing, 118; model of self-reliant community of believers, 118–120, 152; movement, 158; mysticism, 137; Olson's critique on, 1–2, 4; as person of unsound mind, 2, 96, 131, 141; polity fluidity, 158; popularity, 42; prophecy, 40–41, 109, 136–137, 159; racial sermons/preaching, 50–51; and Rastafari, 149–155; remand in custody, 128, 130; return to Jamaica from Colón, 33–35; revised lunatic law and, 83; Revivalism, 11, 145; rights to the holdings, 142; sermons, 137, 152, 159; social welfare programmes, 118–119; trial, 11, 58, 115, 131–133, 141, 150

Bedward, Alexander, sedition case of, 57, 58, 81; arrest, 2, 9, 57; case for the defence, 64–68 (Steele, Alfred, evidence of, 71–73; Stern, Philip, address to the jury, 73–74); Prosecution's closing speech, 74–75 (Judge's charge, 75–78); Prosecution's evidence, 59–60 (Calder, William Jameson, 62–63, 66, 72, 76; Lanigan, John, 60–62, 76; Nelson, Robert, 68–74; Taylor, James Rainford, 63–64; Wilson, Daniel, 64); release from, 79; verdict of the jury, 78; vindication on, 78–80

Bedwardism, 1, 2, 5, 24, 51, 54–55, 95, 97, 99, 104, 105, 136, 137, 143, 145–147, 151, 155; Bedwardite stations, 55–56; birth and development, 31–43; and community of Saints, 115–121; consolidation of, 107–110; as flexible movement, 54; international, 55–56; interpreting, 6–14; membership, 54–56; national, 56; religious-racial philosophical ideas, 41; and Revivalism, 149, 155–160; and Revival religions, 155–160; stability and growth, 104, 107–109; and three days of fasting, 49. *See also* Revivalism

Bedwardites, 4–6, 9, 10, 12, 37, 38, 41, 42, 44–49, 84–87, 91, 92, 96, 104, 115–121, 123–125, 135–137, 142, 143, 145–150, 158–161; belief in three heavens, 136; charged with Vagrancy Law, 128–131; earnings, 120; as followers of Rastafari, 153, 155; living in August Town, 164; marching orders, 125–128; members, 161; millenarism and Ethiopianism, 151; movement, 161; punishment of, 130; Revised Obeah Act for, 100; Revival meetings of, 90–92; rituals, 156–157; self-identity, 52–56; social protest for rights of blacks, 142; social welfare fund, 119; trial of, 128–131; Vowing Ceremony, 156, 157

belief of flying home, 123–125
Bell, David, 160
Bellevue: criminal lunatics, 87 (asylum's recovery rate, 87; transfer of, 87); incarceration of people as insane, 89–90
Besson, Jean, 158
Bible, 45, 47, 49, 50, 108, 136, 138, 154, 158, 159
Black: fighting for the rights of, 142; identity, 12, 145; indigenous movement, 146; nationalism, 12, 13, 51, 148; race, 46–47, 50–51, 148–149, 151
"black Christ", 12, 116, 125, 135, 136, 138, 144–146, 149, 151, 154, 155, 160
Black Power movement, 135

black theology, 135; Bedward, Alexander and, 143–147
Blake, Henry Arthur, 82
Bogle, Paul, 9, 12, 23, 141, 142
British colonialism, 1, 46, 115, 123, 146
British Guiana, lunatic asylum, 84–85
Brooks, A. A., 6, 32, 33, 39, 49, 136, 156
Brooks, Asher, 132–133
"Brother Sal". *See* Hewitt, Solomon J.
Brown, Uriah, 107
Bryan, Patrick, 10
Buckridge, Steeve, 54
"Burial Scheme", 119
Burke, Sam, 127, 128, 130, 131

Calder, William Jameson, 59, 62–64, 66–69, 71–76, 192n52
Campbell, Caleb, 140
Carter, Stewart, 99–100
Chevannes, Barry, 9, 47, 53, 145, 149, 151, 152, 157, 158
Christianity, 19, 22, 51, 53, 108, 109, 136, 143, 151, 158–160; indigenous, 20, 21; Pentecostal, 162
Christian Trinity, 22, 45, 46, 161
colonialism, 13, 111; British, 1, 46, 115, 123, 146; social injustices of, 144
colonial resistance, 11–14, 134, 145, 152
colonial thinking, 90, 92
colonial violence, 13
colour white, 52–54
Cone, James, 135
Convention of 1920, rules and report of, 179–181
convince, 187n50
convinced doctors, 30
Cox, Cyril Lionel, 139–140
criminal lunacy, 94
criminal lunatics, 82–84, 87; acquittal of, 87–88; funding of, 94–95; recovery rate per cent, 89
Curtin, Philip, 23

Daily Gleaner, 7, 10, 30, 42, 67, 105, 106, 108, 114–116, 120–123, 134, 141, 150–151, 153, 165
Daniel 10:5, 136
district medical officers (DMOs), 24–25
divine healing, 161

divine revelation, 44, 47
Dixon, Sister, 39, 49
DMOs. *See* district medical officers (DMOs)
Doreman, Theophilus, 103
Dougal, W.F., 107

Edwards, Charles, 131–133
Elkins, Stanley, 136
Elkins, W.F., 30, 35
Emancipation Act of 1838, 19
eschatology, 144
established churches, 162
Ethiopianism, 12, 146, 148, 151, 160
European Christianity, 20
European colonialism, 13, 111

Fanon, Frantz, 13
fasting, 44, 46–49, 158. *See also* prayer
Ferguson, Richard, 132
Fisher, Samuel, 133
Florence Hall Pen incident, 23
flying home belief, 123–125
folk: culture, 112–115; medicine, 27; songs, 112–114, 125
Foote, 17
Forbes, George, 102–103
Forbes, Rose-Ann, 103
Foucault, Michel, 111
funding for healthcare, 25

Gardner, William, 17–19
Garvey, Marcus, 9, 11, 12, 14, 143, 147–149, 151; movement, 148; theology relating to Christ, 134–135
Garveyism, 9, 11, 12, 143, 146
Genesis 49:10, 136
Gifford, Lawson, 92
Gooden, Isaiah, 129
Gordon, 4
Great Revival, 10, 12, 15–17, 143, 145, 159; evaluation of, 17–22 (crises of the 1850s, 22–24; health crises of 1860s–1890s, 24–28); social protest and justice, 146

Hancock, Henry Burford, 58
healing, 158, 159, 161; preaching and, 104; Revivalism and, 28–30;

traditional, 27–28; water rituals for, 22, 30, 36–39, 41–43, 105, 159
healing streams, 30, 36–39, 42–43, 108, 109
health crises, 24–28
Henry, Roman, 37, 39, 46, 50, 55, 115–117, 120, 129, 136, 147–149
herbal medicine, 28–29
heredity, 91, 111
Hermitage Pen, 163
Hewitt, Solomon J., 100–101, 104; trial for lunacy, 101–102
Hickling, Frederick, 111, 112
Higgins, John, 106–107, 160
Hill, Garvey Robert, 150
Hinds, Robert, 149–151; Bedwardite practices, 155; beliefs about a "black Christ", 154; conversion to Rastafari, 153; King of Kings, 154, 155; trials, 153–155
Hines, Robert, 132
historical Jesus, 50, 137, 154
Holy Spirit, 22, 45, 161, 162
Hope River, 37, 38, 108, 157, 159
Hopewell Baptist Church, 102, 194n58
Howell, Leonard P., 150–155; destruction of property of, 153
Hurricane Charlie of 1951, 165
Hutchinson, Gerard, 111, 112
Hutton, Clinton, 21, 23

imbecility, 87
indigenous black theology, 145
indigenous Christianity, 20, 21
insanity, 6–10, 12–14, 42, 81–84, 87, 89, 111, 141; African Jamaicans, 91–92; high rate of, 89–90; religious excitement as a cause of, 91–92
"Instrument of Obeah", 97, 98
Isaiah movement, 22

Jamaica: black religion, 160; black wall of Revivalism, 104–107; culture, 114; Great Revival. *See* Great Revival
Jamaica Native Baptist Church, 31, 41–42, 119, 159; baptism in, 45–46; churches of, 171–173; complete dependence on divine revelation, 44–45; inward cleansing/purification of soul, 45–49; millenarianism, 49–51; symbol of, 125, 126
Jamaican law, 25, 26, 57, 79, 82
Jeremiah 8:20–22, 154
Jerry, Bongo, 155
Johnson, Michelle A., 5, 11, 107
Jones, Margaret, 92
Judaism, 136

Kerr-Jarrett, F.M., 134
Kingston and St Andrew parochial board (KSAC), 95–96, 105
Kingston Police Laws of 1881–1887, 104
KSAC. *See* Kingston and St Andrew parochial board (KSAC)
Kumina, 22, 52, 124

Lanigan, John, 59–62, 65–68, 74–76, 192n52
Latimers Pen, 163
Lee, Hélène, 152
"legitimate church", 162
Leile, George, 17
Lewis, Rupert, 9
Love, Robert, 9, 13
lunacy, charge of, 109
lunatic asylum, 81, 84; admission of persons to, 85–87; age-group profile of persons sent to, 93; cause of detention in, 91–92; reports of, 91–94
The Lunatic Asylum Law: of 1861 (sections 1–4 of, 81; section 13 of, 81);of 1896 (amendments, 82–83, 94; funding for, 94–97; goal of the legislation for, 84; Law 26 of 1914, 96; revised law, 82–85, 87, 95; section 16, 83; sections 1 and 2, 84; sections 1–9, 83; sections 11–13, 83)
lunatics, high rate of, 90–91

madness, 111, 112
"Mama Forbes." *See* Forbes, George
Manley, Michael, 148–149
Manley, Norman, 165
marching order, 131, 139, 142, 150, 155, 157, 160; of females and imprisonment, 177; of males and imprisonment, 174–176

Maroons, 26, 27
Marriott, Louis, 10
Martin, Ezekiel, 133
material poverty, 30
Matthew 3:3, 144
Matthew 15, 144
Matthew 16:1–7, 137–138
Matthew 23 and 23:4, 144
Mbiti, John S., 20
McGuire, George Alexander, 134, 135
Medical Act of 1908, 82, 102–104
mental illness, 92
millenarianism/millenarism, 49–51, 146, 149, 151–153
Miller, Kei, 10, 34
miscarriage of justice, 83
missionary Christianity, 20
Mona Estate, 163
Mona River, 30, 32, 36, 41, 109
"Mongoose Slide", 113, 114
Moore, Brian L., 5, 11, 107
Morant Bay War of 1865, 15, 23, 24, 41, 51, 60–63, 70, 73
morbidity rates, 25
mortality rates, 25–26
myalism, 18–19, 97, 98, 105

Native Baptists, 146–147; religion, 22
Negro World, 134
Nelson, Robert, 66, 68–75, 138
New Testament, 151; Church of God, 161; theology, 10
Nuttall, Enos, 4

obeah, 18–19, 28; criminalization of, 97; definition of, 98, 99; legislation for, 100; practice, 98
Obeah Act of 1898, 82, 97–102, 105
Old Testament, 151
Olson, George, 1, 4, 92, 148
Opoku, K Asare, 21
Orthodox Christianity, 10
Osterhammel, Jurgen, 13
Oughton, T. Bancroft, 59–60, 62, 70, 74–75, 83

Papine Estate, 163
parochial boards, 94–96
Paton, Diana, 100

Paton, Joseph, 140
Penfield, Bigelow, 16
Pennock, 158–159
Pentecostal church, 161–162
Pentecostalism, influence of Revivalism on, 160–162
Phillippo, Mursell, 17
Pierson, Rosco, 55
Platt, William, 163
Plaxton, 79
Poco Revival, 21
Post, Ken, 51
post-1865 Great Revival, 158
poverty, 27, 30
practising the obeah, 98
prayer, 44, 46–48
Prince Makaroo. *See* Brown, Uriah
Probyn, Leslie, 127
Psalm 68:5, 137
Psalm 68:31, 9

race, 46–47, 50–51, 146, 148–149, 151
racial identity, 51
racial politics, 50
Raderford, 35
Rastafari, 9, 11, 12, 143, 145, 146; Bedward, Alexander and, 149–155; community, 137; doctrine, culture and rituals, 155; members, 87, 100, 145, 153; preaching, 155; teaching, 151
reader-response approach, 137
Reid, Samuel, 29
religion, 20–22
religious excitement, 91–92
religious fanaticism, 105
religious rituals, 24
Revelation 7:9, 49
Revelation 11, 61
Revelation 11:3, 138
Revelation 12, 154
Revelation 12:1–6, 136
Revivalism, 11, 21, 97, 104, 109, 137, 145, 155, 160; Bedwardism and, 149, 155–160; black wall of, 104–107; and healing, 28–30; influence on Pentecostalism, 160–162
Revivalist groups, 157, 158, 161
Revivalist/Revival movements, 22, 30, 157–161

Revival meetings of Bedwardites, 90–92
Revival religions, 21, 22, 24, 104, 110, 111; Bedwardism and, 155–160
Revival Zion Sixty, 21, 155–157
Revival Zion Sixty-One, 21, 155–156
rituals, 156–157; water for healing, 22, 30, 36–39, 41–43, 105, 159
Robinson-Smith, Maria, 21
Roman Catholic Church, 157
"Run Mongoose Run", 113

Satchell, Vermont, 8–9, 11, 55, 107, 130, 136, 142
Schuler, Monica, 124
sedition, 57–59, 65, 66, 68, 75, 77–79, 81
Selassie, Haile, 46, 149, 151, 155
self-identity of Bedwardites, 52–56
Shakespeare. *See* Woods, Harrison E.S.
Sharpe, Sam, 9, 12
Sheridan, Richard, 27
Sherlock, Philip, 13
Simpson, George Eaton, 30, 156–157
Skervin, Samuel, 116, 126–127
"Sly Mongoose", 112–113
Smith, Leonard, 94
social defiance, 111–112
social (in)justices, 144, 146, 159
social welfare fund, 119
Sonderman, Theodor, 15
song and dance culture, 112–114
spiritual healing, 28
spiritual power, 48
Stafford, E.H.B., 26–27
Steele, Alfred, 71–73, 75
Stern, Philip, 57, 64–68, 72–74, 77–79, 192n52
Stewart, 28
Stewart, Robert, 158
Sugar Duties Act of 1846, 22
superstitions, 4, 18, 19, 99, 105

taxation, 22
Taylor, James Rainford, 63–64, 66, 73
Thomas, Alexander, 8
toll-road taxes, 22–23
traditional healing, 27–28
traditional religion, 21
"Trelawny Riots", 23
Trinidad, lunatic asylum, 84
tri-weekly fasts, 44, 47–49
Turner, Henry McNeal, 135

Union Temple, 54, 109, 116, 164
Universal Negro Improvement Association/African Communities League (UNIA/ACL), 134, 147, 148

vagrancy, charge of, 101, 109, 128
Vagrancy Act of 1833, 82, 97, 129–131
Verley, Lewis, 163
violence, 13, 112
Vow ceremony, 156, 157

water rituals for healing, 22, 30, 36–39, 41–43, 105, 159
Watson, Roxanne, 10
Webb, W., 26
West Indian Review, 8
White: oppression, 51, 144; race, 46, 121, 145
White, Edward, 5, 42, 50
Williams, D.J., 53, 87, 90–91, 133
Williams, J.J., 28–29
Williams, Major, 97, 131, 138–139, 141–142
Williams, Rudolph, 7
Wilson, Daniel, 64, 66, 73
Woods, Harrison E.S., 31–33, 35, 40, 138, 159, 163
Wright, 129, 130, 132, 133

Yoshiko Nagashima, 9, 136–137
Young, George Leslie, 130–131